Illegal, Alien, or Immigrant

The Politics of Immigration Reform

Lina Newton

NEW YORK UNIVERSITY PRESS

New York and London

NEW YORK UNIVERSITY PRESS
New York and London
www.nyupress.org

Library of Congress Cataloging-in-Publication Data
Newton, Lina.
Illegal, alien, or immigrant : the politics of immigration reform /
Lina Newton.
p. cm.
Includes bibliographical references and index.
ISBN-13: 978-0-8147-5842-7 (cl : alk. paper)
ISBN-10: 0-8147-5842-8 (cl : alk. paper)
ISBN-13: 978-0-8147-5843-4 (pb : alk. paper)
ISBN-10: 0-8147-5843-6 (pb : alk. paper)
1. United States—Emigration and immigration. 2. United States—
Emigration and immigration—Government policy. 3. Immigrants—
United States. 4. Immigrants—Government policy—United States.
I. Title.
JV6465.N498 2008
325.73—dc22   2008008059

New York University Press books are printed on acid-free paper,
and their binding materials are chosen for strength and durability.

Manufactured in the United States of America

c 10 9 8 7 6 5 4 3 2 1
p 10 9 8 7 6 5 4 3 2 1

Contents

Acknowledgments

The evolution of this book benefited from the support of several people. My husband, best friend, and scholar of American politics in his own right, Anthony Salvanto, deserves first mention. He brought a sharp and critical eye to the manuscript as I worked to clarify the main arguments. I am grateful to him for his uncanny ability to see clarity in spaces where I often see distracting complexity. He has been a wonderful (if sometimes captive) audience, and has served as a constant sounding board for my ideas. I am fortunate to have his intellectual and emotional support in all of my endeavors.

Three people have been elemental to ensuring that the project did not languish. Jane Junn at Rutgers University made herself available to read the inelegant versions and graciously shared her knowledge of American politics and literature on race, ethnicity, and immigration. I thank her for her humor and her generosity of time and spirit. Anne Schneider at Arizona State University was also a champion of the project, as was Helen Ingram, who has continued to be a valuable mentor. She is retiring this year, and I sincerely see my own professional successes as a tribute to her outstanding and unwavering support.

Others who deserve mention and thanks for their assistance with substantive and technical aspects of this project include Dan Tichenor from Rutgers University and my colleague at Hunter College, Andy Polsky, each of whom offered helpful critiques of the proposal. Ilene Kalish of New York University Press has been consistently enthusiastic about this project, and I appreciate her expert counsel and humor. I am likewise grateful to the anonymous reviewers whose insights and thoughtful criticisms served to improve the work.

This project required time to complete, and time is expensive. The production of the manuscript would not have been possible without funding from Hunter College's Gender Equity Project. I also benefited from funding from the City University of New York's PSC-CUNY grant program. In addition, I wish to thank Hunter College and the political science department for granting me the time to work on this book.

Finally, I am grateful for the unconditional support of my friends and family, and for the warm well wishes with which they responded when their inquiries into my progress were met all too often with "almost." I would like especially to thank my sister, Windie. She has been ready with words of encouragement at each step of the way.

A Note on Terminology

In this book I employ the term "illegal immigrant" to describe immigrants of any nation who have entered the United States or remained in the United States unofficially. Thus, I use "illegal" interchangeably with the descriptors "unofficial," "unauthorized," and "illicit" when discussing the immigration activities or status of those people who have entered or overstayed without official federal recognition. While I recognize that the term "undocumented" is often favored for political reasons (and grammatical reasons, since the word "illegal" is an adjective that technically describes actions or things, but not people), the term "undocumented" often proves problematic in a policy analytic context. Since the passage of the 1986 Immigration Reform and Control Act many immigrants who are in the country unofficially are, in fact, documented—although they may have false social security numbers, alien cards, and so on. The reality of false documentation provides its own set of policy problems that would not be captured by the term "undocumented." Likewise, readers will note from the titles of the numerous government and scholarly studies listed in the bibliography that my use of the term "illegal immigrant" often simply reflects its widespread use in official reports, journalistic accounts, and academic research.

Finally, and most importantly, this is a study of publicly oriented official rhetoric offered in support of government policy. Exploring how elected officials speak of immigration issues, the book presents and analyzes symbolic language, or specific iterations of immigration imagery and narrative structures; this endeavor requires that I pay attention to political language as it appears in official records. However, I have produced this book as an effort to show how official rhetoric ensures that policy nomenclature is often not politically neutral, and to provide critical analysis of immigration discourse where warranted.

Introduction

The Power of a Good Story

> Let me state the following premise about which there is little
> disagreement. It is the obligation of the Federal Government to
> secure the borders of the Nation from illegal entry and unauthor-
> ized invasion. . . . It is not a question of being anti-immigration.
> This country was founded by immigrants. I am the son of one
> of them.   —Rep. Steven Horn (R-CA), August 9, 1996

In these opening remarks to a hearing on federal border control efforts, immigrants appear simultaneously as villainous invaders of
the nation and as its heroic founders. That Americans view and treat the
immigrant population with both veneration and fear is an accepted peculiarity of the nation's history. However, Congressman Horn's remarks
also reveal four themes that have become the hallmarks of contemporary discourse on immigration policy, which blends old and new sensi-
bilities about the benefits and harms of immigration to the nation. For
example, Mr. Horn reminds his audience that the only entity with the
power to engage in national defense is the federal government. This first
theme, the tendency in political discourse to describe immigration with
the crisis language of "war" and "invasion," is as old as the immigration
phenomenon.[1]

Similarly, the congressman's reminder that the federal government has a
responsibility to control immigration alludes to another historical theme,
the dispute over state versus federal fiscal responsibilities in immigration
administration and settlement. State and local governments have peri-
odically complained that they bear the costs of large-scale immigration
policies that they do not design, but are mandated to implement. In 1882,

for example, the city of New York threatened to close down immigrant processing centers at Castle Garden (where immigrants were processed prior to Ellis Island) until the federal government made funds available to cover administrative costs of immigration! Over one hundred years later, in 1994, the governors of Arizona, California, and Florida appealed to Congress to reimburse their states for the fiscal costs of immigration.[2] Concern about un-funded federal mandates and the fiscal burdens of immigration even led states to take matters into their own hands: in 1994 California voters passed Proposition 187, designed in part to limit illegal immigrant access to state-funded social services, and in part to send a clear message about California's unwillingness to follow in lock-step with policy devised in Washington, D.C.[3] Since the passage of Proposition 187, a growing number of states and cities has legislated responses to what they perceive as failure of control at the federal level.[4]

The third and fourth themes in the congressman's statement are modern. The desire to avoid appearing anti-immigrant and, perhaps inadvertently, appearing racist, reflects the constraints lawmakers feel when embarking on immigration reform in a post–Civil Rights era. Mr. Horn tries to assure his audience that asserting control over immigrant invasions and unauthorized entries is not "anti-immigration." He simply wishes to keep out the unauthorized, the invaders—the bad kinds of immigrants. To further the distinction, he alludes to his own immigrant past: clearly, there are good immigrants out there; in fact, he is the product of such good immigrants who "founded this nation"—the son of the right kind of immigrants. While it may not be his intent to do this, Congressman Horn's statement also reveals the fourth theme of contemporary immigration debates: the privileging of the European immigrant experience. The congressman appeals to his own European (white) heritage, credits European immigration with the founding of the nation, and in so doing, engages in modern American mythmaking at the expense of American history. Although immigration from Latin America and Asia is not new to the United States, this immigration (which is presently dominated by immigrants from Mexico) is sidelined in favor of stories that establish European immigration of the nineteenth and early twentieth centuries as the "immigration experience." With the so-called First and Second Wave immigrants (mainly Europeans arriving between 1840 to 1880, and 1900 to 1920, respectively) having supposedly become fully assimilated, the question of whether current immigrants have what it takes to assimilate and be as successful as those who came before has become common.

Over the last two decades there has been a proliferation of research on immigration and its impact on population trends, economics, and labor markets, as well as on national security and territorial sovereignty. However, when policy choices are defended in the public sphere, science inevitably takes a back seat to stories and myths that play to the fears and prejudices, as well as the positive biases and interpretations, of the American immigrant experience. Hortatory language, a term that Murray Edelman employed to describe political posturing on behalf of policy, remains crucial to crafting immigration policy.[5] Political elites rely on emotion in justifying policy choices; they employ stories that are instinctually appealing to their audiences, packing them with language and symbols that tap into widely understood notions of who and what comprises the American immigrant experience. The symbols and myths of immigration are the political capital of policymakers who must build consensus regarding this highly contentious issue.

Congressman Horn's brief statement exemplifies how language and emotive imagery can tell a story of immigration that rationalizes restriction, but his speech is only one of many examples I might have chosen. In fact, the types of stories that politicians tell to build support for immigration reforms are so ritualized and basic in argument that my analysis of congressional debates and hearings on immigration reform in the 1980s and 1990s distilled thousands of pages of transcripts (often representing days, months, or even years of continuous discussion) into fewer than a dozen narrative types. These few policy narratives, in turn, reveal that immigration policymaking occurs within a narrow field of options largely dictated by images of the groups these laws target for reform. Elected officials identify policy goals as solving widely perceived problems in the control and administration of immigration, but an examination of the process of policy design unmasks its unstated purpose: these policies offer assurances that the right groups receive due rewards, while the socially unpopular are blamed for persistent problems and punished.[6]

The narratives that comprise contemporary immigration rhetoric offer dramatic tales with heroes and villains, but they also condense information, reduce uncertainty, and provide heuristics for decision-making in a field for which conflicting or incomplete evidence may provide no definitive course of action. Indeed, these narratives often supplant consistent findings. Most remarkably, policy narratives often rationalize the continuation of immigration policies that are, by scientific accounts, failures. As the following chapters will show, stories often replace studies, and emotion is the currency of Congress as it engages in policy debates. In essence, policy designs rest on a national mythology about what types of immigrants made America, and which ones lack the values, traits, or contributions that would earn them inclusion in that story.

Such story-telling is more than political theater—it is purposive activity in policymaking. These stories serve as foundations for building consensus for massive policies with multiple, often conflicting components; successful narratives can mollify critics' claims that legislation channels rewards in an unjust manner. And, while it might be tempting to treat discursive activities as political window dressing for the real behind-the-scenes business of devising legislation, I propose that policy narratives and the social constructions of the target populations embedded in these narratives are essential to understanding how lawmakers divide and subdivide the immigrant population to achieve policy goals. In turn, this activity of constructing divisions that indicate who is assimilable and who should be kept out allows policymakers to placate champions of immigration restriction while channeling labor to specific segments of the economy.

1

Considering Unlikely Outcomes
The Peculiar Politics of Immigration

This is a study of the public face of congressional lawmaking that focuses on the official function of imagery, stories, and symbolism in the policy process. It employs specific methods of discourse analysis and Anne Schneider and Helen Ingram's social constructions of target populations theory to explore how public officials use these stories and images in defending legislative solutions to immigration problems.[1] The research focused on two policy periods (1981–1986 and 1994–1996) characterized by significant policy changes. Such significant policy changes include alterations in approaches to dealing with a problem (mechanisms referred to as policy tools) and redefinitions of which parties (target populations or groups) should be implicated in these new approaches. I am specifically interested in revealing how legislators justify pursuing policies that narrowly favor very unpopular groups.

Viewed from a historical perspective, policy change is a recurring feature of immigration administration. The criteria and regulatory tools utilized to control immigration have shifted from the establishment of qualitative criteria designed to keep out those unable to support themselves (1875–1917), to overt restriction by race and national origin (1880s–1960s), to the post-1965 system that emphasizes family reunification, labor force needs, and humanitarian considerations. Furthermore, the 1986 Immigration Reform and Control Act (IRCA) represented a significant departure from past policies, marking the first time businesses faced federal penalties for their role in encouraging illegal immigration. It was also the first time that the United States offered resident unauthorized immigrants the chance to regularize their status. By contrast, the 1996 Illegal Immigration Reform and Immigrant Responsibility Act eased compliance requirements for employers while restricting access to public benefits such as housing, food stamps, and Temporary Aid to Needy Families (or TANF) available to legal and illegal immigrants.

In reviewing our history of immigration restriction efforts, we may find the reason public officials regularly target immigrants with restrictive or punitive policy tools fairly obvious: the public often blames immigrants for social ills, and elected officials can expect to mobilize public opinion against immigrants in support of policies reflecting immigrant unpopularity. However, it is less obvious why Congress would offer a consistently maligned group like illegal immigrants the option to correct their status and enter the social mainstream, as occurred in 1986. In fact, given that the political payoffs for supporting policies favoring a non-voting, criminalized population are indirect or elusive, we might ask why Congress would ever pass policies that undo discriminatory immigrant policies, let alone one that would extend full legal protections to people who, by definition, are law-breakers.

Immigration scholarship has mined the trends of conflicting goals, particularized benefits, and codified xenophobia that characterize this complex issue; the range of explanations for the peculiarity of immigration politics and policies reveal the influence of the various disciplines that researchers have brought to bear on the subject. Within the discipline of political science, the scholarship on immigration policy is quite diverse. Political theorists, for example, have explored the challenge of immigration to Americans' definition of the nation and its people as well as its civic culture and unity, and they have studied the specific challenges that illegal immigration poses to the liberal democratic order.[2] Political economists and security specialists have focused on immigration control as the assertion of security and market-driven prerogatives of American and European nation states.[3] Only more recently have scholars of American politics attempted to pry apart the various interests, actors, ideologies, and political circumstances that impel policy outcomes. While an evaluation of existing approaches shows important progress toward explaining why certain interests and ideological strains dominate immigration policymaking, the evaluation also reveals that important questions about the specific nature of group power and its influence on policy outcomes remain unanswered.

Influence of Interest Groups

Change in interest group power is a common explanation for change in policy. Policies that reward groups provide evidence of that group's political power; thus, a change in policy that favors previously ignored or sidelined groups would indicate a change in their ability to influence the legislative process. For example, immigration policy scholars often point to the influence of business groups on the policy process, invoking this influence to explain the weakness of restrictive policies amidst demands for control from American labor unions or other restrictionist interests.[4] Evidence of business influence abounds in analyses of agricultural lobbies that have had disproportionate abilities to secure labor for their industry, even when the goal of Congress has been to restrict labor migrants.[5] More recently, the activities of the high-tech industry in securing highly educated skilled workers has captured attention as the arrival of a new interest intent on shaping guest-worker policies in 1990 and 1996.[6]

However, while business would enjoy unfettered access to foreign labor, Congress has repeatedly taken steps to regulate access to such labor. This suggests, contrary to the assertions above, or those of neo-Marxist analyses of policymaking, that business interests do not reign exclusively in the policymaking process.[7] New analyses of policymaking after the passage of the 1965 Immigration and Nationality Act are emphasizing the growing power of other pro-immigration interest groups such as the American Immigration Lawyers Association, ethnic and religious organizations, and, more recently, certain labor unions, which have been increasingly successful in achieving and maintaining expansive admissions policies and ensuring that laws account for immigrants' rights.[8] In fact, the alliances these groups have forged with business interests help explain why Congress has not acted to restrict such immigration despite public demands to do so.[9]

One example that illustrates the influence of pro-immigration interests emerged during immigration reform efforts in the 1990s. Senator Alan Simpson (R-WY) fought to ensure that immigration reform would cut down family reunification visas, which constitute the largest number of immigration visas issued to foreigners each year. However, the proposed cuts never made it to the final bill. Simpson found his efforts defeated by an alliance between business interests (fighting for access to foreign workers) and various ethnic and legal pro-immigration interest groups that had benefited since 1965 from the family reunification preference system.[10]

Even earlier, the legalization component of the 1986 IRCA represented a substantive victory for Hispanic interest groups, signaling their arrival on the scene as advocates for liberal immigration policies.[11] Carolyn Wong's research on immigrant advocacy suggests that a combination of non-profit advocacy groups and growing, ethnic-based electorates in key congressional districts has ensured that legal immigration policies remain progressive, rights-oriented, and inclusive, much in the traditions of the 1964 Civil Rights Act and the 1965 Immigration and Nationality Act.[12] For Wong and others who document the rise of the pro-immigration lobby, the fact that the later, 1990 Immigration and Nationality Act increased legal immigration and that 1996 policy reforms did not reduce caps is solid evidence of the influence enjoyed by this powerful coalition of immigration advocates. However, the other components of the 1996 Illegal Immigration Reform and Immigrant Responsibility Act (IIRAIRA), such as border fortification and benefits restriction for legal and illegal immigrants and their children, represent a substantial loss of the protections for immigrants instated with IRCA. Many of the immigrants who had benefited from legalization in the late 1980s would face substantive rollbacks in their entitlements as legal permanent residents under the 1996 reforms. An estimated 935,000 legal immigrants, many of whom were either minors or had been admitted legally as refugees, were cut off from food stamps.[13] Although a portion of these benefits was re-instated for some immigrants in 1998 and again for others in 2003, these policy corrections occurred under the radar, and without the political spectacle that accompanied the passage of the IIRAIRA.[14] By contrast, business interests faced no parallel restrictions or sanctions for their role in encouraging immigration.

The Latino voting population has only grown since the 1986 IRCA, and the type of pressure tactics that Wong and James Gimpel and James Edwards attribute to the growth of Latino political clout and ethnic group lobbying ought to have increased. Yet the numerous immigrant restrictions of the IIRAIRA and the difficulty Latinos and ethnic lobbyists have had recently in securing a new legalization program for the estimated ten to twelve million resident illegal immigrants in the United States imply that policy victories for Latino immigrants are not only tenuous, but also do not necessarily provide a solid base upon which to build further victories. Business interests, by contrast, have not witnessed such rollbacks or challenges to their policy victories, and compromise does not erode their foundation for securing further victories.

Contextual Change and Ideological Ruptures

The competition among interests and alliances forged by immigration policy offers a strong explanation for differences in policy outcomes, but explanations driven by their focus on interest groups often overlook contextual shifts and accompanying ideological changes that activate new approaches to intractable social issues. During the periods under study here, Congress changed its explanations for why illegal immigration occurs, and in doing so, lay the blame on different factors. Most significantly, this change occurred without any significant alteration in scientific knowledge about the social phenomenon of illegal immigration, why the problem occurs, or why it persists.

A change in contexts such as external shocks to the political system can force political actors to approach an old issue in a new manner, or it can open opportunities for previously sidelined interests to find an audience or influence policy design.[15] Thus, a change in party control of Congress can impel untried alternatives to social problems, or create an institutional environment that favors approaches that are in keeping with the ideology of the ruling party. To illustrate, the 99th Congress, which was controlled by Democrats, would have been open to an immigrant civil rights agenda; it also supported measures such as employer sanctions to regulate businesses. But when the 1994 midterm elections gave partisan control to the Republican Party, this change created an opening for new approaches to the problems of illegal immigration. The 1996 Illegal Immigration Reform and Immigrant Responsibility Act fit with the new Republican governing philosophy set forth in the "Contract with America." The so-called Republican Revolution signified a shift in how all groups viewed as "dependents" of the national government stood in relation to federal policy—an ideological expression of fiscal conservatism pitting "taxpayers" against "tax recipients" that had been gaining traction among white middle class voters since the 1970s.[16] Under the leadership of House Speaker Newt Gingrich (R-GA), the 104th Congress would pass a more punitive welfare reform bill than that originally proposed by President Bill Clinton, and the IIRAIRA in many ways overlapped with the 1996 Personal Responsibility and Work Opportunity Reconciliation Act (PREWORA).[17] In this new policy context, immigrants (legal and illegal) were no different from citizens relying on federal assistance: they were not pulling their weight, and, more significantly, they were doing so at taxpayers' expense.

However, there were limits to how far advocates of the "Contract with America" could go in applying its reform prescriptions to immigration policy: even though public opinion polls in the 1990s showed a public in favor of restriction on all immigration, and the new Republican Congress was amenable to restrictive approaches to immigration, an alliance of business and pro-immigrant lobby groups successfully checked efforts to cut family reunification visas (as discussed earlier). Such particular outcomes suggest that even under conditions of systemic shock, differences in the nature of group power still matter; they also suggest that some forms of immigration may be beyond the reach of restriction.

Daniel Tichenor, whose longitudinal study of immigration policy shifts from laissez-faire style openness to restrictionism based on nationality and then to a rights-based openness, offers an explanation for the combined consequence of ideology and policy context in enabling group power. He argues that different institutional contexts have produced conditions that can facilitate policy victories for groups wielding different types of power.[18] Demonstrating a trend since the 1960s towards expansionist legal immigration and refugee policies, Tichenor suggests that the legacy of the Civil Rights movement and growing political activism among pro-immigrant lobbies (including a relatively recent about-face by some key labor unions) have provided ideological as well as institutional contexts more favorable to immigrants and their advocates in all branches of government. Likewise, he argues that increasing naturalization and new voter registration rates have thus far served as disincentives to officials who would otherwise pursue extreme restrictionist agendas. The fact that Governor Pete Wilson, a champion of California's Proposition 187, found himself ousted in 1998 by Democrat Gray Davis suggests that overt anti-immigration stances alienated a growing block of voting Latinos. Tichenor finds further proof of limits to the Republicans' restrictionist agenda in the election of President George W. Bush, who took a decidedly less anti-immigrant position than typically associated with Republicans at the time. As close as the 2000 election was, there is no question that George W. Bush enjoyed a significant increase in support from Hispanics.[19] Furthermore, while contemporary restrictionism parallels past efforts to initiate immigration bans, the practice of banning immigrants from particular nations is no longer a feature of U.S. immigration policy. Tichenor argues that the ideologies of civil and human rights have taken a firm hold in American politics, creating an infertile environment for restrictionists who pursue policies that single out groups by race or nation or who would institute across-the-board cuts in family immigrant admissions.

What is alluring about context-driven explanations of policy change is their collective acknowledgement that arenas of policymaking are not open to all groups, interests, or ideologies at all times, and that different issues and policymaking institutions (or venues) lend distinctive advantages to groups seeking influence.[20] Tichenor's study of immigration policy change recognizes that in addition to organization and access, policy contexts can favor different ideological commitments or definitions of social problems that can, in turn, produce changes in immigration law. However, when the 1986 IRCA and 1996 IIRAIRA are viewed in their entireties, it appears that contextual changes, whether external to the system or internal to institutions, seem to affect some groups more profoundly than others. When contrasted with the proliferation in the 1990s and early 2000s of state and municipal legislation devised to restrict the movement and behaviors of foreigners living in U.S. communities, Gary Freeman's characterization of the expansionist bias in contemporary U.S. immigration policy appears overstated. For a despised group like illegal immigrants to be deemed worthy of consideration for full membership at one point, and then emerge vilified once again within the span of ten years, suggests that human rights or minority civil rights approaches to immigration may have more limited traction in the legislative arena than does restrictionism. This, in turn, implies that some immigrants and their advocates are simply more vulnerable to contextual changes than are employers, who are also implicated in immigration reform. The passage of the 1996 IIRAIRA so shortly after IRCA indicates that immigrants face specific barriers to securing *enduring* policy victories.

Groups, Race, and Policy Reaction

In the political system of the United States, groups appear as agents structuring immigration policies, but they appear as policy recipients as well. Policy is not simply reflective of dominant modes of power or prevailing ideologies; policy can reinforce how social groups interact, and it can structure and maintain systems of inequality. Policies that reward groups differently may reflect the modes of influence that various groups wield in the political process, but they may also reflect the status of those groups in the broader social and political order. Literature focusing on immigration policy change from a race perspective notes that periods of exclusion and expansion are the function of changing racial ideologies in the United States, and that different groups have either gained status or been denied membership in accordance with ideological shifts or ruptures. Instances of change in immigration administration and control have often coincided with official efforts to delineate social and political membership for immigrant groups along race lines.

Excludable Groups

Much of the nineteenth- and early twentieth-century rationalization for barring some immigrant groups involved discussions accentuating the problematic distinctiveness of certain groups; race, national origin, cultural and religious differences were framed as disruptive to the social order and threatening to the existence of a majority Anglo-Saxon racial stock.[21] Immigration policies such as the 1882 Chinese Exclusion Act, the creation in 1917 of an "Asiatic barred zone" that banned immigration from Asia, India, and parts of eastern Africa, and the 1921 and 1924 National Origins Acts each named source countries and specific races for exclusion or severe restriction. For non-Anglo, non-Protestant immigrants already living in the United States, the Americanization movement sought to correct their deficiencies and resolve the problems many reformers of the Progressive era feared would ensue without proper education in American political ideals and social values.[22] Some groups, deemed beyond the reach of assimilation projects, were systematically denied political and social membership in the United States. In addition to being barred from immigrating, Chinese, and later, other Asian-origin groups falling within the barred zone, were denied the right to naturalize. In a post-quota era, Filipino and Mexican immigrants recruited work in the United States faced repatriation campaigns and selective application of deportation policies because these immigrants' skin color, facial features, behaviors, and concentration in the working classes marked them as inassimilable. Filipino immigrants, who initially enjoyed the right to naturalize as citizens of a U.S. commonwealth, later found the right rescinded when the United States granted the country its independence and decided that barring Filipino migration was necessary to maintain consistency with the nation's general exclusion of Asian immigrants.[23]

Erika Lee argues that as race policy, the 1882 Chinese Exclusion law and its enforcement apparatus mark a crucial point in American state-making.[24] The 1882 law began a process in which the American identity was defined in racial terms, and this definition was actively protected via state efforts.[25] The exclusion of Chinese not only set the stage for exclusion of other Asians, but also provided the ideological justification, administrative institutions, and legal apparatus to exclude other groups. Mexican immigrants, for example, who took the place of Chinese and Asian Indians after their exclusion, came to be racialized in ways that emphasized the group's foreignness, racial inferiority and racial unassimilability. Likewise, Chinese exclusion set the policy foundation for exclusion of specific Europeans, who would continually be compared in terms that harkened back to the Chinese: Italians were referred to as "the Chinese of Europe," and French Canadians were referred to as "the Chinese of the Eastern States."[26]

In light of the role that race and nativism have historically played in immigration policy, some scholarship features these elements to discuss contemporary policy in a type of racial/nativist path-dependency argument. [27] Thus, these scholars contend that modern policies, while written race-neutrally, still contain elements of past policies. State-level initiatives such as Proposition 187 represent the legal outgrowth of public distaste for third world (read "brown") immigration. Likewise, the increasing militarization of the U.S.-Mexico border and the 1996 IIRAIRA's strict deeming requirements exemplify how the United States exerts dominance over Latin American immigrants through the legal production of race-based criteria that determine both rights of access and individual rights.[28] While laws emphasizing a crackdown on "public charges" may, on their face, seem to promote a class bias against poor immigrants, Kevin Johnson warns that more often than not, legal interpretation and actual application of these laws have historically had a strong, if not overriding, racial bias to them.[29]

While any effort to discount the power of racism and nativism as either overt or underlying forces in determining policy outcomes would clearly be mistaken, accounts that grant primacy to racism and nativism as policy determinants can rarely move beyond descriptions of policy contexts and socio-cultural trends. These conceptualizations of immigration policy then prove unsatisfying when contrasted with empirical evidence of legislative measures that dismantle racist policies. In other words, while it is not problematic to identify the many ways in which entrenched ideologies about race and nation resurface even in a post–Civil Rights era, the question remains how to engage race and nationalism in a discussion of policy change that can account for policy efforts that either dismantle racist policies or use alternative criteria to define social and political membership.

The dynamism of race and nationalism in policy formulation is better captured in policy accounts that apply Michael Omi and Howard Winant's racial formation theory to immigration policy; such accounts have offered ways to conceptualize past policy shifts, as well as a lens through which to view current policy efforts.[30] According to Omi and Winant, laws and the institutions that produce and interpret them have organized resident and immigrant racial and ethnic groups into a hierarchy via legally constructed racial categories.[31] Omi and Winant address the interaction among group racialization, power, and policy change in this manner: when laws change to favor powerless racial or ethnic minorities, they have done so in response to social movements that successfully contest the racial order.[32] The 1965 Immigration and Nationality Act, according to this perspective, would be an outgrowth of the Civil Rights movement and a new ideology of racial accommodation taking hold in the public and solidified in the social policies of Presidents Kennedy and Johnson.[33] Likewise, we might interpret legalization as a victory for previously disengaged ethnic groups whose vision for immigration policy draws upon the Civil Rights legacy, and a new context of race accommodation that validated their concerns, championed expansive immigration policies, and expanded definitions of social membership.

Yet, this otherwise compelling framework for understanding immigration policy change falters when matched against recent transformations in immigration legislation. Seen in light of the racial formation account, the decisive move in the mid-1990s towards immigration restriction at the federal and local levels suggests the unraveling of the Civil Rights consensus that lay at the foundation of Great Society programs, and, by extension, contributed to expansive immigration policy. And yet, it is difficult to make this case when the 1990 Immigration and Nationality Act increased legal admissions overall, and even after the 1996 IIRAIRA, family reunification remains the foundation of immigrant admissions, accounting for approximately three-quarters of them annually.[34] Moreover, given that the current admissions system for legal immigrants and refugees maintains a flow of non-white people to the United States, it is clear that more is at work in immigration policymaking than traditional American-brand restrictionism.

Desmond King, whose work also engages Rogers Smith's multiple traditions approach, offers an alternative possibility. King argues that it is not

so much that racist and xenophobic elite responses to immigration pe-
riodically resurface as different groups holding these ideologies gain or
lose power, but rather that such ideologies are continually competing with
alternative, liberal egalitarian ideologies.[35] Liberal notions of equality and
ascriptive equality enjoy resonance in the polity, making each a suitable
justification for immigration reforms at any given time. King also offers
some insights into the uses of race in justifying both restriction and social
and political expansion and incorporation of immigrants. For King, the
immigration debates of the early twentieth century and resultant policies
represent a "convergence of alleged scientific authenticity with populist
stereotypes, which, in the hands of unreflecting promoters enabled it to
influence legislation."[36] He contends that rhetoric and concepts that arose
from the late-nineteenth and early twentieth centuries—namely, the concern over immigrant quality, and the promotion of a constricted definition of "American" as "white," as well as the conception of the "melting
pot" as the definitive immigrant experience—would all remain features of
political discourse on immigration into the twenty-first century.

The challenge remains, nonetheless, to examine group racialization in
a post–Civil Rights era in which overt expressions of racism do not enjoy
the same claim to legitimacy they did in the nineteenth and early twentieth centuries. It is unclear whether current immigration restriction efforts
are simply variants on an illiberal American theme, or whether ascriptive citizenship has morphed into a new and different ideological stance
in response to changes in the relationship among citizens, aliens, and the
modern nation state occurring against the backdrop of globalization, as
others contend it has.[37] In light of the patterns of restriction emerging in
the United States and Europe, some have pushed for a conceptualization
of modern policies in which race *and* legal status operate in tandem to
marginalize immigrant populations.[38]

Race: Its Function and Limitations in Policy Formulation

Race, while particularly significant in the American context, is not the
only axis of division in American immigration policymaking. A practical example that speaks to the limits of race is the comparatively favorable policy treatment of Afro-Cubans arriving on U.S. shores since the
1980s, versus the executive mandates for interdiction, detainment, and
deportation of black Haitians. In this case, national origin trumped race
as foreign policy considerations produced different stances towards these

groups. The 1986 IRCA's legalization program also reveals alternative axes of division: as later chapters will discuss in detail, legalization policy made length of continuous residency in the United States and/or employment in perishable agriculture (not racial or ethnic group membership) the criteria for individual eligibility. One study of print media coverage of legalization applicants showed that the primary distinctions that news stories drew among applicants simply mirrored archetypes such as "hard workers," "stable," and "family men" that were in use when the law itself was being debated.[39] Those who studied the implementation of legalization noted that women—particularly single women—had a harder time applying for green cards. The bias against women resulted from social and employment network differences between the sexes.[40]

The practice of "culling" from a target population is hardly limited to immigration policy: the invocation of race, class, values, gender, and other indicators of division serve as discursive strategies in policy formulation. Most interesting are those cases in which race can appear or fade away within an issue area depending on the goals of a policy. For example, Mara Sidney's study of federal housing policies demonstrated how congressional elites constructed a class of deserving, middle-class blacks in seeking support for the 1968 Fair Housing Law. As Congress debated the merits of the law amidst a climate of urban riots and the decisively militant turn of the Civil Rights movement, the creation of a hard-working, professional middle-class black target population that needed to "escape" the ghettoes and their inhabitants was crucial to the bill's passage. Later, policy measures designed to channel federal funds into urban areas with large minority populations would succeed because congressional advocates strategically removed people (and therefore race) from the discussion, and focused instead on more abstract "neighborhoods" and "community" entities as deserving federal funds.[41]

Sidney's findings are instructive about the strategic uses of race in policymaking, particularly in circumstances for which there is little public consensus that a particular group merits government protection or funding.[42] Given that laws can essentially divide broad populations and redefine their component parts to signal that specific populations merit differential policy treatment, we need to account for the multiple ways in which populations are defined as meritorious. Thus, rather than ask whether group racialization is a policy determinant, I believe a more useful question to ask is when is group racialization employed to justify policy designs, and under what circumstances does race recede or disappear from these discussions? Answering this question will also grant better insights into the specific political challenges that immigrant advocates face in securing benefits for this population.

Policy Change: Remaining Questions

Each of the approaches above engages a different perspective on the impact of groups on the policy process in order to explain policy change. What unifies the interest group, contextual change, and race-based frameworks is the notion that policy evolves as a resolution for conflicts among competing groups or competing ideological forces. Policy outcomes, and policy change, for that matter, reflect either similar contexts in which new groups have striven for influence, or different ideological or institutional contexts that have opened the door for new groups, or new articulations of policy goals to influence policy design. While each perspective offers significant insights for our understanding of immigration policy change, these perspectives are somewhat less satisfying in their treatment of (or outright inattention to) unlikely policy outcomes—particularly those in which relatively politically weak or systemically maligned groups reap significant benefits.

Moreover, the following observations remain unaccounted for: some groups seem to win favorable policies built on foundations of sand, while other groups' claims to favorable outcomes appear firmly entrenched. While Civil Rights values of equality and race-blindness may continue to justify generous immigrant admissions policies, as Freeman, Wong, King, and Tichenor have each argued, these values have not been successfully mobilized to cement immigrants' rights of access to either the material or the membership benefits of the modern American welfare state. In fact, immigrants in the 1990s found themselves written out of these benefits with a new and broadly resonant ideology that attacked the welfare state writ large and that forged deep divisions between those seen as milking the welfare state, and those seen as paying for it. At the same time, while Gimpel and Edwards have argued that competing views of redistributive politics and not racism form the major social and partisan cleavages over approaches to immigration, I disagree with a conclusion that discounts race as a force in the crafting of contemporary immigration policy. In fact, group racialization as encoded in policy serves the larger political goal of managing immigration by reaffirming an existing consensus about who can make claims upon the welfare state.

This activity of political division and development of consensus is the lynchpin of contemporary immigration policy. If we consider that even the most restrictive nineteenth- and twentieth-century immigration policies never completely shut the door to immigration, the utility of such group divisions is even clearer. If the nation never has and, for the foreseeable future, never will stop all immigration completely, the management of immigration will perpetually be about constructing typologies of acceptable and unacceptable immigrants. By focusing on this process of classification, or the social construction of policy target groups, we can better grasp how group power and group image serve to affirm or collapse our definitions of who is worthy of reward through immigration policies.

Deserving and Undeserving: Recasting the Politics of Immigration

To the extent that government output reflects institutional biases and an existing distribution of power, policies can communicate that some groups will regularly gain access to the system and receive benefits while others will regularly face barriers in having their interests heard.[43] However, since immigrant groups have been conferred with significant political victories, the question is not whether these groups have a seat at the table, but rather why immigrants groups see their victories more easily eroded than do other stakeholders in immigration reform. I believe the answer lies in the dual social construction of immigrants, and in the operation of this duality in the drafting and justification of immigration policies.

In selecting policies, lawmakers as well as citizens are more likely to support definitions and solutions to social problems that are in sync with the way they view the world as well as the way they assume their constituents view the world.[44] Anne Schneider and Helen Ingram have argued that elected officials cement public support for policies by assuring people that government "does not give anyone more than they deserve" nor does it contribute to "unfairness or injustice."[45] Therefore, even in favorable political contexts, those advocating policies that reward immigrant groups face an additional struggle, which is to present these groups as *deserving* benefits.

Murray Edelman, who considered the instrumental functions of myth and symbol in politics, identified how condensation symbols serve to induce "an attitude, a set of impressions, or a pattern of events associated through time, through space, through logic, or through imagination with the symbol."[46] To illustrate, the word "immigrant" has long served as a condensation symbol for both related and contradictory views, such as economic uncertainty, poverty, immorality, hard work, social mobility, remaking of the self, and the embodiment of the "American dream." The category "illegal immigrant" is a legal designation for people who have entered the United States without inspection at a designated port of entry (POE). However, "illegal immigrant" has become a condensation symbol for an invasion of the American Southwest, fiscal crisis, welfare abuse, crime, and Mexican immigration.

Such mixed symbolism provides a wealth of political capital for legislators designing policies that selectively confer such benefits as legal status, public benefits, or even access to entry. In their social constructions of target populations theory, Schneider and Ingram assert that legislators select the groups expected to comply with policy (or "target populations") in light of the popular perceptions (social constructions) of these groups. According to Schneider and Ingram, "there are strong pressures for officials to provide beneficial policy to powerful, positively constructed target populations and to devise punitive, punishment-oriented policy for negatively constructed groups."[47] If, as Edelman argued, political support is dependent upon how the mass public understands symbols attached to issues, then it follows that the policies intended to solve the problems will also depend on emotional appeal, political drama, and pre-existing myths and images about the people, groups, or institutions relevant to the issue area. The social construction of target groups is important not only in determining policy tools, but also in developing rationales that ensure political consensus for policies.[48]

Viewed from this perspective, rationales for restricting different immigrant groups at different times correspond to each group's political and social construction as "undeserving." Historically, restrictionism has coincided with the social instability produced by economic downturns, but the fact that it also takes on in-group/out-group overtones indicates a more fundamental divide over which groups should be considered part of the national fabric, and which groups are marked as undeserving of access or of the naturalization option, which would ensure that access. Michael Shapiro notes parallels between nativism past and present:

The contemporary political climate, which encourages attacks from various segments of the social and political order—right wing journalists, nativist groups, regional labor organizations, state governors, national leaders, and legislative bodies—is part of a venerable American tradition. . . . Alien-others, who, in various periods have been "Indians," French speakers, Irish, southern Europeans, eastern Europeans, Asians, and third world immigrants, and most recently, "illegal aliens" crossing the U.S. border with Mexico, have been constructed as threats to valued models of personhood and to images of a unified national society and culture.[49]

Contemporary pleas to limit immigration whose justifications refer to the qualitative deficiencies of today's immigrants do recall restrictionist ideologies and policy efforts of the past. The anti-immigrant movement and resultant policies of the Progressive era were documented in John Higham's classic study of American nativism, *Strangers at the Gates*. As Higham explains, to policymakers of the era, "race often meant little more than national character. It usually suggested some sort of innate impulse."[50] Higham's analysis explains the passage of the 1924 National Origins system, and, in his account, Italian, German, Irish, and Jewish immigrants were cast in terms of their linguistic (with the exception of the Irish), religious, cultural, and moral differences.[51]

There are limitations, however, to drawing parallels between the National Origins system's European targets and all groups that have at some point been considered "others." Higham's account of the historical period that produced the National Origins system provides an excellent account of European restriction, but it took additional scholarship to establish clear patterns of difference in policy treatment of Europeans and Asians. The differences in policy treatment of those of European and Asian origin would, in turn, produce varied possibilities for group integration and membership as the nation limited citizenship by race rather than ethnicity.

As historian Erika Lee notes, it is significant that the quota system categorized Europeans by nation of origin. By contrast, those hailing from the Asiatic barred zone were not permitted to naturalize due to qualities ascribed to their membership in the politically conceived racial category of "Asian." Likewise, "Asia" was conceived not in accordance with its component nations, but rather as a region hosting people of recognizable physical traits that were "Mongolian" and not "White." Significantly, Italians, Slovaks, and other Southern and Eastern Europeans, while strictly limited numerically, were not defined racially in one key area: naturalization and political participation rights—the quintessential avenues by which immigrants have integrated into the American polity. Mae Ngai observes that in essence, the National Origins system reified the difference between race (which cannot be changed) and ethnicity (at once tied to national origin, and which yet can fade away): the 1924 National Origins Act tied Europeans to their national origins, created ethnicities, and thus made it possible for them eventually to become "White." For the groups restricted (and, notably, not *banned*) with the National Origins Act, race was decoupled from nation. However, the same act collapsed the ethnic and racial identities of Japanese, Chinese, and Filipinos.[52]

Like Asians, Mexicans came to occupy a racialized position of alien other that in turn shaped a migration and citizenship experience distinctive from that enjoyed by Europeans. State-supported labor policies, southern border enforcement, and repatriation policies combined to produce the notion of "illegal" as being the primary marker of the Mexican in the United States.[53] This connection between nation of origin and status would emerge as a stigma, a lingering question of right to physical presence in the United States that would follow someone of Mexican origin regardless of whether he or she was born in the United States.[54] Fundamentally, this relationship between Mexicans and the terminology "illegal" is the product of a specific relationship between Mexico and the United States, which includes the United States' conquest and acquisition of the Southwest, the protection of labor migration routes by U.S. growers and government in that region, and the geographic proximity and permeability of the U.S.-Mexico border. As the largest and therefore most visible group of immigrants today, Mexicans are often the subject of discussions of immigrant criminality, as well as being attributed other characteristics such as laziness, poverty, and dependency. As Mexican immigration is conflated with illegal immigration, official status has become yet another mark of difference for Mexican immigrants.[55] Significantly, the construct of illegality, so central to the contemporary immigration experience, simply finds no parallel in the European immigrant experience.

Another facet of contemporary immigration politics that has no analogy in earlier expressions of nativism is a melding of immigration restrictionism with "balanced budget conservatism," which involves an ideological attack on the state as allocator of public goods. According to this view, the state exists as an arbiter of "taxpayer funded programs," or goods presumed to be paid for by some and drawn on by others. The policy expressions of balanced budget conservatism are to be found in efforts to bring fiscal discipline to federal expenditures through budget cuts in welfare and other federally funded programs. In contemporary discourse, immigration has been recast as a domestic policy issue that is now subject to the larger debate over redistributive policies.[56] Moreover, race is deeply enmeshed in the discourse of deserving and undeserving, the leitmotif of contemporary social policy.[57]

In terms of public policy designs, when elected officials identify immigrants—particularly those from Mexico—as a problem population, these immigrants face an additional barrier of illegitimacy in claiming that their demands upon the polity are rightful claims. While legislative outcomes are written race-neutrally, the discourse employed to sell the legislation is often race-laden. As the following section will show, this notion of *what* constitutes a legitimate claim has everything to do with prevailing beliefs about *who* is making this claim. Mexicans have been constructed through processes of conquest, citizenship, and immigration, and the population has a specific set of social constructions that appear as archetypes in immigration policy rhetoric.

Constructing a Mexican Other

The assimilation model that Robert Dahl employed in describing the political experiences and social mobility of European immigrants who came to the United States in the mid-nineteenth and early twentieth centuries assumed that groups lose their outsider status once they adopt the language and values of the dominant culture and participate in civic life.[58] The straight-line assimilation model, however, appears inappropriate in describing the Latino and Asian-American experiences. Despite the long histories of these populations in the United States, these groups continue to be viewed as foreign and unassimilable, due to their physical identifiability and public use of languages other than English.[59] In the case of Asian Americans, racial difference and continued immigration that adds to population growth of Asian America, along with an absence of distinction in American culture of the multiple and varied nationalities comprising the term "Asian," have served to construct this group as less than American, permanently foreign.[60]

The "permanent foreigner" concept is likewise applicable to the Mexican-American experience: the distinctive language, traditions, history, and culture of Mexicans within the United States formed the core of political solidarity and ethnic consciousness as this population internalized and developed its status as "different" from the dominant Anglo-American population.[61] At the same time, I would add that American perceptions of Mexican migration add yet another dynamic to the relationship between this population and the greater polity, by infusing this relationship with the expectation of temporality. The characterization of Mexican immigration as "temporary" or "sojourner" immigration, and the codification of this idea in policy, have further curtailed broader recognition of Mexican-origin people as a permanent, longstanding feature of the American experience. This multifaceted reality of the Mexican immigrant experience simply finds no parallel in the European immigrant experience, and yet, the European experience has become the de facto yardstick by which the experience of the Mexican-origin population—whether citizen or immigrant—continues to be measured.

These three characterizations of the Mexican-origin population, the "permanent foreigner," the "temporary Mexican," and the "criminal alien," merit further exploration since these will appear as archetypes in immigration policy rhetoric. The following section develops and explains some of the origins of these characterizations and attests to their present-day prevalence in general immigration discourse. Again, these social constructions are significant because they resonate in the broader public arena, offering assurance that we are admitting the right people and restricting those who may not/will not/cannot become Americans. Insofar as they mark Mexican immigrants and the Mexican-origin population as qualitatively different from past immigrants, these are constructions of undeserving people.

The Mexican American as Permanent Foreigner

In 1848, the stipulations of the Treaty of Guadalupe Hidalgo ended the Mexican-American War and made United States citizens of tens of thousands of Mexican nationals living in conquered territories.[62] Historians Matt Meier and Feliciano Ribera pinpoint the difference between the historical experiences of European immigrants and those of Mexican heritage in the following manner: "Without moving, these people became foreigners in their native land," subject to a dominant Anglo language, culture, religion, and legal system.[63] As a result, attitudinal and structural biases against this population stymied their claims to full citizenship. Relationships between Anglo-American migrants to the region and

Mexicans living there had been hostile long before the war. As one historian has described,

> bitterness and hatred toward Mexicans stimulated by the recent war in many ways intensified Anglo Americans' hostility toward "Mexican"—including those who, at least in theory, had become members of American society.[64]

These new citizens did not acquire the full protection of civil and property rights. Land seizures, economic and legal barriers, and overt discrimination from a growing Anglo settler majority, marked interracial relations in the Southwest, particularly in California and Texas.[65] The result of these encounters was both the affirmation and internalization of difference, and the forging of a distinctive Mexican-based identity. In describing the emergence of this distinctive identity of the disparate newly incorporated population, David Gutiérrez takes note of the irony involved:

> In technical, political terms, although Mexican Americans, by virtue of their new status as American citizens, were no longer Mexicans, American racism and Mexican Americans' de facto subordinate status in the new social order encouraged them to consider themselves Mexicans in a way they never had before.[66]

In time, as immigration from Mexico drove population growth of the Mexican-origin population in the region, this population would appear even more different from mainstream America.

The "alien" or "foreigner" construction continues to mark the Mexican-American population even 150 years after the annexation of Texas and the territorial expansion of the United States towards the Pacific. To cite just one recent and well-known example, in a 2004 *Foreign Policy* article that attracted much academic and media attention, Samuel P. Huntington advanced a view of Mexicans, and Hispanics more generally, as a threat within the United States. Huntington outlined the many ways in which Mexican, Mexican-American, and Hispanic/Latino culture (terms he often employed interchangeably) are too contrary to American culture to allow for Hispanics' complete assimilation. He also listed ways in which Mexican Americans, unlike their European counterparts, actively resist assimilating an American work ethic, standards of educational achievement, and norms of individualism.[67]

While Huntington did acknowledge that the territorial history of the American Southwest is unique for the Mexican immigrant, in his view this historical fact also poses an internal threat, laying the foundations for a claim to *reconquista* by both Mexicans and Mexican Americans:

> History shows that serious potential for conflict exists when people in one country begin referring to territory in a neighboring country in proprietary terms and to assert [*sic*] special rights and claims to that territory.[68]

Throughout the article, Huntington conflated the Mexican and Mexican American to suggest collusion on the part of both groups to make Spanish an official language of the United States, to loosen immigration control laws, and to move to reclaim the American Southwest on behalf of Mexico.

Response to Huntington's article was unprecedented according to the editors of *Foreign Policy,* and most scholarly researchers' responses to his article and follow-up book, *Who Are We?,* were overwhelmingly critical.[69] At the same time, Huntington's perception of the "alien" Mexican American, his view that the American immigrant experience is the Ellis Island/ East Coast immigrant experience, and his perception that Latin American immigration undermines a very narrowly conceived (Anglo-Saxon Protestant) "American culture" is neither new nor confined to his opinions. Ten years earlier, journalist Peter Brimelow's polemic, *Alien Nation,* advanced the same ideas to argue for a halt to liberal immigration policies.[70] The political and policy expressions of the threats detailed in such writings have taken the form of state and local-level English-only initiatives, ballot measures in California (1994) and Arizona (2004), efforts to bar unauthorized immigrants from accessing publicly funded educational and health benefits, and border policing campaigns like the "Minuteman Project," launched in 2005. However, while immigration alarmists such as Pat Buchanan and CNN's Lou Dobbs often focus on an external but penetrating threat of alien invasion, Huntington focused on the internal threat of a Latino population with a contempt for a narrowly construed American culture. A further distinctive feature was the stature of the author, an esteemed Harvard University professor, one-time president of the American Political Science Association, and former advisor to and member of the National Security Council. As one notable American historian and reviewer of *Who Are We?* remarked, "he is not just some loopy professor

. . . His conjectures, however bizarre and unfounded, unfortunately carry some weight."[71]

The population of Mexican origin is different from the European groups to which it is often compared in that its history and its migrations have been inextricably linked to the United States through battle, invasion, conquest, colonialism, citizenship, and U.S. policies that have encouraged—and in many cases facilitated—large-scale inflows of people. Yet often, as we will see, immigration from Latin America is not valued or venerated in the manner that now characterizes discourse about the European immigrant experience. Mexicans are not the "immigrants who built this country" or who fought and continue to die in U.S. wars. The fact of this population's presence in the United States for over a century and a half is forgotten, as is its role in the development of the nation. Currently, the word "Mexican" in the United States is pejorative; it automatically conjures a vision of something un-American, even menacing.

The Temporary Mexican

Large-scale labor migration from Mexico began only a few decades after war with the United States. From early on, agriculture and industry looked to Mexico to provide temporary labor solutions, and to the U.S. government to assist in acquiring it. U.S. mining and railroad industries faced labor shortages following the exclusion of Chinese in 1882 and all Asian laborers in 1917, and labor shortages would only increase with the quantitative restrictions placed on immigrants of Eastern and Southern European origin in 1924. Mexico, Puerto Rico, and the Philippines together provided a solution to these shortages. The Mexican laborer earned favor in the Southwest specifically because the proximity of his homeland ensured that he would return to Mexico. As one labor official put it at the time:

> In the event that [the Mexican] did create serious racial or social problems, he, unlike Puerto Ricans or Filipinos . . . could easily be deported. No safer or more economical unskilled labor force was imaginable.[72]

This ideal Mexican sojourner would provide the cornerstone for U.S. immigration policy towards Mexico during the first half of the twentieth century. Violence and social dislocation caused by the Mexican Revolution, as well as a long period of turmoil following efforts at federal consolidation in Mexico, would also lead to large-scale emigration from Mexico to the United States and create opportunities for U.S. industries seeking labor.[73] From 1917 through 1929, negotiations between the Mexican government and U.S. state governments encouraged labor migration with the expectation that workers would return to Mexico at the end of the harvest. From 1942 to 1954, the U.S. government federalized the temporary farm worker program with the Bracero program.[74] When the official termination of the program did not automatically result in full out-migration of Mexican laborers, the U.S. government charged the Immigration and Naturalization Service (INS) with deporting them. In 1954, Operation Wetback resulted in the INS rounding up and "repatriating" over one million Mexicans— including several hundred U.S. citizens of Mexican descent.[75]

Although the Bracero program ended, the concept of a "temporary Mexican" continues to retain its strength as a workable policy solution to the surplus of labor that Mexico produces and that the United States needs. However, the U.S. experience with the Bracero program and the guest-worker experience in Europe suggest that it is difficult to maintain truly temporary contract laborers so long as contracts are continually renewed and people settle and develop roots where they work even when their intent may be return.[76] Research on unauthorized immigrants in the United States has also shown that community ties and sense of settlement can develop even among this most marginalized immigrant population.[77] Such realities of course prove problematic for nations as they try to manage membership claims among large numbers of people who end up "temporary" for decades at a time, as has been the case in Europe.[78] Since the Bracero program, the United States has not engaged in large-scale guest-worker programs equivalent to those seen in Germany and Switzerland in the latter half of the twentieth century. However, temporary labor programs do exist, and, as later chapters will discuss, they were integral to immigration control policies in the 1980s and 1990s.[79]

Most notably, the notion of the "temporary Mexican" was the cornerstone of the 2004 Bush administration proposal for a large-scale Mexican guest-worker program. Many of the mechanisms proposed, including a 10 percent wage reduction to be paid contingent upon a worker's return to Mexico, recall the Bracero program.[80] Past and proposed federal policy has ascribed to Mexican immigrants the expectation of temporality. This expectation, along with inducements for Mexicans to return to Mexico after the extraction of their labor, sends a clear message: quite unlike European immigrants who came before and are viewed as the engine of industrial growth, the Mexican is simply a fleeting need and not a permanent feature of the United States' economic, political, or social structures.

The Limits of Official Status

The 1965 Immigration Act, which removed the old quota system and installed a multi-tiered preference system that prioritized family reunification, allowed for increased migration from Latin American and Asia and enlarged the resident Mexican immigrant population in the United States. While most illegal immigrants are from Mexico, most Mexican immigrants are not illegal. Unauthorized immigration from all nations accounts for approximately 28 percent of all immigration.[81] Until quite recently, most of the Mexican immigrants who came to the United States arrived legally.[82] Spoken of as an inclusive entity, the Mexican-origin population encompasses a full range of membership statuses: there are generations of U.S.-born citizens, naturalized citizens, legal resident aliens, temporary workers, and unauthorized immigrants. However, this complexity of statuses has become subsumed as the United States has grown consumed with the specter of illicit Mexican immigration.

The blending in the American mind of illegitimacy and criminality with Mexican immigration has its roots in institutional changes in the U.S. government's approach to managing its frontier with Mexico.[83] The establishment of the U.S. Border Patrol in 1924 created illegitimate immigration, or immigration without inspection at an official port of entry and, in so doing, also imbued pre-existing cyclical migrations between the United States and Mexico with unlawful activity.[84] In discussing how newly developed legal statuses, while themselves invisible, would function as a mark upon Mexicans, Jorge Bustamante explains the shift in the lexicon pertaining to Mexican immigration to the U.S., and the changing governmental approach to managing it:

> [T]he illegal immigrant's status was not visibly distinct from the legal immigrant's. The appearance of the Border Patrol in 1924 altered the primary deviance of the illegal entrant by crystallizing a new social reaction to the violation of immigration laws. The new police force was to reveal those primary deviants, violators of immigration laws. In this process, the term "wetback," previously purely descriptive, acquired a new meaning. It became the "label" or "stigma" by which the illegal immigrant was made visible.[85]

Bustamante draws our eyes to the nexus of criminality, power, and stigma, which has served to maintain these "wetbacks" as a subject category of people:

> As an outsider [the wetback] has no legitimacy since he is not eligible to stay in the country, unless he is in jail. He is also not eligible for other benefits because of the stigma of having broken the immigration laws.[86]

In Bustamante's analysis, legal statuses that are written neutrally to apply universally, can have selective effects—even to the extent that the word "illegal" now conjures "Mexicans" as automatically fitting this status.

Mae Ngai ventures deeper into the application of immigration law to elucidate the processes by which immigration law and its application led to the association of Mexicans with "illegals." For Ngai, a historian, the Mexican case presents a paradox. Southern and Eastern Europeans who entered the United States in violation of the 1921 and 1924 National Origins laws designed to restrict them managed to escape the label "illegal." By contrast not only were Mexicans omitted from the national origins caps, but also state and federal policies of the period largely facilitated Mexican labor migration to the United States during the quota period. That Mexicans became the group associated with illegal immigration, as Ngai thoroughly documents, is a result of selective deportation practices and interior policing efforts (which increased during the 1930s and 1940s and culminated with Operation Wetback in 1954) in which administrative application and adjudication relied on "racial presumptions about Mexican laborers, not law."[87]

The Border Patrol, whose original role was to pursue smugglers and their contraband, developed into the agency charged with immigrant pursuit and apprehension. The prevalence of this agency in managing labor in the Southwest further associated the Mexican migrants of the region with criminality—this despite the agency's official task of upholding civil (not criminal) administrative laws.[88] While the quota policy created excludable groups, the interpretation of the policy, and the mechanisms for its enforcement, created the category of "illegal." Those who administered this new immigration regime favored correction of status for European and Canadian illegal aliens and pursued individual and mass removal for Mexicans. The result of this uneven implementation of policy was that "Europeans and Canadians tended to be disassociated from the real and imagined category of illegal alien," which, in turn, facilitated their acceptance as white American citizens. By contrast, Mexicans "emerged as iconic illegal aliens," transformed during this historical period into a group racialized by their physical markers as members of the laboring class, their presumed illegal status, and their national origin—a group perceived as alien and excludable from the nation.[89]

U.S.-Mexico border scholarship augments these critical analyses of the juridical and legal categories that Mexicans have occupied by incorporating concepts of the border as a distinctive space. The border, now more than a geo-political boundary, looms large in contemporary immigration discourse, and its pathologies (real and imagined) follow the people associated with its transgression. Nestor P. Rodriguez has written that the border between the United States and Mexico appears to be immutable because people perceive it as a barrier between two distinct cultures and "social qualities."[90] This perception persists despite the longtime melding of people and cultures in this region, and the economic interdependency between the two nations now fostered through the North American Free Trade Agreement.[91] Oscar Martinez has also highlighted the historical association of the southern border as a region of lawlessness and refuge for criminals and banditry.[92] The border itself, with all of its connotations of chaos, crime, crisis, immorality, and militarism, figures in depictions of illegal immigrants and enhances the criminal characterization of people hailing from that region as being too morally and culturally distinct for consideration as assimilable immigrant stocks.

Considering how policy shapes the relationship between the United States and the Mexican-origin population means accounting for the ways in which an individual or group's official status functions as yet another marker of otherness. Michael Omi and Howard Winant have proposed that race and racial categories have provided the primary system of categorization to justify differential ascription of rights to groups, and achieve social control in the United States. They contend that management of the immigrant population within the United States has hinged upon the elite racialization of particular groups as either white or non-white.[93] Others focusing on the role of race in determining social order have noted that the privileges of political and social membership and the guaranteed protection of individual rights do not necessarily correspond to the technical legal status of foreigners.[94] In conjunction with race, legal status becomes particularly important to consider as an indicator of qualitative delineators; it is not simply an objective description of an immigrant group's mode of entry. According to Kitty Calavita's analysis of Spanish immigration law, "race, exclusion and economic function are of one piece. The law pays a central role in this alchemy" by writing different ethnic and racial groups into or out of the definition of "members" of the European community.[95] In this version of immigration law, legal categories produce hierarchies of access, and racial categories regularly subsumed by or collapsed under designations of "legal" and "illegal" serve as the primary marginalizing agents.

Paradoxically, as discussions of immigration policy have grown increasingly obsessed with the illegality of Mexican immigration and restoring the rule of law to the southern border, the discursive and policy lines between legal and illegal immigrants have blurred. For example, Proposition 187 in California called for doctors, teachers, and other public servants to deny education, housing, or healthcare to those *suspected* of being in the United States illegally. Likewise, at the federal level, policymakers often do not distinguish Mexican legal and illegal immigration, and, ultimately, the 1996 Illegal Immigration Reform and Immigrant Responsibility Act further clouded longstanding legislative distinctions between legal and illegal immigrants through measures intended to restrict public benefits to both groups.

Race and the Symbolic Politics of Entitlement

While 1965 may have eradicated the racist quota system and discredited the odious ideologies that kept it in place, modern immigration policies still symbolically communicate who fits a "good immigrant" and "potential citizen" ideal, and who does not. These categories also clearly coincide with specific immigrant nationalities. Politicians regularly judge immigrants against a model that stipulates labor, taxpaying, and *derivative* citizenship (or having citizen parents) as markers of group deservedness. This mark of approval translates into policies that offer direct benefits, or that grant protection and acknowledgement from the state. By contrast, the discourse about groups that do not meet this standard casts them as meriting punishment. The immigrants about whom legislators speak positively are often their own (European) ancestors, and attributes of family-orientation, labor, and self-sufficiency emerge as the markers of assimilation. By contrast, much of the discourse about modern immigration deals with issues of immigration from Latin America, specifically, Mexico. Legislators often and freely describe these immigrants as morally and substantively deficient, lacking the qualities that led to the success story of the European immigrants who came before them.

In her theory of racial triangulation, Claire Jean Kim conceptualizes a process of racialization in which groups are constructed (at both mass and elite levels) in reference to other racial groups. While Kim builds her theory from the shifting legal and political construction of Asian immigrants and Asian Americans, the process that she describes illuminates the position of Mexican immigrants and Mexican Americans when political leaders and other elites construct these groups through immigration debates. Kim envisions a multidimensional process in which groups are constructed in binary terms (insider/outsider, moral/immoral, inferior/superior) and then valued or devalued relative to other groups. This process of comparison occurring through elite political rhetoric is applicable in the Mexican and Mexican-American context. Racial triangulation captures how it is that the Mexican-origin population is constructed relative not only to whites, but also relative to Europeans, who in many cases have only recently come to occupy the position of "white." In critiquing the lack of assimilation and acculturation of the Mexican-origin population, public officials often do not make significant distinctions between citizens and immigrants; rather the Mexican-origin population is constructed collectively as less than American, as non-white, and as a population whose loyalty and standing as citizens is open to question.

This mark of difference is not merely descriptive. As later chapters will demonstrate, this difference constitutes a political disadvantage for supporters of policies that benefit immigrants or efforts to curb punitive measures that will largely affect Mexican immigrants. Legislators wishing to target immigrants for benefits face the task of both building support for policies around their technical merits and convincing their peers and the public that maligned immigrant groups merit policies that favor them.

Official Rhetoric and the Contest over Social Constructions

Policy change requires that supporters construct target groups in new ways, and they must develop stories that make untried or unpopular solutions appear both reasonable and legitimate. How these target group constructions and stories function in the political process—and exactly how these serve as political currency for elected officials—requires further clarification. Likewise, the design of the study put forth in this book and the methods employed to systematically analyze discursive aspects of policymaking require further attention.

Elite Uses of Symbolic Politics

Research on symbolic politics and scholarship on single-issue politics have offered some important touchstones for understanding the political utility of stirring emotional response to certain groups. Murray Edelman originally argued that "mass publics respond to currently conspicuous political symbols: not to 'facts,' and not to moral codes embedded in the character or soul, but to the gestures and speeches that make up the drama of the state." Accordingly, it is up to political actors to play upon the otherwise latent fears and emotions of the mass public, and depict issues as either "symbolically threatening or reassuring."[96] Edelman argued that through their depictions of social conditions, elites come to shape what the citizenry believes to be its "self-interest" even when the public may not have any interest at stake at all.

Specialized research on public opinion and single-issue politics has empirically developed Edelman's original contention that politics is about emotional appeal rather than about individual calculations based on experience or grasp of facts. Analyses of other redistributive social policy areas like busing, English-Only laws, and the state-level tax revolts of the 1970s and 1980s, provide compelling evidence that these single-issue campaigns provide a focal point for the mass public's anxieties about the people and the topics represented in, and by, these issues.[97] Of course, there is a debate within this field as to whether these issues gain popularity through grass-roots activism, as David Sears and Jack Citrin argue was the case for the tax revolt, or through elite manipulation of the issues, which is the larger argument Raymond Tatalovich draws from his study of the English-Only movement. However, research on public opinion on immigration both in the United States and Europe suggests that elite manipulation of the issue explains public obsession with it.[98] This interpretation finds support as well in the patterns of adoption of English-Only legislation —a closely related issue area. While four states with large Spanish-speaking populations (California, Colorado, Florida, and Arizona) have passed English-Only laws, ten Southern states without large non-English-speaking minority or immigrant populations have also passed such laws.[99]

The assertion that elites in government and the media amplify anxieties about immigration provides a compelling explanation for the periodic surfacing of anti-immigrant opinions in the public, as do the counterintuitive findings which contend that some of the public's anti-immigrant sentiment is not based on interaction with immigrants or direct job or housing competition with immigrants. Notably, post-election analyses of vote distributions on California's Proposition 187 found that support among the electorate was considerably higher in counties with few immigrant residents.[100] Researchers have shown that anti-immigrant sentiment at the national level has less to do with individuals' economic circumstances than it does with those individuals' perceptions about the state of the national economy as well as how individuals perceive immigrant groups.[101] To understand how it is that immigration problems and issues move from the realm of elite to public concern, and how it is that lawmakers generate consensus on single issues that cross partisan lines or that seem curiously salient for the public, requires a specific understanding of how immigration problems play out in the public sphere.

Social Constructions and Immigration Policy

Conceptually, "social constructions" are defined as "socially mandated perceptions" of groups implicated in policy, or "the cultural characterizations or popular images" of these groups, or "social representations" whose meanings are shared within a society.[102] As elements in the political process, social constructions may seem disembodied from political institutions and political actors.[103] Increasingly, though, scholarship that applies Schneider and Ingram's theory of policy design to areas such as entitlement policies, housing policy, and welfare policy have demonstrated that lawmakers employ existing group images or recast groups according to alternate images in justifying redistributive policies.[104]

Schneider and Ingram initially proposed that the selection of target groups is a value-laden process that incorporates the positive or negative perceptions of particular groups. According to them, even seemingly neutral target population designations such as "the elderly," "people on welfare," "college students," or "farmers," are permeable to the assumptions and predispositions that people have towards these groups.[105] "Immigrant" is a legal designation for foreigners with a green card, but "immigrant" also serves as a condensation symbol for economic uncertainty, high fertility rates, criminality, welfare usage, as well as values such as hard work, social mobility, and a national experience.

Social constructions of groups do not originate with political leaders. Like the rest of us, members of Congress are familiar with commonplace views about a group or an issue; they are literate in the nationalist credos that describe the United States as a "nation of immigrants" and a "melting pot." What distinguishes legislators in their uses of these images and stories, though, are their positions of authority. As popularly elected leaders, moreover, they can claim to represent a democratic consensus, or the will of the people, in pursuit of solutions to immigration problems. By selecting which issues to attend to, Congress communicates which issues matter most, and when the nation faces a crisis, elected officials may be the ones who provide the first official designation of that crisis.[106] When legislators deploy social constructions to identify problem groups and to rationalize how policy will deal with these groups, these characterizations are transformed from being commonplace stereotypes to having the status of official, even legitimate ways of discussing people and issues.

The social constructions of target populations perspective allows us to see U.S. immigration lawmaking as an exercise in assigning blame to some groups while absolving others from responsibility. This perspective is indispensable to studies of immigration policymaking as immigration is not always viewed as a problem, nor is it viewed as a problem for all relevant players. The past contract labor system and current temporary worker designations affirm that international labor migration is desirable so long as it is designated as temporary and narrowly relegated to specific industrial sectors. Legislators faced with drafting immigration control laws must function in an environment in which powerful groups like agriculture and the high-tech industries contend that labor migration is essential to their competitive functioning and survival. As a result, when legislators seek to restrict and control immigration, they must take care to employ a causal story that highlights the ills of immigration and obscures the fact that labor migration persists with the direct encouragement (or lax discouragement) of the federal government. The construction of these groups will involve strategic uses of symbols and imagery that the society (both elites and the mass publics) associates with these groups. How successful legislators are in their endeavor will depend on their ability to construct relevant groups as deserving of the benefits and punishments of a restrictive immigration policy.

Narrative Policy Analysis: Tracking and Categorizing
Social Constructions

Rhetoric is elemental to the conduct of politics, and the discursive activities of Congress are where political ideas and values are expressed, exchanged, and challenged. Floor debates provide lawmakers with a forum to discuss and contest the merits of policy for the public record. The *Congressional Record* represents the prepared public stances of members of Congress, and the institution is a venue in which discordant values compete for primacy. As discussed earlier, immigration policymaking has historically involved the definition of nation, people, and national interests, and the *Congressional Record* offers one window for observing the clashes and negotiations about the direction of the nation and its interests as defined through immigration policy. The data analyzed for this book represent what Murray Edelman referred to as hortatory language, a particular form of publicly oriented political language that legislators use in seeking support for their policy position.[107]

Congress conducts its floor debates with the public in mind—indeed, its members are mindful that they must explain their policy choices to the public. In addition to broadcasts on C-SPAN, newscasts often disseminate footage from debates on especially contentious legislation. Furthermore, the *Congressional Record* is the official historical record of the body's proceedings; while the roll call votes represent the final position of individual members on legislation, the debate record represents the clash of values, goals, and interests involved in the production of federal policies. This makes the *Record* invaluable in analyzing the use of social constructions in policymaking.

SYSTEMATIC DISCOURSE ANALYSIS

This study engages in narrative policy analysis. Emery Roe, who introduced narrative analysis to policy analysis, argued that understanding argumentative structures is integral to understanding policy outcomes for issue areas characterized by high levels of uncertainty and deep disagreement regarding the appropriate course of action.[108] Accordingly, policy "stories" or "narratives" emerge under such conditions precisely because they simplify complexities and provide the sense that a difficult problem is manageable. In essence, these stories provide a foundation of assumptions on which to build plausible (if not workable) solutions.

To avoid arbitrariness and de-contextualization of these remarks, this method requires that a researcher systematically identify the narratives and catalogue them by type. In this respect, the process resembles content analysis, except that the analyst is looking for recurring themes and patterns in the discursive representation of people rather than recurring words. The goal is to maintain a regularized, detached approach to the text, and yet retain meaning and context that often disappear when only content analytic methods are employed.

To begin this type of analysis as Roe prescribes in *Narrative Policy Analysis*, I began by disaggregating each speaker's statement into its component, or discrete, problem statements. Discrete problem statements assert a causal relationship or sets of causal relationships such as "immigrants come here because they are looking for work," or "immigrants come because employers hire them." This step was conducted without regard to whether contradictory testimony or another framing of a problem emerged later in the transcripts. Using Microsoft Excel, I constructed a database of discrete problem statements and their frequency of occurrence during the length of the hearing or debate.[109] The *Record* clearly distinguishes between statements made on the floor and comments that members later edited, posting the latter types of changes to the transcript in all capital letters. As my goal was to capture the iterative and interactive nature of policy narratives, I limited the transcript data to those statements made on the House or Senate floor, rather than those that were later edited or those that were written and submitted by absentee members.

These discrete statements were then grouped together into policy narratives that encompassed related problem statements. A policy narrative identifies a problem, states or implies a cause of the problem, and also (very importantly) provides a solution for this problem. An example will illustrate both what this means and why problem statements are noteworthy elements of the policy process. Consider a problem with multiple causes, like persistent unauthorized immigration. If someone believes that illegal immigration persists because employer sanctions are not enforced, the solution that follows would be different than it would be were someone to argue that illegal immigration persists because undocumented women can give birth to citizen children once on U.S. soil. The solution implied in the first formulation calls for further enforcement against employers; what follows from the second version is further enforcement against pregnant women in U.S. hospitals or a reconsideration of birthright citizenship for the children of unauthorized immigrants. The important aspect of both statements is that solutions to the problem flow logically from the cause-effect relationship that the narrative establishes. This logical flow is what gives the story its rationality and its credibility.[110] It can be addressed by a counter-narrative that not only challenges the original story but also provides a story of its own that is equally believable and straightforward. Such a counter-narrative is not the same as a critique: a critique simply raises an objection about a policy without offering an alternative solution. By contrast, a counter-narrative offers an alternative reading of the same issue as well as an alternative solution to the problem that is put forth in the policy narrative which it challenges.[111]

Insofar as the goal of this study is to position social constructions theory more firmly as a theory of policy change that draws its strengths from its attention to group image and political power, I have supplemented the narrative analysis methods with critical discourse analysis (CDA), a method designed to explore power dynamics as relayed through elite discourse. This method requires the identification of linguistic patterns and strategic uses of rhetoric. I have employed principles of text analysis developed by Tuen A. van Dijk and have used several of the typologies he developed from his extensive and comparative analyses on themes of racism and immigration in parliamentary debates in Europe and North America.[112] In his discussion and application of critical discourse analysis, the method proves to be useful in uncovering power biases reflected in elite discourse: these are the people who not only have access to public expression, but also control such access. Van Dijk focuses on language as a reflection of an individual's cognitive orientations, as well as a reflection of collectively held ideologies that enable the marginalization of minority groups.

Those who employ CDA tend to focus on rhetoric as maximizing the power of those in the position to produce official talk, and to emphasize the role of language in reconstituting and rationalizing elite power. However, approaching elite discourse from this vantage point alone can obscure our understanding of why some ideological expressions are marginalized while others enjoy broad appeal among various sectors of society. In the United States, there is no denying that immigration has positive and negative connotations; elite discourse on immigration necessarily reflects and amplifies these struggles, and public policy outcomes reflect an effort to manage this ambivalence. Moreover, the capture of immigration issues by a single interest is not absolute, and the use of CDA alone would not provide the means by which to observe linkages between rhetorical strategies and policy outcomes.

NARRATIVES AND SOCIAL CONSTRUCTIONS OF TARGET GROUPS

Policy narratives comprise a strategic rhetorical tool. A strong, believable narrative affects understanding of a problem and promotes the suitability of a particular solution. But a narrative's credibility also depends upon how well it taps into preconceived ideas about who is to blame for the problems or who is deserving of resources or punishments from government action. For this reason, the narratives become the vehicle for reproduction of social constructions, and, as official pronouncements validated in policy, the narratives amplify these constructions. Schneider and Ingram contend that policy tools are based on these constructions and that policies amplify social constructions by communicating which groups are worthy of benefits and which groups merit strict regulation or curtailment of rights.[113] Drawing on their views, I have mined and analyzed debates to show how the nation's elected leadership discusses immigrants as policy targets and evaluated the rhetorical treatment of these targets against the expectations of Schneider and Ingram's theory of target groups and social constructions. The study considered narratives in terms of how they framed problems, how they distributed blame among targeted populations, and how target group constructions served in defense of particular policy solutions.

Emery Roe had intended that his methods be applied to qualitative data drawn from interviews, and, in this respect, I am taking liberties with his method by applying it to political debate transcripts. In doing so, I am broadening the methodology to account for social constructions of target populations, which I view as inseparable from the qualities that give narratives and counter-narratives their command. I am also testing the effectiveness of the method by applying it to an intractable social policy issue. Roe's test case, the California medfly crop infestation, had a clear start and finish to it, although the causes and solutions to the problem were complex. Moreover, in Roe's test case, there was little disagreement on the fact that there was a problem; disagreement flourished about the extent of the crisis, and around potential solutions. Needless to say, immigration is quite different as a policy problem: the defined nature of the problem can change from one period to the next. For that reason, I focused on policies whose primary goal was the control and abatement of unauthorized immigration.

Aside from these differences, I have thoroughly engaged the process that Roe described precisely because the method provides a rigorous structure and systematic mode for approaching large amounts of text containing multiple interpretations of a policy area and its related policy problems. Moreover, Roe's method is in keeping with other approaches to political discourse analysis that regard argumentative structure as a means for exploring the expressive nature of political power.[114] In the case of policy narratives, the power lies with political actors who are best able to develop a full story that both minimizes complexity and offers reasonable solutions to simplified problems.

Overview of the Study

The next chapter covers the backgrounds of the Immigration Reform and Control Act and the Illegal Immigration Reform and Immigrant Responsibility Act, including the social and economic contexts in which these laws emerged and the types of problems Congress believed each new immigration reform bill should address. The chapter looks at the conditions that led to the planning and development of these policies, outlines which groups stood to gain or lose from each policy, and explores the relationship between policy tactics, or tools, and how elected officials portrayed problems and target groups in designing immigration restriction policies. The chapter considers contextual explanations for policy change, the role of task force research and recommendations during each period, and the distinctive problem definitions that arose at the time. The chapter also presents a comparative content analysis of problem statements made during each period to illustrate how definitions of the same problems changed from one policy period to the next.

Chapter 3 presents a narrative analysis of the 1986 Immigration Reform and Control Act. The chapter details how political elites played upon existing biases for or against the target groups involved (in this case, illegal immigrants, legal immigrants, American businesses generally, and agribusiness particularly) in justifying legislative design. The IRCA's employer sanctions regulated the hiring practices of U.S. businesses; opponents of sanctions relied on the liberal economic argument that justifies minimal regulation of business practices, while proponents of sanctions uniformly sought to depict employers as "bad guys" exploiting workers and flouting wage floors. In the case of legalization, opponents juxtaposed illegal immigrants with legal immigrants to highlight the criminality and injustice of illegal immigration. Supporters of legalization needed to de-emphasize the criminality of undocumented immigrants and create an alternative narrative that explained why this criminal population deserved legal recognition and protection. The narrative analysis presented in this chapter demonstrates that the social constructions of target groups are not fixed, but negotiable, and that legislators employ this flexibility to their advantage in promoting policy choices and generating policy consensus.

Chapter 4 presents the narrative analysis of debates over the 1996 Illegal Immigration Reform and Immigrant Responsibility Act. The IIRAIRA was designed to crack down on a category of people who are criminals by statutory definition (illegal aliens). However, the law also penalized *legal* immigrants, thereby lending legislative credence to the idea that all immigrants were damaging the nation. But legal status was not the only set of qualities believed to separate the right kind of immigrants from the wrong kind. As my research on the 1996 IIRAIRA reveals, the distribution of penalties and resources to immigrants rested upon the persistent measurement of immigrants against an ideal that spoke to their potential to make good Americans. The chapter provides a fascinating contrast to the IRCA debates. Justification for punitive and coercive policy measures that typify immigration reform in 1996 lay in the repetition and promotion of negative immigration rhetoric. While their illegal status facilitated the portrayal of undocumented aliens as undeserving of access to the welfare state, legal status *did not* guarantee which immigrants could make claims on their host nation. Rather, the policy debates portrayed all immigration as being out of control and all immigrants as draining resources.

Chapter 5 and the conclusion to the book build on the findings in the narrative analyses in previous chapters by exploring the symbolic language of race and gender in immigration debates. Chapter 5 considers the relationship between social constructions and how the boundaries delineating who may be considered a potential citizen changed between 1981 and 1996. The concluding chapter presents American citizenship as an identity that lies at the nexus of different axes of in-group and out-group construction; the images of immigrants that emerge from these divisions are then examined in terms of their symbolic potency in the policy process. Both chapters consider the impact of legislative manipulation of immigrant constructions—specifically constructions of Mexican immigration —on how nation, membership, and constituencies continue to be defined in the American context.

2

Cases, Contexts, and the
Puzzle of Policy Change

> In addition to reducing the "pull" of U.S. employment, we should
> try to change the conditions abroad which "push" people toward
> our borders. That would be accomplished by assisting people to
> improve the quality of life in their own country. . . . It is no co-
> incidence that America has been a symbol of both freedom and
> prosperity. This is a theme which should be fully developed and
> communicated to the world in a much more effective way than we
> have been able to date.
>
> —Senator Alan Simpson (R-WY), Opening Statement to
> Joint Hearings, Final Report of the Commission on
> Immigration and Refugee Policy, May 5, 1981

> This sends a signal to the world: Don't come here illegally and
> think the American taxpayer will take care of you.
>
> —House Speaker Newt Gingrich (R-GA),
> *New York Times,* September 26, 1996

As the statements above demonstrate, legislators are quite
aware that they are not simply writing laws, but communicating values to
a broader audience. The quotations reveal two very different definitions
of the illegal immigration issue. Senator Simpson, who was an original
force driving the bill that would become the 1986 Immigration Reform
and Control Act (IRCA), defines illegal immigration as a dynamic process
involving both domestic forces (employers) and international problems
(poor economic policies and conditions abroad). Solutions to illegal immigration, according to Simpson, would need to address conditions in the
United States and abroad. A decade later, House Speaker Newt Gingrich,

who presided over the debates concerning the Illegal Immigration Reform and Immigrant Responsibility Act (IIRAIRA), would frame the need for immigration reform quite differently: illegal immigrants are attracted to the United States by the prospect of living off public programs. The implication is that the solution to illegal immigration lies in restricting access to those programs.

What happened to produce such different understandings? As this chapter will discuss, these different problem definitions are the result of an ideological shift that would produce different policies to deal with the same problem. This ideological change does not correspond to partisan divisions, nor does it relate to new discoveries about the phenomenon of illegal immigration. The ideological shift represents a change in the way members of Congress allocated blame among groups implicated in the illegal immigration problem. While the tales of blame that emerged during each period would dictate acceptable solutions, the images and themes that imbue these causal stories with plausibility have roots that run more deeply than the policies under examination.

Changing Contexts of Immigration Reform

A brief exploration of the unemployment conditions preceding each case of immigration reform provides a window into the economic contexts of the immigration reform policies of the 1980s and 1990s. Figure 2.1 shows a chronology of key events in immigration reform in relation to the national unemployment rate from 1970 to 2000 as reported by the U.S. Department of Labor. The points on the graph represent the average for the year based on the monthly figures from the Department of Labor's Bureau of Labor Statistics. While unemployment rates alone are insufficient to fully capture economic downturn and recession, these rates do capture the facet of poor economic performance most apt to generate economic insecurity among the broader public. Even when people do not face direct competition with immigrants for work, conditions that produce economic insecurity have been widely credited with the politicization of immigration, and the treatment of immigrants as sources of competition and wage depression.

In reviewing Figure 2.1, we see that the introduction of immigration reform in the 1980s coincides with peak unemployment. In the case of the IIRAIRA, the situation is a bit more complex. While it appears from

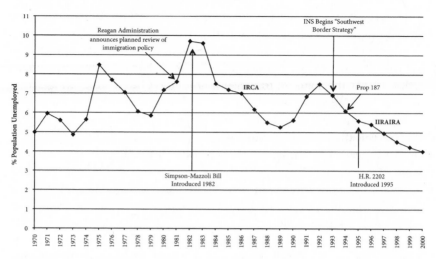

Fig. 2.1. U.S. unemployment rates, 1970–2000. (U.S. Bureau of Labor Statistics)

a glance at Figure 2.1 that unemployment levels were falling at the time that the Clinton administration began a large-scale policy of border deterrence, and had fallen further at the introduction of H.R. 2202 (the bill that would become the IIRAIRA), the roots of the IIRAIRA actually appeared earlier in the 1990s, when the economy was in worse shape and unemployment levels were higher. According to this graph, the final bills appeared after economic crises had diminished. However, this lag between high points in unemployment rates and the appearance of immigration reform laws represents the slow pace of congressional lawmaking; responses to social crises take time to move through the process from introduction to federal law. The graph also shows that major developments that led to the final laws occurred in conjunction with high unemployment rates: the introduction of the Simpson-Mazzoli Bill (which became IRCA) in 1982, the start of the Immigration and Naturalization Service's (INS's) Southwest Border Initiative in 1993. An important caveat to Figure 2.1 is that it provides national data. It does not show, for example, that California remained in recession long after the rest of the nation. Illegal immigration control efforts such as Proposition 187 and Operation Gatekeeper applied only to California, but received national attention. The governor of California, Pete Wilson, made highly publicized overtures to Washington in which he demanded federal money to alleviate the costs of illegal immigration, and Operation Gatekeeper represented the INS response to the California segment of the southern border. As we will see, the tone of the immigration debate and the logic that bolstered supporters of Proposition 187 and Gatekeeper would color federal reform efforts.

Given the familiar historical pattern of economic recession breeding immigration reform, the fact that Congress undertook the immigration issue during these periods is not surprising. Both Congresses pursued immigration reform in the midst of strong public sentiment against immigration. However, what is interesting is that IRCA and IIRAIRA represent two distinct approaches to the same problem of "too much immigration." Literature on policy change expects external forces such as the economic climate or public opinion to force policy change. A shift in party control and leadership can change not only the institution's agenda, but also the types of solutions sought and considered by policymakers.[1] The IRCA was the product of a Congress under the control of Democrats, while the IIRAIRA emerged from a Republican Congress. However, a shift in party control, even differences in partisan ideologies, cannot fully account for a basic difference in how legislators understood the causes of and the appropriate solutions to the immigration problem. Even though partisan change can contribute to a shift in the congressional agenda, a change in how a problem is defined and which solutions are believed to be most effective requires a more fundamental shift in how policymakers understand the sources and solutions to the problem.[2] Thus, an analysis of the bipartisan task force reports that Congress requested for the purposes of informing each reform effort provides an alternative perspective on the causal stories that the legislative body would produce.

Framing the Immigration Problem: The Select Commission on Immigration and Refugee Policy

The Select Commission on Immigration and Refugee Policy (SCIRP) was created in 1978 under the directorship of the president of the University of Notre Dame, Father Theodore M. Hesburgh. The Select Commission held twelve hearings on topics related to immigration and secured the testimony of over 700 witnesses on the topic of immigration reform. The SCIRP submitted its final report, *U.S. Immigration Policy and the National Interest*, to Congress in 1981.

According to the Select Commission, the United States was at least as much to blame for its illegal immigration problem as anyone else: lack of visa enforcement and of labor standards enforcement, as well as an absence of uniform hiring regulations at the national level all allowed employers free reign and thereby facilitated illegal immigration. Additionally, the SCRIP saw immigration as an international problem with roots in both the United States and sending nations; the economic disparities between them and social dislocation in sending nations produced contexts ripe for mass migrations, and any attempt to resolve the problems of illegal immigration would require an international approach. In response to this multi-dimensional problem, the Select Commission recommended two new methods for addressing domestic practices in the United States that resulted in the illegal immigration problem. The first was the legalization of undocumented people who met a certain set of eligibility requirements. The rationale for legalization rested in part in humanitarian concerns for a population living in the society without the protection of law enjoyed by citizens and legal aliens. The Select Commission also reasoned that U.S. employers had long benefited from undocumented workers that they were able to recruit and hire under protection of existing laws.[3] Sanctions would remove this legal protection for employers and would establish guidelines for punishing employers who knowingly hired unauthorized workers.

The Select Commission advised keeping the annual ceiling of 350,000 immigrant visas, plus allowing additional visas to clear backlogs. Rather than target legal immigration for restriction, the report recommended that efforts to limit immigration should focus on controlling illegal immigration. According to the report, this focus represented an acknowledgment of "the widespread dissatisfaction among U.S. citizens with an immigration policy that seems to be out of control."[4] Thus, the Select Commission's report framed the illegal immigration problem in two important ways. First, it located the cause of the problem within the United States —namely, in the hiring practices of U.S. businesses. It is one thing to say that illegal immigration happens because immigrants are looking for work, but it is quite another to say that illegal immigration occurs because they can easily find jobs in the United States and because U.S. employers face no barriers in hiring them. The difference is more than semantic: in the former case, immigrants are the actors motivated by jobs; in the latter, employers are the actors motivated by the benefits of hiring an illicit workforce and the absence of constraints to hiring illegal immigrants as employees. Such a shift in causal logic demands a shift in tactics to deal with a problem, and efforts to regulate hiring practices would require the promotion and acceptance of the view that business had a part in creating and maintaining illegal immigration.

Secondly, the report added an ethical dimension to the issue of illegal immigration by highlighting the potential for human rights abuses should the U.S. government continue to ignore this unprotected population living within its borders. While the focus on undocumented labor had often emphasized the deleterious effects of this population on wages, on national sovereignty, and on U.S. minority groups who competed with it for housing and jobs, the SCIRP report offered an alternative vision of a population living and working in U.S. territory, unprotected by labor laws, vulnerable to abuse, and taken for granted.

The 1986 Immigration Reform and Control Act

Late in 1980, the incoming Reagan administration and the newly elected Congress announced that immigration reform would be a priority, and proposed controlling illegal immigration using the dual approach that the SCIRP had recommended. One news article characterized the urgency of the problem that faced the Reagan administration and Congress in the following manner:

> . . . there are growing indications, in public opinion polls and in angry letters from constituents, that many Americans, convinced that immigrants are taking their jobs, draining the treasury and dividing cities into isolated and increasingly hostile ethnic communities, are demanding a solution.[5]

The article cited polls by the Roper Organization showing that "nine of 10 of those surveyed supported an 'all-out effort' to halt illegal immigration," and that slightly fewer (eight of ten) favored a reduction in legal immigration. The article detailed the dual sanctions and legalization approach, and cited evidence that the public had a mixed reaction to the policy as described in an earlier Gallup poll. In this poll, 76 percent of Americans agreed that hiring illegal aliens should be against the law, but only 37 percent of Americans favored a legalization program.[6]

The proposed immigration reforms were no less controversial among legislators, and the IRCA would face a tortuous route to passage. Co-sponsors Senator Alan Simpson (R-WY) and Representative Romano Mazzoli (D-KY) introduced the bill to Congress in 1982. In the four years following its introduction, the bill endured lengthy and heated debate and the consideration of numerous amendments. The bill included four components: employer sanctions, legalization, border enforcement, and foreign aid, which combined to create a multi-pronged campaign against continued illegal immigration. The first part, employer sanctions, would be a national expansion of efforts already underway in twelve states, including California. Program evaluators described state-level sanctions programs as fruitless and warned that to be effective at the national level, employer sanctions would require a greater commitment to enforcement than the state programs received.[7] Witnesses called to testify before the Senate Subcommittee on Immigration and Refugee Policy cited low threat of enforcement and minimal fines (in some cases, only $100), as well as legal loopholes (such as the Texas proviso, which exempted the hiring of an unauthorized worker from the otherwise illegal activities of "harboring" or "transporting" them), with the failure of the state-level initiatives to dampen employers' preference for illegal immigrants.[8]

As a tool meant to accomplish immigration control, employer sanctions faced opposition from Republicans concerned that sanctions would introduce onerous regulations. Most notable among those opposed were members representing grower interests who suddenly faced scrutiny for their role in luring and hiring undocumented workers. Sanctions also proved problematic for Democrats representing racial and ethnic minority interests and members representing civil libertarians. Hispanic-based interest groups opposed sanctions because "foreign-sounding" or "foreign-looking" persons would face discrimination and additional scrutiny under new hiring rules.

Bitter battles in Congress also emerged in response to the legalization component of the bill, as opponents protested a law that would reward those who had purposely circumvented legal avenues to immigration to the United States. The bill died once when time ran out at the end of 1982, and there were still 300 amendments pending. The Simpson-Mazzoli bill was introduced again in 1983; it passed through the Senate in May, but was eventually blocked from further consideration in the House in October. The bill re-emerged once more for full consideration after the presidential election of 1984. Both employer sanctions and legalization remained contentious measures upon which to build comprehensive reform.

When Congress finally passed the 1986 Immigration Reform and Control Act on October 17, 1986, the law's provisions for employer sanctions introduced a new approach to the problem of illegal immigration. As a regulatory policy tool, sanctions focused attention on the role employers play as pull forces in the international labor market. As Representative Romano Mazzoli (D-KY) explained while introducing the final conference report to the House, "Quite simply, until the magnet that draws people here—jobs—is removed, we will never be able to effectively control our borders."[9] Until IRCA, American businesses had been exempted from punishment for having undocumented employees. The Texas Proviso, which had been added to the 1952 McCarran-Walter Act as an appeal to agricultural interests, made employment a legal exception to the otherwise illicit acts of harboring or transporting undocumented immigrants. Thus, IRCA represented a significant change from more than a century of immigration policymaking which either did not mention employment as a draw for immigration or that explicitly protected employers' access to undocumented laborers.

The IRCA's legalization component was also groundbreaking in terms of U.S. approaches to illegal immigration. Legalization was supposed to work in tandem with sanctions to control illegal immigration. The legalization program essentially recognized that a population of undocumented people was residing and working within U.S. territory, and gave those people who could prove continuous residence in the United States since 1981 the opportunity to correct their status. In his introduction, Representative Romano Mazzoli presented the legalization program to his fellow legislators as a way to save a shadow population from exploitation at the hands of employers:

> I submit that having within our borders millions of people living under this dark cloud of constant fear is not in the best interests of the United States. Once it is known that an individual is incapable of asserting his rights, there will always be those who are all too ready to exploit their advantage over that individual. In short, we are talking about made-to-order victims, and until these individuals are either removed from the United States or legalized, this utterly unacceptable situation will continue to exist.[10]

Legalization would endow its recipients with the right to work and live in the United States (and, eventually apply for citizenship), as well as covering them with labor protections such as wage floors. Legalization would remove the incentive for employers to hire illicitly as a way to dodge existing labor and workplace regulations.

An overview of policy provisions and agency responsibilities appears in the following table. It outlines the major components and requirements of IRCA. While IRCA's dual sanction and legalization provisions made this policy a unique approach to controlling illegal immigration to the United States, other aspects of the act look familiar—namely, the components of IRCA designed for the benefit of U.S. agriculture. Agriculturists feared that legalization and documentation of worker eligibility would decimate its labor pool. The IRCA streamlined the existing H2 visa program, which provided agriculture with temporary workers during peak seasons, and provided legalization for seasonal agricultural laborers. The new program, H-2A, facilitated access to foreign labor by streamlining the request process and setting narrower time periods for the Department of Labor to determine the validity of employers' requests. The agricultural labor provisions represent a compromise—originally, members of Congress from western growing states like California and Washington pushed for the passage of the Wilson amendment that would have allowed 350,000 temporary foreign workers into the United States annually.

TABLE 2.1

Major Provisions of the 1986 Immigration Reform and Control Act (IRCA)

I. Control of Illegal Immigration—Employment

- Employer Sanctions
  1. Establishes civil and criminal penalties for the knowing employment/recruitment of illegal aliens; civil penalties for 1st and subsequent offenses; criminal penalties for pattern/practice violations.
  2. Required 6-month period of public education of employers.
  3. Determined that only citations shall be issued in the 12 months following the 6-month education period.
  4. Mandated GAO investigation and triennial reporting to Congress on sanctions enforcement.

- Establishment of Worker Eligibility Requirements
  1. Established that employers must document that employee's work status has been verified by examination of a passport, birth certificate, Social Security card, or alien documentation papers which attest that s/he is a U.S. citizen or national or and authorized alien.
  2. Established that employers may not discriminate against individuals in hiring, but that hiring a citizen over an equally qualified alien is not a violation of the anti-discrimination clause.

II. Control of Illegal Immigration—Enforcement

- Improvement of Enforcement and Services
  1. Authorized increased FY 1987 and 1988 appropriations for the INS and Border Patrol.
  2. Authorized more funding for improved immigration and naturalization services and for enhanced community outreach and in-service personnel training.
  3. Authorized a $35,000,000 immigration emergency fund for state and local reimbursements.
  4. Extended Fourth Amendment to cover farms and fields.

TABLE 2.1 (*continued*)

III. Legalization

- Adjustment of Status

1. Allowed attorney general to adjust to temporary resident status those aliens who a) apply within 18 months; b) establish that they entered the U.S. before January 1, 1982 and have resided in the U.S. continuously in an unlawful status, and c) are otherwise inadmissible.
2. Prohibited legalization of anyone convicted of a felony or 3 or more misdemeanors, as well as anyone who has taken part in political, religious, or racial persecution.
3. Allowed attorney general to adjust status of temporary resident aliens to permanent resident if the alien a) applies during the one year period beginning with the 19th month following the grant of temporary resident status; b) has established continuous residence in the U.S. since the grant of temporary resident status; c) is otherwise admissible and has not been convicted of a felony; d) either meets the minimum requirements for an understanding of English and a knowledge of American history and government, or demonstrates the satisfactory pursuit of a course of study in these subjects (exception for those aged 65+).
4. Made legalized aliens (other than Cuban/Haitian entrants) ineligible for federal financial assistance, Medicaid, or Food Stamps.

IV. Reform of Legal Immigration

- Temporary Agricultural Workers

1. Reformed H2 visa program for agricultural workers: shortened application period to 60 days prior to need, assured timely approvals by the Department of Labor, and established that employers must provide or secure housing for H2A laborers. Number of workers is exempted from numerical caps.
2. Provided for Special Agricultural Worker program which allows for the adjustment to permanent resident status for aliens who a) apply during a specified 18-month period; b) have performed at least 90 man-days of seasonal agricultural work during the 12-month period ending May 1, 1986; and c) are admissible as immigrants.

- Other Reforms

1. Established Commission for the Study of International Migration and Cooperative Economic Development to study the conditions that contribute to unauthorized migration to the U.S. and to consider trade and investment programs to alleviate such conditions in Mexico and other sending countries.
2. Expedited deportation of aliens convicted of crimes.

Source: 99th Cong., 2nd sess., *Statutes at Large*, P.L. 99-603.

Another aspect of IRCA that represents an effort to appease representatives from farming districts was the extension of Fourth Amendment search-and-seizure protections to fields. Historically, law enforcement did not need a warrant to search fields, since these did not represent physically enclosed areas, and the waiver of warrants in field raids was supposed to facilitate investigations of drug-growing operations, as well as INS round-ups of illicit workers conducted in open-air situations. With the passage of IRCA, the INS (as well as other law enforcement agencies) would need to secure and present warrants before raids; essentially, open fields, for legal purposes, were to be treated like a home or office building.

Finally, the Immigration Reform and Control Act provided additional resources for the INS and Border Patrol, increasing its operating budget by 50 percent. In addition to funding and equipping the INS and Border Patrol in its continued efforts at apprehending illegal aliens along the nation's southern border, the INS would be the agency charged with implementing both sanctions and the legalization program. These responsibilities justified the increases in manpower and funding for the agency. However, even though the authorization of $850 million represented a 70 percent increase in the agency's operating budget, most of the money would go to the Border Patrol and legalization, and not to sanctions. This was purposeful: employer sanctions were not designed to be a major policing effort; rather, the expectation was that employers would regulate themselves and only repeat offenders would face serious fines.

As a result, and by all accounts, employer sanctions failed. Most INS resources were not channeled into sanctions implementation. According to one implementation study's calculations, in New York, the INS District Office had 27 staff members assigned to monitor 500,000 businesses, while in Los Angeles County, a ratio of 2 INS staffers per 10,000 businesses characterized the low-level priority of enforcement.[11] As Kitty Calavita notes, one of the basic contradictions of employer sanctions is that they try to curb the flow of immigrants to industries that have a history and habit of hiring outside of the legal labor force. Calavita suggests that the failure of IRCA's employer sanctions lies in the way the law produced a low-risk crime, whose penalties were unable to deter the illicit hiring practices of sectors relying on low-wage labor.[12] Other evaluators have also noted that employers did not see much risk in non-compliance.[13] Because sanctions were poorly enforced, they hardly deterred employers from seeking undocumented workers; moreover, since the law simply required that employers ask for documentation, not verify its authenticity, fake documents and the use of labor contractors who assumed responsibility for worker eligibility enabled old practices to flourish despite new regulations.[14]

By contrast, the legalization program did serve its goal of allowing for long-term residents to regularize their status, though its other goal, the further reduction of illegal immigration, was not achieved. Nearly 3 million illegal immigrants pursued legalization, and accounts of the process cited improvements in day-to-day living for those who did. Those who pursued regularization enjoyed greater geographic and employment mobility, and could apply for credit and bank accounts.[15] While legislators opposing legalization argued that the possibility of legalization would lure others to come illegally, researchers in this field attribute the continuance and growth of illegal immigration post-IRCA to an array of factors related to IRCA's implementation, as well as economic conditions in Mexico at the time.[16] To some extent, legalization did provide the opportunity for newly documented immigrants to gain a toehold in U.S. society, thus strengthening networks for migration of family members (legally and illegally) from Mexico. IRCA's border enforcement efforts contributed as well, by making return migration to Mexico and Latin America more difficult.[17] Related to this reality was the fact that many illegal immigrants were not eligible for legalization even when the INS reduced eligibility requirements. The INS policy was that it would not deport ineligible family members of clients applying for legalization.[18]

The 1996 Illegal Immigration Reform and Immigrant Responsibility Act

A decade after the failure of either sanctions or legalization to end unauthorized immigration to the United States, the topic of illegal immigration returned to the congressional agenda. This time, the Republican Party had recently taken control of the Congress, while Bill Clinton, a Democrat, held the White House. The November 1994 midterm election was touted as a "Republican Revolution" which ended decades of Democratic control. The partisan breakdown in the House was 230 Republicans, 204 Democrats, and 1 minor party representative. In the Senate, the much closer vote breakdown was 52 Republicans to 48 Democrats.

In 1990, Congress passed an immigration act that adjusted the preference system for admitting legal immigrants in family-sponsored, employment-based, and refugee admissions. The 1990 act also established the Diversity Program, the intent of which was to offer visas to immigrants from countries that were underrepresented in the U.S. immigrant population. The increases in legal admissions caps were not implemented until fiscal year 1992, and therefore their effects on immigration levels had not yet revealed themselves before the introduction of a new bill in early 1995.

Furthermore, while we generally see immigration reforms undertaken in response to economic recession and public backlash, by the time Representative Lamar Smith introduced H.R. 2202 (the bill that would become the IIRAIRA) to Congress on August 4, 1995, the nation was solidly on its way to economic recovery following the recession of the early 1990s (see Figure 2.1).

The 1990 Immigration Act had mandated the formation of a bipartisan commission, which was scheduled to provide evaluative reports on the 1990 act in 1994 and 1997. The 1994 report of the Commission on Immigration Reform, *U.S. Immigration Policy: Restoring Credibility*, made recommendations to Congress to increase border deterrence, sanctions enforcement, and deportation order enforcement, and to improve interagency cooperation in immigration efforts. However, the report's executive summary also advised against a policy of benefits restrictions for illegal immigrants and suggested instead that the federal government define immigrant eligibility for benefits more clearly and that it enforce existing public charge provisions prior to admission. H.R. 2202 seemingly ignored the commission's advice regarding legal immigrants; a chief component of the new bill would limit immigrant access to public benefits.

Other agency reports were available to Congress prior to its embarking on immigration reform that in retrospect challenged the utility of some of IIRAIRA's most fundamental provisions. For instance, in July of 1995, the General Accounting Office released a report at the request of Senator Alfonse D'Amato and Representative Lamar Smith as well as others. The report surveyed all of the empirical studies of the fiscal costs of illegal aliens written between 1984 and 1994, and included an extensive evaluation of three studies attempting to estimate the "national net cost" of illegal immigration to public funds. According to the GAO report, the findings of studies existing at the time "varied considerably, ranging from $2 billion to $19 billion," leaving the GAO to pronounce "a great deal of uncertainty remains about the actual national fiscal impact of illegal aliens."[19] According to the report, the greatest discrepancy occurred in how researchers calculated Social Security costs and rates of usage in their estimates.[20] The GAO concluded that better data and more conclusive studies were needed before estimates of national net costs of illegal immigration would be of use to lawmakers. Despite these discrepancies in efforts to calculate fiscal costs, supporters of H.R. 2202 pushed ahead with benefits restriction as though the fiscal drain argument was a proven fact. Clearly, since the

IIRAIRA quite simply did not follow the recommendations of the Commission on Immigration Reform, it is important to consider what other events drove the 104th Congress to draft a law that emphasized border enforcement over sanctions enforcement and viewed benefits restriction for all immigrants as a practicable policy approach.

The passage of the IIRAIRA occurred shortly after the passage of a landmark welfare reform law in August of 1996, the Personal Responsibility and Work Opportunity Reconciliation Act (PREWORA). The latter's emphasis on "personal responsibility" carried over into the continued quest for immigration control, as was evident in the full title of the Illegal Immigration Reform and Immigrant Responsibility Act. In early 1995 Speaker of the House Newt Gingrich and Representative Lamar Smith (R-TX) announced that the new Congress would undertake major immigration reforms that would include benefits restriction and border enforcement. H.R. 2202 would restrict benefits access to legal immigrants, limiting Supplemental Security Income (SSI) payments and housing assistance. It called for a renewed emphasis on a century-old immigration law which restricted immigrants "likely to become a public charge" by requiring that families sponsoring immigrants show proof that they could support them at 125 percent of the national poverty level.[21] While the failure of the 1986 IRCA to curb illegal immigration and the persistence of undocumented migration and residence in the United States provides some rationale for the legislative return to immigration reform, explaining why Congress would pick this particular juncture in the 1990s to embark on massive legal and illegal immigration reforms is much more complex.

CALIFORNIA AND THE "CONTRACT WITH AMERICA": FRAMING IMMIGRATION FOR THE NATIONAL AGENDA, 1990–1996

The renewed interest in immigration and a new concern over fiscal costs of immigration were propelled to the national agenda by events at the state level, as well as by maneuvering on the part of a resurgent Republican Party that cultivated immigration as a wedge issue. The tactics of border deterrence and limiting welfare as a way to deter immigration originally emerged as policy topics in the state of California during the early 1990s. The U.S.-Mexico border had witnessed rising levels of military presence over the 1980s as the federal government's War on Drugs focused efforts on the southern border as an entry point for illicit drugs as well as illegal immigration.[22] However, in California, the southern border increasingly became a focus for local activists concerned with illegal immigration. One example of grassroots activism occurred in 1990, when hundreds of demonstrators from San Diego County began the "Light Up the Border" campaign. Participants parked their cars along the U.S. side and flashed their headlights south in an effort to deter crossings and criminal activities that the activists associated with illegal immigrants such as drug smuggling, assault, and robbery.[23] Some participants claimed they simply wished to bring the problems of illegal immigration to the attention of the federal government.[24] The Border Patrol eventually responded to the campaign by installing lights and rebuilding fences along the Tijuana River in 1990.

The INS response to anti-immigrant protests in San Diego County foreshadowed the deterrence approach that would characterize immigration control efforts in the 1990s. In 1993 and 1994, the INS instituted pilot programs in El Paso, Texas (Operation Hold-the-Line), and Imperial Beach, California (Operation Gatekeeper), which used a combination of agents, stadium lighting, fortified or re-built fencing, and tracking technology both to increase apprehensions of unauthorized border crossers and to deter others from crossing. The INS continued to expand these efforts and installed new patrolling initiatives—efforts known comprehensively as the Southwest border strategy. By the end of the decade, INS efforts to choke off major border-crossing routes had expanded to Nogales, Arizona, Eastern San Diego County, and Brownsville, Texas, and similar initiatives would persist into the early 2000s.

The focus on the southern border was not the only way in which immigration politics in California directed federal attention to the issue of illegal immigrants. While the rest of the country was climbing out of recession and unemployment levels were dropping, California actually remained in an economic slump. In 1993, three initiatives restricting illegal immigrant access to state resources vied for inclusion on California's upcoming general election ballot. This push to define the immigration problem as a problem of fiscal costs—which identified an undeserving class of people as the locus of misplaced government spending—took hold among voters. Ultimately, Proposition 187, the most restrictive of the three initiatives, made it to the November 1994 general election ballot. Supporters of 187 viewed medical care, education, Aid to Families with Dependent Children (AFDC) and other supplemental income, and housing and citizenship for children of immigrants born on U.S. soil as magnets for illegal immigration. Moreover, California voters sensed that any illegal immigrants availing themselves of public benefits were doing so at a ballooning cost to citizen taxpayers. Surveys conducted prior to the 1994 election by the California Field Institute, a state-wide polling agency, showed that Californians perceived the initiative as an answer to the negative fiscal impact of illegal immigration. For example, when asked how likely it was that 187 would save the state of California millions of dollars spent on illegal immigrants, most respondents (57 percent) felt that the initiative would be very or somewhat likely to save state money. Similarly, when asked if Proposition 187 would free money used to educate the children of illegal immigrants and make it available for educating citizens and legal residents, most respondents (54.7 percent) felt that this was a likely outcome. At the same time, most supporters also felt that the significance of 187 was the message it would send to the federal government about the crisis in illegal immigration.[25] Thus, Proposition 187 not only turned an otherwise dull governor's race into a referendum on illegal immigration as Republican Pete Wilson's flagging candidacy received a boost from his decision to support 187, while Kathleen Brown, his Democratic challenger, opposed it. The passage of Proposition 187, as well as Wilson's re-election, also reverberated beyond California. Republicans had taken careful note of the currency of the illegal immigration issue in the electorally significant state of California and moved to make immigration an issue in the 1996 presidential election by pushing for immigration reform in Congress.[26]

Nineteen ninety-four was also politically significant in that congressional elections brought on the Republican takeover of both chambers. House Speaker Newt Gingrich (R-GA) and other party leaders construed their majority as indicating public support for the Republican agenda as set forth in the "Contract with America."[27] The contract not only outlined the Republican agenda, but also set out the party's staunch ideological stance against public expenditures that it believed had produced a bloated, wasteful welfare state. Welfare reform, a chief policy priority, allowed the new Congress to identify a swath of the population as undeserving of government assistance, and a fair target on the road to trimming the federal budget. The financial responsibility requirements for sponsors of legal immigrants and the capping of social services reflected a broader philosophy that identified public-sector spending on the undeserving poor as problematic and encouraged fiscal discipline through cuts in such spending. The focus on border deterrence in the final law was an extension of border enforcement efforts that the INS had already undertaken along the southern border. Likewise, the other objective of the reform bill, reducing the costs of immigration, reflected the impact of California's popular Proposition 187, which had passed two years earlier. H.R. 2202 was replete with the same fundamental logic appearing in Proposition 187—namely, that the way to control legal and illegal immigration is to remove the lure of public benefits. Unlike Proposition 187, however, the announced reforms would extend benefits restrictions to legal immigrants and propose a lower cap on legal immigration.[28]

This expansion of the targets from unauthorized aliens to all aliens is partly attributable to federal welfare reform efforts that Congress undertook in 1995 and that President Clinton signed into law in August 1996. The welfare law restructured eligibility guidelines and devolved welfare program administration to the states. Most notably, the law limited entitlements to U.S. citizens of working age and narrowed the number of years that adults could remain on social assistance before having to enter the work force. Title IV of the Personal Responsibility and Work Opportunity Reconciliation Act of 1996 (PREWORA) barred legal aliens from receiving SSI and Food Stamps unless they had worked in the United States for ten years. Legal immigrants entering the United States after 1996 would be ineligible to receive any social services (except for emergency medical care) for their first five years in the country, and their sponsors would have to provide an affidavit of financial support (the "deeming" requirement) for those first five years. The determination of alien qualification for many means-tested programs, such as Temporary Aid to Needy Families (TANF, or the block grant program that replaced the AFDC) and Medicaid, was a decision that would now fall to the states.

On August 4, 1995, Representative Lamar Smith (R-TX) introduced the Immigration and the National Interest Act (H.R. 2202) for congressional consideration. While the bill called for stricter enforcement of the employer sanctions and document verification provisions of the weak 1986 Immigration Reform and Control Act, it also added border-tightening efforts, including the extension of triple fencing and the addition of several thousand border agents per year through fiscal year 2001. In addition to controlling illegal immigration, the 1996 law also addressed the social costs attributed to illegal immigrants residing in U.S. territory. House consideration of the bill included testimony from state witnesses regarding estimated costs in medical care and public assistance (housing, SSI,

AFDC, and Food Stamps). Among the more contentious amendments in this bill was one proposed by Elton Gallegly, a Republican representative from California, which would have allowed states to deny public education to the children of illegal immigrants. The threat of a presidential veto ultimately forced a removal of the amendment from the final version of the bill, but not before the House spent hours debating its merits as a way to control education costs.

The Illegal Immigration Reform and Immigrant Responsibility Act passed in the House with a vote of 333 to 87 and in the Senate by 97 to 3 during the spring of 1996. The act was finally included as Division C of the 1997 Omnibus Appropriations Act, which passed in the House 370 to 37 and in the Senate, 84 to 15, on September 30, 1996. The breakdown of the votes clearly reflects bi-partisan support for the effort. On October 1, 1996, with President Clinton's signature, the IIRAIRA became the fourth significant piece of immigration legislation to pass into law since the 1965 Immigration and Nationality Act, and its expansion of Operation Gatekeeper represents the most comprehensive effort the U.S. government has undertaken to enforce its southern border since the establishment of the U.S. Border Patrol in 1924. In combination with the 1996 welfare reform package, the IIRAIRA was also the first time federal law addressed the premise that access to public benefits played a substantial role in encouraging legal and illegal immigration. A summary of the key components of the IIRAIRA appears in Table 2.2, p. 60. The table shows that the benefits guidelines of the IIRAIRA expand many of the provisions of Title IV of the welfare reform laws. For example, deeming of sponsors of legal immigrants was extended from five to ten years, and the level of support was set at 125 percent above the federal poverty line. These provisions were actually stricter than those in the PREWORA.

The IIRAIRA is unusual when compared to post-1965 U.S. immigration policy because its provisions extended the notion of negative fiscal impacts to the category of *legal* immigrants. In the end, the legal immigration cap proposed by the Commission on Immigration Reform and that Alan Simpson (R-WY) would promote in the Senate version of an immigration reform bill was dropped for lack of political support. While the law did not affect legal immigration in absolute numbers, the law did restrict immigrants already present legally in the United States from accessing benefits. Later studies would show a significant decline in legal immigrant households that enrolled in Medicaid, Food Stamps, unemployment insurance, or Temporary Aid to Needy Families.[29]

TABLE 2.2

*Major Provisions of the 1996 Illegal Immigration Reform and
Immigrant Responsibility Act (IIRAIRA)*

I. *Enhancement & Enforcement of Immigration Control*

More Agents	Increased number of Border Patrol agents by not less than 1,000 per fiscal year beginning in 1997 through 2001. Also provided for an increase of up to 300 support personnel for the same period.
More Barriers	Called for the reinforcement of existing barriers along the U.S. border and construction of second and third fences along the 14 miles stretching eastward from the Pacific Ocean. Authorized $12,000,000 to carry out construction, and waived the Endangered Species Act of 1973 and National Environmental Policy Act of 1969 to "ensure expeditious construction of the barriers and roads."
More Facilities	Called for increase in INS detention space of 9,000 beds.
More Equipment	Authorized the attorney general to use "any federal equipment (including fixed wing aircraft, helicopters, four wheel drive vehicles, sedans, night vision goggles, night vision scopes, and sensor units) determined available for transfer by any other agency of the Federal government upon request of the Attorney General."
Streamlined Procedures	Reduced documents employees can use to demonstrate work eligibility. Facilitated interagency cooperation with the INS by authorizing local agencies to assist in immigration enforcement. At ports of entry, allowed for removal without hearing (excepted: asylum claims). Removed discrimination barrier stating that employers do not engage in unfair employment practices unless they show intent to discriminate.

II. *Limits on Access to Public Benefits*

New Public Charge Exclusion	Established sponsors of legal applicants must provide affidavits of support at 125% of the federal poverty line for the duration of 10 years (40 quarters) of employment by admitted legal alien, or until his or her naturalization.
Ineligibility for Public Benefits	Determined that persons unlawfully in the U.S. are not eligible for Social Security benefits or post-secondary education benefits. Called for transition of ineligible immigrants out of public housing.

Source: 104th Cong., 2nd sess., *Statutes at Large*, P.L. 104-132.

The Limits of Path Dependent and Economic Cycle Explanations of Immigration Reform

It is an accepted feature of U.S. immigration history that restriction follows economic recession and that public backlash against immigrants accompanies rising economic uncertainty. While the contextual factors explored briefly here suggest that the IRCA and the IIRAIRA followed this pattern, the design of these policies—the tools and target groups selected

—did not simply play to anti-immigrant backlash. Even as the IRCA did not accomplish its ultimate goal of reducing illegal immigration, its legalization and employer sanctions provisions reflect a re-definition of the causes of illegal immigration, the problems associated with this phenomenon, and, in turn, different policy solutions. The IRCA is an unexpected outcome given the economic conditions and the anti-immigration stance of public opinion at its inception. Although the IIRAIRA appears to be the type of policy one would expect from a restrictionist social and economic context, I propose that its design reflects a broader movement on the Right to pit those who pay taxes against those who purportedly do not. In the 1990s, immigration policy became the final frontier in a conservative agenda that had been waging battles against federal policies viewed as rewarding undeserving poor at taxpayer expense since the 1970s. Seen from this perspective, it is not simply a restrictionist policy; it is part of a broader ideological movement that has been underway in American politics since the 1960s.[30]

While the IRCA represented a rupture in immigration policymaking, in several respects, the IIRAIRA represented a continuation of the IRCA insofar as the latter continued employer sanctions and largely relied on employers to voluntarily determine employment eligibility of workers. The fact that the IIRAIRA did not cut family-based reunification preferences and that it did increase highly skilled labor visas is cited as evidence of the continued strength of pro-immigrant and ethnic lobbies in shaping immigration reform since the 1980s.[31] In addition, however, the IIRAIRA marked a significant departure in contemporary U.S. immigration policy because it defined both legal and illegal immigration as problematic for the United States and because of the way it framed the immigration problem in terms of fiscal costs.

One factor that can often force policy change is new data or evidence that forces a re-evaluation of existing methods for dealing with problems.[32] However, advances in scientific analyses of immigration and policy implementation did not inform the shift between 1986 and 1996. Nor was the shift based on existing scientific analyses of the costs of immigration, since available studies on federal costs (as reviewed by the General Accounting Office) were inconclusive and lent support to both sides of this debate. In comparing the IIRAIRA to the policy recommendations of the GAO and Commission on Immigration Reform, we find that lawmakers actually did the opposite of what was recommended: they cut off benefits

TABLE 2.3
Comparison of Problem Statements for Each Policy Period

Statement Category	As Percentage of Statements Made*	
	1985–86 (N = 159)	1994–96 (N = 557)
Indicators for Immigration Reform		
Task force report (straight mention)	22.6	3.1
The public wants something done about immigration.	6.3	7.1
The border is lawless and out of control	2.5	2.2
Illegal immigration is out of control	7.5	3.9
Immigrants are not assimilating	0.1	0.1
Problems Associated with Illegal Immigration		
Illegal immigration is a burden to taxpayers	5.7	16.7
Illegal immigrants are criminals	3.8	13.3
Illegal immigration is unfair to those who came legally	3.1	3.1
Illegal immigration has a negative environmental impact	1.3	4.5
Causes of Illegal Immigration		
Illegal immigrants come because they find work here	11.9	7.0
The INS/Border Patrol don't have necessary resources	2.5	3.8
The Mexican Government/Army isn't cooperating	1.3	0.01
U.S. benefits are a magnet for illegal immigrants	1.3	18.1
Employers are hiring illegal immigrants	4.4	1.4
The federal government has failed to enforce the border	3.1	4.8
Problems with the legal admissions system	1.3	1.8
Poverty, war, socio-economic instability abroad	13.2	0

* Some categories (such as legal immigration problems) are missing because they applied only to their specific policy debate and thus did not overlap.

to legal immigrants (including many classes of refugees), and they did not wait for further evaluation of existing border initiatives before calling for their expansion.

The different designs of the IRCA and the IIRAIRA represent an ideological shift in causal stories about the problem of illegal immigration. To demonstrate this shift, Table 2.3 presents a content analysis of the *Congressional Record* that compares the simple cause-effect statements and their frequencies. By briefly reviewing variations in the problem, cause, and effect definitions for each policy period, we can begin to see where shifts in discourse associated with each legislative period emerged, as well as where discourse would remain unchanged. It is important to note that this table is missing some of the categories that provide the basis for the narrative analyses put forth further on in this study. Some portions of the discussions, such as legal immigrant use of public services, were policy-specific, and therefore are not included in the table. However, by combining most relevant statements into categories that did recur, this table captures nearly 90 percent of all statement categories appearing in the *Record* for each period.

Indicators for Immigration Reform

Starting with the first subset of statements, those that offer rationales for Congress to engage in reform, we find that the most substantial shift occurs in references to the task force reports. That 22.6 percent of all statements made in 1984–1986 made some reference to the work of the Select Commission is evidence that legislators at least symbolically referred to available research and recommendations produced by a body assigned to the task of inquiry into immigration issues. The much lower number of references to the Commission on Immigration Reform's efforts in the 1994–1996 period, 3.1 percent, suggests that the available research and recommendations by a similar specialized inquiry did not matter as much to Congress as it pursued reforms. Instead, public opinion—and the need of elected officials to appeal to it—appeared more often as a rationale during the 1994–1996 period.

Problems Associated with Illegal Immigration

This next subset enumerates the troubles that legislators attributed to both the phenomenon of illegal immigration and to the immigrants themselves. In this case, there is a palpable rise between the 1980 and the 1990 periods in the proportion of statements made linking illegal immigrants to a variety of social problems, with the fiscal burden and crime dominating the statements.

Causes of Illegal Immigration

The final subset of statements compared in Table 2.3 shows there was a difference in how Congress understood the sources of illegal immigration. Job availability was offered as a reason for the persistence of illegal immigration far more often in the first period than in the second. Likewise, while the role of employers was downplayed during both periods, it was much lower in 1994–1996. This is significant because this reading of the issue framed employer behavior as problematic, and, in turn, required a policy solution that would target employers.

Taken together, the 1984–1986 set of illegal immigration causal statements depict a classic "push-pull" immigration causal story in which international factors (poverty, war, and instability abroad) push illegal immigrants out of their home countries, and available jobs (immigrants come because they find work here) and employers who are "hiring illegal immigrants" pull immigrants into the United States. Because jobs and employers seem impervious or indifferent to the status of immigrants, undocumented immigration persists. Thus, during the 1980s, illegal immigration was framed as a systemic problem with elements in domestic and international factors. By contrast, in 1994–1996 we see a much heavier emphasis on the role of benefits in "pulling" illegal immigrants, and a decrease in emphasis on the role of available jobs. Moreover, for whatever reason (lack of resources, lack of inter-governmental cooperation or efforts on the part of the U.S. federal government), the border is unattended.

The causal story for 1994–96 reads uni-directionally: the United States offers many incentives to would-be immigrants, and because the border is not enforced as it should be, immigrants can come here illegally to take advantage of these incentives. Viewed in this way, illegal immigrants are no longer potential workers in a system that is willing to hire them regardless of their status, and American jobs are simply one more benefit available to these transgressors. In this interpretation of the immigration problem, its source is the illegal immigrants themselves. They are the ones who are willing to transgress the law in order to take advantage of the good life in the United States. Accordingly, theirs is a selfish, immoral twist on the classic immigration story in which people come to America to better their lot in life and their children's.

The Causal Stories of 1984–1986 and 1994–1996, in Brief

In comparing the major differences in how Congress defined the immigration problem over both policy periods, we begin to see how it is that the same problem can be redefined to give the audience (the public, particularly constituents) a very different understanding of who or what is to blame for a social condition. In the 1984–1986 period a complex story explained why illegal immigration happens: people migrate because of conditions in the home country, and they are drawn to the United States because of available jobs and complicit employers. Interestingly, this push-pull story could also easily apply to legal immigrants and refugees. Told in this manner, the causal story portrays illegal immigrants as no different from legal immigrants or refugees; these are classical immigrants motivated by dreams of self-improvement for themselves and their children. The aberration lies not within the people themselves, but rather in their status and resultant relationship with the state.

By contrast, what we see emerge in 1994–1996 is a causal story in which illegal immigration is an illegitimate avenue to a "good life" that is not earned (and, by implication, not deserved). With no consideration for the "push" factors, and a heavy emphasis on the many "pull" factors drawing immigrants to the United States, this is a story about a group of people with no regard for the law, and strong desire to take advantage of benefits at whatever cost. A nation that does not or cannot control its borders will find itself prey to aliens willing to defraud the system for jobs, welfare, and free schools and health care. Moreover, because the 1996 IIRAIRA also charged legal immigrants with the same selfish motivations, this rationale dominated arguments in favor of restricting benefits to all non-citizens.

It is worth noting, though, that a significant source of undocumented immigration—student and tourist visa overstays—were largely absent from the collective set of problem statements associated with both policies. Not surprisingly, where student and tourist visa overstays were absent from the problem definition stage, they were also absent from policy solutions. These groups are more difficult to portray negatively, and therefore, it is politically difficult to include these two groups among the problematic immigrants. Not until the events of September 11, 2001, would the issue of visa overstays filter into the public discourse. Even so, discussion of the issue has been limited, focusing on students originating from terror watch-list countries with little comprehensive attention granted to the students and tourists who stay past their authorized time.

With the evidence of problem re-definition established, the next step requires adding discursive depictions of the implicated target populations to these causal stories. The group depictions, when combined with problem logics, will supply the policy narratives that legislators used to defend the designs of the IRCA and the IIRAIRA. The chapters that follow focus on how the depiction of key target populations including employers, farmers, legal immigrants, and illegal immigrants, as "good guys" and "bad guys" in combination with these causal stories, produced distinctive policy narratives that would define people as deserving or undeserving of the treatments that the 1986 IRCA and the 1996 IIRAIRA would deliver.

3

Contesting Illegalities

The 1986 Immigration Reform and Control Act

In August of 1984, an in-depth article on immigration reform appeared in *Newsweek* along with a poll of American opinion on immigration and aspects of the proposed reforms. The results showed that Americans had "mixed feelings" about the policy proposals and revealed "ambivalence about all immigration, legal as well as illegal."[1] The poll had asked Americans to rank issues according to their perceived importance: unemployment ranked highest (84 percent), inflation was second (73 percent), and threat of nuclear war was third (70 percent). A majority of Americans (55 percent) also ranked immigration as a "very important" issue; still, *Newsweek* deduced that compared to the rancorous congressional debates that lay ahead, "the public's view of all of this is somewhat less impassioned—but it is fair to say that immigration reform is a serious national concern."[2]

In addition to ranking issue saliency, the poll asked respondents to assess a number of claims about immigrants, which are reproduced in Table 3.1. The poll did not ask that respondents differentiate between legal and illegal immigrants, but the findings reveal that Americans viewed immigrants as simultaneously injurious and beneficent. While nearly two thirds of Americans believed that immigrants took jobs from U.S. workers, 80 percent believed that immigrants were industrious and resourceful, taking

TABLE 3.1
Public Evaluations of Immigrants, 1984

Do you agree or disagree with the following statements?	Agree	Disagree
Immigrants take jobs from U.S. workers	61%	36%
Many immigrants work hard—often taking jobs that Americans don't want	80%	17%
Many immigrants wind up on welfare and raise taxes for Americans	59%	33%
Immigrants help improve our culture with their different cultures and talents	61%	35%

Source: *Newsweek*/Gallup Poll, June 1984. The telephone survey (conduced between June 1 and 3) had 751 respondents and a margin of error of plus or minus 4 percent. *Newsweek* did not report responses of "Don't Know" in its write-up.

jobs that Americans didn't want—even in a context in which unemployment loomed large for many. People believed that immigrants "wind up on welfare" at cost to Americans, but nearly the same amount of people viewed cultural contributions as favorable outcomes of immigration.

The fact that Americans held ambivalent attitudes about immigrants meant that policymakers could pursue different avenues in justifying approaches for immigration regulation; there were different policy stories that they could expect to resonate with both their peers and the public. In the following analysis of congressional speeches on the IRCA, we can observe just how significant the social constructions of target populations are to the stories that politicians develop to explain why a particular course of action is preferable to an alternative one. Policy narratives are stories that rationalize policy outcomes; they not only sell solutions to problems, they assure us that target groups are getting what they deserve.

The Narratives of the 1986 Immigration Reform and Control Act

The interplay of narratives and group constructions is particularly critical when policy dispenses benefits to new groups, or when policy channels benefits to very narrowly defined populations. Anne Schneider and Helen Ingram propose that policy tools will align with a group's social construction: politically powerful and positively constructed "advantaged" populations receive resources and rarely punishments; politically powerful, but negatively constructed "contender" groups will receive sub rosa benefits; politically weak, but positively constructed "dependent" populations will receive symbolic policies, and benefits will be under-subscribed; politically weak and negatively constructed "deviant" populations will be targets for punitive and coercive tools.[3] What the following discourse analysis reveals is that while various groups may have certain images ascribed to them already, much of the deliberative process surrounding the 1986 Immigration Reform and Control Act amounted to contests over these images and how they could be employed in justifying specific policy tools. But the analysis also reveals that larger recurring themes concerning the expansion (or contraction) of social membership, signifiers of immigrant contribution, and the expansion of federal power structured debates about specific policy measures. Meanwhile, narratives depicting private-sector efficiency, hard-working immigrants, greedy big business, and traditional families were intended to stir emotional responses to policy measures. The rhetoric deployed in these debates was only partly about arguing the technical merits of a policy tool as a solution to a problem. The narratives produced in the debates also represent the attempts of legislators to assure their audiences that specific groups were receiving appropriate treatment from the government.

The Government-Off-Our-Backs Narrative

The government-off-our-backs narrative is an anti-regulation narrative with three instantly recognizable components: it portrays employers as bearing too many regulatory burdens; it represents agricultural employers in particular as victims of excessive expectations and regulations; and it predicts disastrous results for farmers and the American public should measures designed to curb employment of unauthorized workers pass.

Throughout the employer sanctions debates, opponents of sanctions highlighted the numerous ways in which the law would encumber employers. In the examples that follow, these opponents argued that by passing employer sanctions, Congress would saddle employers with policing immigrant behaviors:

(1) . . . The sanctions shift onto business the burden of enforcing our immigration laws. We already have a governmental agency, the Immigration and Naturalization Service, which is properly charged with preventing entry of illegal immigrants into the United States. Yet, while retaining that agency and its border patrols, this legislation essentially forces upon employers the responsibility of halting undocumented immigration.[4]

(2) As far as employer sanctions are concerned, I don't think that employers should be put in the position of protecting our borders from illegal entry. The provisions of the bill, while not mandatory, will in practice be unnecessarily burdensome on employers. More importantly, however, I don't think that employers should be subject to criminal penalties for hiring illegal aliens except in those instances where they have abused the workers.[5]

(3) I feel strongly that we need a system that does not require the employer to be judge and jury in determining the worker's status.[6]

In each statement, the requirement of the new law, which involved employers verifying that their workers were authorized for employment, appears unfair, taxing employers with enforcement activities. In statement 1, a Republican senator from Idaho claims that with sanctions, "employers are forced to become police officers"—an unnecessary expectation since "we already have a governmental agency" that has the job of stopping illegal immigration. In statement 2, Senator Domenici (R-NM) reiterates the argument, suggesting that legislators are putting business "in the position of protecting our borders from illegal entry," and that employers should not face criminal penalties for hiring illegally.[7] In statement 3, Senator Lawton Chiles (D-FL) claims that verification forces employers to act as "judge and jury." Opponents of sanctions favored measures to ease verification for employers and shift responsibility for workforce compliance back to the federal government. Senator Chiles supported instituting a phone verification system akin to a credit check that would facilitate verification of a worker's eligibility. The final hiring decision would also come from the Department of Labor, making a federal agency, and not employers, the final arbiter of worker eligibility.

Opponents of stricter guidelines portrayed the new regulations for obtaining guest workers as bureaucratic and hampering businesses' ability to function smoothly. Concerns for the special needs of agriculture—particularly the segment of the industry producing perishable crops and dairy products—dominated arguments against the tougher guest-worker application program, the H-2A program. The excerpt below shows how one Senator from a western farming state portrayed the bureaucratic nightmare farmers would face when applying for temporary foreign labor:

(4) . . . H-2's existing 72 hour emergency provisions . . . [are] simply inadequate in light of the nature of the industry. . . . There is always the possibility that the Department of Labor couldn't render a decision within 72 hours.

Even if the Department of Labor made a decision within 72 hours the necessary paperwork, such as visas, documentation, and the employment contract would have to be approved. Foreign workers would also have to be recruited. It is highly unlikely that this could be done within 1 week. . . .

As I have mentioned, cherries are highly susceptible to rain. Last June in Washington State, farmers in the Yakima Valley had to triple their work force in a matter of hours because an impending rainstorm threatened the harvest. The crop would never have been harvested if the farmers used H-2.[8]

This Senator's anecdote depicts the plight of farmers already operating under standards too stringent to accommodate the volatile circumstances of the industry. Reminding his colleagues that the bill under consideration, S.1200, included even stricter controls, he would go on to say that the proposed H-2A would place crippling constraints on farmers.

The quotation above also portrays regulation as wreaking havoc on American employers. The senator from Washington State describes the volatile world of the farmer, where inadequate or inefficient guest-worker programs lead to crop losses. The debates over guest-worker reforms prompted many opponents to forecast disastrous results for agribusiness. In response, Senator Pete Wilson (R-CA) countered with an amendment that would streamline existing prerequisites for farmers to petition the Department of Labor for foreign workers and allow employers to withhold 20 percent of workers' earnings as insurance of their return to their country of origin. In petitioning for leniency instead of stricter controls, Senator Wilson presented the following crisis scenario:

(5) Mr. President, at some time, probably within a month, but at some time later this fall, this body will take up any numbers of proposals that have to do with trade. They have to do with the loss, Mr. President, the virtual hemorrhaging of American jobs offshore. It is no exaggeration to state that without this amendment, we face an additional hemorrhage within a narrow segment of perhaps America's most basic industry, agriculture; because without the workable provisions that ensure a timely harvest, we will see farmers decline to subject themselves, their families, and their workers to the kinds of procedures that inevitably will drive them out of business.

My guess is that many of them will begin farming in other nations.[9]

This statement offers one example of the rhetorical construction of members of the agricultural industry as victims. Alluding to the collapse of American manufacturing, it suggests that such a collapse could also affect agriculture. Without changes, Senator Wilson argues, immigration reform would result in "an additional hemorrhage" of American jobs. By linking the fate of agriculture to the declining fates of other industries, Wilson tapped into the existing insecurities that Americans began to feel in the

1970s and 1980s as forces of economic restructuring sent industries abroad and effected the displacement of American workers in the United States. The irony—that Wilson is complaining of loss of American jobs overseas while arguing in favor of laws that would facilitate the importation of foreign workers to do these jobs—is muted by his warning that American farms will go the way of the steel mill or automobile plant without the importation of foreign labor.

According to opponents of sanctions, the only way to avoid such crises was for Congress to address the special labor needs of agriculture in immigration reform. Anything short of this would cause farmers to make some hard choices:

(6) . . . If S. 1200 is not amended with respect to the seasonal workers' provisions, this country's perishable crop growers will have to decide between hiring undocumented, and probably illegal workers, or losing their crops. A well-balanced immigration reform package should not force perishable crop farmers to make that choice.[10]

(7) . . . We are thoroughly and 100 percent convinced that the system proposed in this bill will not work for our States. It will result in one of two undesirable consequences: either we will continue to have employers who violate the law, or we will have a large number of farms which simply have to go out of business. They simply will be unable to plant, to grow, and to market the kind of products they do at the present time.

. . . The perishable commodities industry has relied heavily on foreign workers for approximately 50 years. Once the flow of illegal immigration has been stemmed there is no guarantee that adequate numbers of domestic workers will fill such jobs.[11]

The senators quoted in statements 6 and 7 predicted that Congress would, in essence, force farmers to choose between continued hiring of an illegal workforce and the loss of their crops. The only solution to this dilemma was to include seasonal worker provisions in the new policy. Statement 7 is a testament to the dependence of agriculture on illegal labor. Congressional efforts to control illegal immigration would subsequently lead to inadequate numbers of laborers and farmers going out of business. Statements 6 and 7 also depict the agricultural industry as a victim of regulatory attempts. Interestingly, the farmers who were hiring undocumented workers to ensure their economic gain are not referred to as being law-less themselves—rather it is government regulation of the workforce that compels farmers to continue hiring undocumented immigrants.

The Family Farmer Narrative

This variation of the anti-regulatory theme deserves separate consid-eration because it deploys an ideal type, the small family farm, which has a venerable tradition in American political culture. The archetype of the self-sustaining small farmer is at least as old as the founding of the na-tion; Thomas Jefferson believed in the virtuous yeoman farmer, idealized as the engaged citizen with a stake in self-governance. Historian Richard Hofstadter discusses the "agrarian myth" as a recurring theme in Ameri-can politics in which "agriculture, as a calling uniquely productive and uniquely important to society, had a special right to the concern and pro-tection of government."[12] As the examples below will show, these attri-butes of virtue, public service, and hard work are invoked to rationalize government protection of agriculture's foreign labor force.

To mention the collapse of agriculture is to strike at a sacred American institution, and the discussion of the IRCA occurred during a decade that witnessed numerous and highly publicized foreclosures of small farms. In statement 5, California Senator Pete Wilson was not off the mark in ap-pealing to fears that American jobs were seeping abroad, or in linking the plight of the American farm to that of the American auto plant or steel mill. Recalling the foreclosures, Wilson and his colleagues peppered their anti-regulatory appeals with images of small farmers who, they argued, would suffer under tighter hiring controls. The ideal of the American farm and its central role in the national life was a common theme among Wilson's supporters, who urged the adoption of the new H-2A program. The statements that follow demonstrate how those supporting a simpli-fied process to hire foreign workers depicted the centrality of the farming industry to all Americans:

(8) Most producers who cultivate perishable commodities are small farm-ers who are susceptible to serious crop losses which can occur under the inflexible and restrictive H-2 provisions of S. 1200.

... Were this [crop losses] to happen, distribution and transportation workers would be lacking quality products to sell, and their business would suffer accordingly. Restaurants would have difficulty in obtaining fresh fruits and vegetables to serve to their customers. But most important, the American consumer would find it difficult to obtain some of this Nation's most valued food products and will pay higher prices from those perishable commodities able to find their way to the marketplace.[13]

(9) [The Wilson amendment] is the only guarantee that the family farms which we represent will be able to harvest their crops and provide them for the good, for the betterment of the American people.[14]

The story in statements 8 and 9 links the viability of American agriculture to instantly available labor. If Congress failed to provide farmers with foreign labor, the result would be disastrous for perishable crop farmers. Furthermore, other industries, including canneries, trucking, and restaurants, would also feel the ripple effects of a labor shortage, as would the American people, who would "pay higher prices from those perishable commodities." In statement 8, Senator Wilson portrays an industry operating at maximum efficiency: produce appears quickly on the tables of American families. But labor availability guarantees not just the quality of products; it also guarantees jobs in related sectors. Thus, in statements 8 and 9 a policy that would actually benefit a narrow target group (in this case, farmers) appears to benefit other groups, with the linkages between the food-processing and service industries being extended, ultimately, to the largest indirect target group, American consumers.

That statements 8 and 9 refer to "small" or "family" farmers merits further attention because supporters of seasonal worker provisions made certain to explain that absent these provisions, the small family farmers in particular would perish:

(10) [Sen. Mentzenbaum, from Ohio] speaks of the benefits provided by the present system, the huge corporate farms. He certainly is not speaking of the farms in my State or in the State of the distinguished Senator from California, where, almost without exception, these farms are small, very, very modest in size, and run by individual families. . . .[15]

(11) I visited those [immigrant farm labor] camps on a number of occasions and have for many years visited, talked with, and I think understand

something of the problems of our orchardists, most of whom, as pointed out by my colleagues, are small framers, small businessmen.[16]

(12) This country cannot afford to attempt immigration reform, while ignoring the vital interests of small farmers who produce our agricultural necessities, including reasonably priced, high quality, fresh fruits and vegetables.[17]

In statement 10 a Republican senator from Washington state reminds his colleagues that these are not faceless, soulless, "huge corporate farms" that would be harmed by legislators' failure to act on their behalf. Instead, this statement, like the two others, asserts that the farms are small, family businesses.

The juxtaposition of the idyllic American family farm against corporate agribusiness in statements 9–12 is deliberate. Historically, clandestine deals and last-minute changes to legislation have facilitated illicit labor migration to labor-intensive sectors of farming industries. Typically the beneficiaries of these hidden rewards have been politically powerful perishable fruit and vegetable growers in the western and southwestern United States, and these growers enjoy entrenched influence in immigration policymaking.[18] Agricultural economist Philip Martin has pointed out that while indeed about two thirds of all U.S. farms are small family farms, the largest 5 percent of all farms accounts for most of agricultural production. The political power of agriculture, he argues, rests not only in the conglomerate farms, but also in the advantaged position of the industry, which Martin describes as "the crown jewel of the U.S. economy."[19]

Perceptions matter, particularly in justifications for special treatment of a target group. Conscious efforts to shift the construction of farms from large enterprises to mom-and-pop ventures reflect a shared understanding of corporate farming clout, as well as acknowledging the benefits of admitting foreign labor in a context of high unemployment and job losses. To be sure, the agricultural industry may be famous for poor working conditions, low wages, and high unemployment and for snubbing jobless citizens in favor of foreign workers. Equally, Congress may be aware of the industry's historical exemption from immigration laws. But such negative realities are eclipsed when speakers instead offer images of the family farmer, and link these images to the many other American families that benefit from its products.

The Corrupt Agriculturists Counter-Narrative

This narrative counters arguments that claim that expanded and restrictive employment regulations would ruin the American farmer, and
it appeared in reaction to the narratives emphasizing the toll that immigration reform would exact on businesses and agriculture in particular.
Examples of the narrative include statements in which legislators charged
farm interests and their congressional allies with trying to pull the teeth
out of immigration reform or with derailing reform altogether. Additionally, this narrative includes reminders of the history of labor abuses, poor
working conditions, and legal exemptions long associated with the agricultural sector. Stories highlight how the agricultural industry habitually
skirts wage protections and workplace standards to reap profits at the
expense of its historically immigrant labor force. In short, the "corrupt
agriculturists" counter-narrative promotes a negative image of agriculture
as engaging in special-interest, shady politicking and as exaggerating the
industry's needs.

In the example that follows, we see the frustration of Alan Simpson
(R-WY), one of S. 1200's original sponsors, as he tries to convince the
Senate to vote in favor of the conference report. At the time of his statement, senators from California, Washington, and other farm states were
holding out for the inclusion of temporary farm labor provisions. Simpson lambasted the influence of agricultural interests in shaping S. 1200
and the ensuing floor discussions:

(13) Of all the constituent groups that grapple—and there are plenty of them
and I have grappled with all of them. I feel like Hercules with the multi-
headed Hydra. I have grappled with them all—there is no way to satisfy
the perishable fruit growers. I can accommodate American Hispanics,
I can accommodate the American AFL-CIO, I can accommodate the
American Farm Bureau, I can accommodate even the ACLU. I can accommodate employer groups, Chambers of Commerce, I can accommodate and work with almost everybody in the whole spectrum of immigration reform, but there is one group that will never ever, ever be satis-
fied and will wait in the wings. If this passes [the Senate], it will not be
enough; they will do a number on the House one more time. That is the
stuff Senators are dealing with then they get to this crew. They are heavy
hitters; they spend big bucks, and they are quite effective, thank you.[20]

Simpson's lament illustrates the number and range of interests that had their hands in immigration reform. Under these circumstances, the bill reflected an accommodation of many opposing interests, but not those of perishable growers who, according to Simpson, refused to compromise. Instead of partaking in the gentlemen's game of interest-group politics, perishable growers were in the less respectable game of strong-arming their opponents.

In the House, members openly reprimanded colleagues from both chambers who demanded that the immigration reform bill include special provisions (such as the Wilson amendment discussed earlier, which was defeated, and the eventual Schumer compromise, which is explained below) to ensure plentiful seasonal labor for agriculture.

(14) The so-called Schumer agricultural guestworker compromise is deservedly one of the most controversial aspects of the bill. I would prefer to see no agricultural guestworker provision in the bill. I don't believe the growers need a special program to provide their labor force; I believe the growers should be subject to the rigors of a competitive employment market like every other industry in this country is. But it has become clear to me that growers will end up either getting a special program in any immigration bill we pass or will use their muscle to keep us from passing one.[21]

(15) There is a provision in this legalization program which is particularly glaring in its shortsightedness and its injustice. That is the so-called Schumer proposal, which would give legal status to 35,000 illegal aliens who had worked for 90 days last year in perishable agriculture. It further allows for admission of so-called replenishment workers, who would be eligible for permanent resident status after working in agriculture for 3 years for at least 90 days per year. Why should we make special provisions for farm workers but not for garment or factory workers? I assure my colleagues that there are many more American farm workers than garment or factory workers who are displaced by illegal aliens. The only difference is that the garment industry does not have the lobby that agriculture does. This is ironic because, after the 90 days of work on the farms, where are these workers going to go for the other 9 months of the year? To the cities, where they will compete with American workers for jobs in the factories.[22]

The Democratic representatives cited above disdain the clout of the agricultural lobby. In Statement 14, Representative John Bryant (D-TX) complains that growers are receiving preferential treatment: they get a "special program to provide their labor force" instead of being part of the "competitive labor market like every other industry." In his comparison of agriculture to the garment industry (statement 15), Representative Matthew Martinez (D-CA) shows that agriculture indeed receives special treatment. Both representatives add to the image appearing in Simpson's depiction of agriculturists as using underhanded and strong-arming tactics: growers "use their muscle" and their strong lobby to secure preferential treatment.

Statements 13 through 15 share a principled argument against having one organized interest highjack immigration reform. Other legislators, though, flatly rejected the argument that growers would suffer dire labor shortages if their workforce were legalized, and thus freed to join the broader labor market:

(16) Will people flock to the cities because they are suddenly legal? Of course not. Will they uproot their families and change their lives totally? Of course not. The growers say that they need a massive pool of foreign workers or the crops cannot be picked. . . . Only if you are totally willing to ignore the interests of American workers, and only if you are willing to guarantee that there will be a huge work force of exploited, poorly treated foreign labor, can you provide any basis to vote for [the Wilson] amendment.[23]

In response to the argument that agricultural jobs are shunned by citizens—even unemployed citizens—some legislators pointed to the ways in which agriculture has enjoyed and continued to demand exemption from labor laws and working conditions that might bring this sector in line with other industries:

(17) . . . The sponsors say this [Wilson] amendment isn't a new Bracero Program, and in one sense they are right: it doesn't even have the minimal protections that the Bracero Program had. They simply throw the door open, making foreign workers look for any job he [sic] can find in the geographical areas in which he is allowed, and fend for himself.

But in another far more important respect, this amendment creates precisely the fundamental flaw of the Bracero Program: Namely . . . it will have the same impact upon American wages and labor conditions that the Bracero program had. . . .[24]

(18) . . . Now, the growers say, "Well, the Americans won't take the jobs in the field." I say nonsense. Unemployment in agriculture is high. Massive employment of illegal aliens only keeps working conditions bad and wages low.

American agricultural workers will accept the jobs that are available, provided they pay a decent wage and provided there are decent working conditions.[25]

In another instance, legislators portrayed agriculturists as a special interest seeking preferential treatment from government. This occurred in discussions of a measure that would extend the Fourth Amendment to cover open fields. Prior to 1986, the police and the INS did not need a warrant to search fields for illegal immigrants, but those protecting agricultural interests pushed for law enforcement to treat open fields in the same way as enclosed workspaces (such as offices, warehouses, and shop floors). This discussion will be addressed further on in the analysis, but the statements that immediately followed show how some Democratic and Republican representatives saw this Fourth Amendment extension as simply one more instance in which agriculture sought special federal protections for its operations:

(19) Mr. Chairman, the effect of adopting this amendment is to completely exempt agriculture from employer sanctions, because requiring a warrant for the Immigration Service to go into an open field will be so cumbersome and so procedurally difficult that there will be no open-field arrests of illegal aliens who are working in the fields.[26]

(20) Mr. Chairman, I think the question is today how much are we going to do for California growers? We are already going to make people citizens basically, so they will have a work force, and then they come to us and ask us to ignore the Immigration Service, to ignore our law enforcement agencies and insert into the law something that has never been there before at any time in our history and that is a requirement that an open field not be searched unless there is a warrant. Those open fields have no such protection at the present time and they have never had that kind of protection at any time in our history.

> This is a major, radical step to protect California growers. I simply ask, how far are we going to go?[27]

(21) . . . What you are talking about is making it virtually impossible to enforce the law against the hiring and exploitation of illegals, because if you have go to and get the search warrant, by the time you show up in the open fields, the law of violation will not be there.[28]

These discussions counter the depiction of virtuous farmers appearing in the family farmer narrative, and they do so in order to undermine efforts to grant agriculture exemptions from law enforcement. Requiring a warrant would make it harder for the INS to conduct searches of farm employers suspected of hiring illegal workers. Similarly, the representative quoted in statement 20 intimates that agriculture is conveniently demanding "something that has never been there before at any time in our history" as a way to exempt itself from the very punishment (sanctions) that is supposed to give immigration reform its teeth.

To briefly summarize, the corrupt agriculturists counter-narrative emphasized the dirty politics of the agricultural (particularly the perishable fruit growers) lobby. It also provided testimony of labor abuses, challenged the image of agriculture buckling as a result of legalization, and indicated that Congress should no longer grant the industry its protection. In the end, however, the IRCA did include two temporary labor provisions, the SAW (special agricultural workers) and RAW (replenishment agricultural workers) programs that were specifically tailored to the needs of agriculture.[29]

The Anti-Discrimination Narrative

This is a victimization narrative, and it emerged from discussions about employer sanctions. This narrative proposed that controls on business and hiring would lead to discrimination against American citizens, legal aliens, and even employers. In the first version of the narrative, those opposing sanctions for their discriminatory potential feared that only people who looked different or sounded foreign would be asked to prove their legal status. Another concern was that the penalties for illegal hiring would be so harsh as to dissuade employers from hiring any foreigners or people of Hispanic or Asian descent.

The following statement offered by a Japanese-American representative demonstrates the concern that this policy would have discriminatory outcomes:

(22) . . . Mr. Speaker, this bill's provision for employer sanctions takes us down the road toward an insidious racial discrimination.

Most Members of this House will never be asked to affirm, let alone prove their citizenship or residency. Looking and sounding American, they will never see these sanctions as an important factor in their lives.

But Mr. Speaker, no matter how many decades and generations non-whites have been here, they will find these sanctions one more unfair and discriminatory burden to bear.

In many ways, Mr. Speaker, I would like to be able to support this bill. . . . But Mr. Speaker, I cannot vote for a bill that will make it harder than ever for non-white Americans to be accepted for what they are: loyal Americans. No more, and no less.[30]

Other members of Congress asserted that the verification requirements would lead to discrimination against those who spoke with accented English or who appeared foreign:

(23) I hope that I can come back, as I said earlier today, and say to every Member in this Congress that I was wrong, that I was wrong, but history, I am afraid, will show that I am right. Three years from now when people who speak or sound different, who do not look the norm, are going to be pulled aside by INS inspectors and asked for identification, then we will come back and we will say, "That was a bad part of the bill."[31]

(24) A major concern of mine regarding S. 1200 deals with the lack of adequate protections to those American citizens who do not "look American," in particular those of Hispanic descent.[32]

Such statements generally came from minority legislators, including Roberto Garcia (D-NY), a Puerto Rican representative, and Norman Mineta (D-CA), an Asian-American representative. However, it was not only members of Congress who happened to be members of racial and ethnic minorities who worried that sanctions might result in discrimination.

Both Democrats and Republicans thought that employer sanctions would lead to discrimination. Thus, for example, one congressman, Steven Bartlett (R-TX), introduced a proposal to scale back the penalties of sanctions, arguing that this measure was essential to curtailing discrimination:

(25) The way the bill is constructed the individual who would be going to jail would be the person who actually does the hiring, the road construction foreman, the high school principal, the manager of the dry cleaners.

Any hint, it seems to me, any hint of jail time or criminal penalties or criminal charges for making a mistake, for making a mistake in the hiring of someone as to whether or not they are eligible to be hired is something that will so chill a manager or someone at the hiring level that they would choose not to make a mistake and they will not consider anyone who appears to be foreign born.

Now, there is no anti-discrimination provision in this bill . . . that could overcome that fear of criminal charges that could be brought. . . .[33]

Note that in this case "employers" are broadly construed: Representative Bartlett comes from Texas, a state long reaping the benefits of minimal government regulation of agricultural practices and generous government policies that facilitate and subsidize southwestern growers. Rather than speak to the narrow interests of agriculture, however, Bartlett argues that sanctions will lead to discriminatory behavior amongst all employers: construction, education, dry cleaners.

Democrats also employed the anti-discrimination argument in support of lowering penalties against businesses:

(26) Criminal sanctions would result in discrimination. The foreman at a construction site or manager at a restaurant would avoid hiring people who look foreign or speak with an accent.

If employers know that they can be handcuffed and arrested if they make the wrong decisions, I seriously doubt that they will take a chance and hire anyone who does not look or sound like Americans.[34]

In this second example, employers are also construction foremen and restaurateurs. Both quotations 25 and 26 offer a scenario in which implementation of sanctions could force employers to discriminate as a way to protect themselves from going to jail. The speakers portray employers and managers as needing to choose between discriminating against foreigners or accepting criminal penalties. In this regard, the anti-discrimination narrative also broadened the pool of those burdened by the law. Whereas the government-off-our-backs narrative spoke to the undue burdens on employers, the anti-discrimination narrative broadened the definition of those who would endure the regulations to include all businesses and the segment of the labor force that was minority or foreign-born. In the end, the IRCA would require employers to verify the eligibility of all prospective employees. In order to address the discrimination issue and to protect employers from lawsuits arising from compliance, the law included a provision stating that hiring a citizen over an equally qualified alien would not be treated as a violation of the anti-discrimination laws. The bill also required the General Accounting Office to review employer sanctions implementation to assess whether discrimination against foreigners and minority job applicants had occurred.

The final manifestation of the anti-discrimination narrative emerged in discussions of the extension of Fourth Amendment search-and-seizure protections to fields and ranches. Prior to the passage of the IRCA, law enforcement did not need a warrant to search fields. The exemption of open fields from the Fourth Amendment protections facilitated search and seizure in drug-growing operations and INS roundups. Members of Congress representing agricultural interests argued for the extension of the Fourth Amendment rights to farmers in a curious manner, as the two statements below illustrate:

(27) . . . The INS can raid the open fields of a farm or ranch without having probable cause to believe that the workers in those fields are illegal aliens.

This practice is arbitrary and discriminatory. It discriminates against ranches and farms and those people who work on ranches and farms. It severely disrupts farming operations, resulting of thousands of dollars in lost crops and man-hours annually.[35]

(28) I contend there is a big difference between entering a field because you have a reasonable suspicion that illegal drugs are being grown there and entering a field simply because the workers on it have brown skin or a national origin from south of our border. . . .[36]

The Republican and Democratic senators quoted in statements 27 and 28 present a tale of unequal treatment of ranchers and farmers at the hands of law enforcement. Note the use of phrases and imagery more likely to be associated with racial profiling on interstates or in urban neighborhoods: field searches occur "without having probable cause," and are "arbitrary and discriminatory" and disruptive. The Democratic senator speaking in statement 28 questioned the basis of reasonable suspicion and whether employers are being targeted because their employees "have brown skin."

According to the narrative, Fourth Amendment protections for farmers operating fields or ranches would correct law enforcement biases and profiling of fields and ranches based on assumptions they have about who works in these fields. Senator James McClure (R-ID), whose amendment would end the discrepancy in Fourth Amendment protections, argued the need for the change in these same terms:

(29) . . . Although this small amount [8–15%] of undocumented workers are employed in agriculture, fully 50 percent of undocumented workers picked up by INS agents in the interior of the country are captured while working in agricultural occupations. . . .

These figures show a distinct bias in INS enforcement activities and serve notice that farmers and farm workers are not receiving equal protection as envisioned in our Constitution. . . . Simply because [the INS] see a group of people working in a field, they operate under the assumption that those people have gained entry into the United States illegally. It is not until the agents enter the field that an illegal versus legal status can be determined.

Harassment of agricultural employers and employees by the INS has gone on for years. . . .

My amendment does not establish protection or set a precedent for farmers; it just guarantees them the same rights and privileges enjoyed by every other employer in our Nation. Likewise, employees will be protected from the humiliation of impulsive interrogation by the INS.[37]

Using an estimate of the numbers of undocumented aliens working in agriculture, Senator McClure makes the case that the INS victimized agricultural enterprises with profiling tactics. Here, the speaker appropriates language commonly associated with Civil Rights, referring on the one hand to the equal protection clause of the Constitution, which "guarantees . . . the same rights and privileges . . . ," and, on the other, to "humiliation" and "harassment" by law enforcement, in order to claim anti-discrimination protections for employers. In this case, the effort is to employ the anti-discrimination narrative to produce a narrow policy benefit for specific categories of agricultural employers.

Nor was this the logic of a few. The same sentiment appears in the following quotations in which employers are further portrayed as victims of law enforcement:

(30) . . . It is right legally because we do have a fourth amendment that prohibits the unlawful search and seizures. That right applies to businesses; it applies to industries; it applies to homes; it applies to citizens. There is one area it does not apply to, to American farmers and American farms.

Surely that double standard ought to be ended.[38]

(31) . . . I think it is clear that a special case is made by S. 1200, one that is not justified by the facts, one that asks us to discriminate against farmers, against those with brown skin. . . .[39]

The California Democrat quoted in statement 30 wished to end an injustice and grant protections enjoyed by all others to the American farmer. In the final call for the extension, this action would benefit not only farmers, but also "those with brown skin."

Two sets of victims appeared in the anti-discrimination narrative: minorities seeking employment and employers. While the narrative follows logically from Democratic concern for the civil rights of minorities who might be denied work by employers fearful of sanctions, it rings oddly when the subject of concern is employers. In representing employers as victims, the second version of the anti-discrimination narrative appears to be a clear attempt by regulation's detractors to find yet another way to avoid government oversight in hiring, and to make an otherwise narrow appeal to a segment of the agricultural industry seem essential to the general protection of civil rights.

The Undeserving Illegal Narrative

This narrative emerged from opponents of the legalization program. While it takes several forms, it is recognizable for its fundamental argument that illegal immigrants, who are criminals by definition or in their behaviors, do not merit a magnanimous policy that would annul their illegality. One form of opposition to legalization emphasized the injustice of a program that rewarded people for breaking the law. Statements to this effect juxtaposed the illegal alien with the legal alien and reminded members of Congress that the policy was an injustice to those who had chosen to abide by U.S. immigration law:

(32) . . . There has been a great deal said about amnesty, and I have a great deal of sympathy for some individuals who have violated the laws of this country and violated our borders on an individual basis. But on a policy basis they are regarded for their illegality. They are preferred over others who try to comply with our laws, who seek entry into our country. Those who have complied with the laws are denied entry and those who violate our laws are granted amnesty. Now why are they granted amnesty? It is not really because of the merit of individual cases. It is because there is such a flood of them.[40]

(33) . . . I think it is a sad, indeed tragic, thing when we grant amnesty to millions of people solely on the grounds that they have gotten here through an illegal act.

That is the common denominator of every one of the people who get amnesty, that they came to this country illegally.[41]

(34) . . . Perhaps the most objectionable aspect of blanket amnesty is the fact that it penalizes those tens of thousands of potential immigrants who are waiting legally to enter our country.[42]

(35) . . . Husbands, wives, and unmarried children of immigrants from Mexico have been waiting for over 9 years to come to America. Brothers and sisters of United States citizens who are attempting to immigrate from Hong Kong have been waiting since 1974, over 12 years, to reunite with their families in our country, and with one fell swoop we are about to legalize all those who illegally crossed our borders, who have been here illegally residing and who have preempted the legal immigration of those who are trying to obey our laws.[43]

Statements 32–35 are all examples of a rhetorical juxtaposition of groups —in this case, of undocumented and legal immigrants—which is a tactic employed to highlight which groups deserve benefits. The speakers develop a portrait of undeserving illegal immigrants by casting the legalization tool as a question of fairness. In comparing the plight of immigrants who have chosen legal channels of entry to their illicit counterparts, the representatives and senators whose statements appear here establish a criterion for the just distribution of legal statuses. The comparison between legal and illegal immigrants intimates that those who have broken the law do not deserve to have their status corrected because of their transgression.

The policy, some argued, was not simply an affront to legal immigrants. In the statement below, one Republican senator asserted that amnesty represented an affront to those who comply with the law:

(36) There is the provision under this bill which rather curiously puts the employer in that rather strange case in which the illegal will be rewarded for his illegality and the employer is subject to penalty while the illegal is improving his right to be present.[44]

In a manner similar to that of the legislators quoted in the preceding four statements, this Senator questions the deservedness of undocumented immigrants who would benefit from naturalization. Here, however, the potential for unjust policy is revealed in the juxtaposition between rewards for the criminal illegal and punishments for the presumably law-abiding employer.

Another version of the undeserving illegal narrative highlights the crisis of illegality using familiar metaphors of floods, military conflict, and invasion that now pervade public discourse about the immigration issue.[45] In their evaluation of IRCA's legalization provisions, opponents also voiced concern that, in addition to rewarding lawbreakers, legalization might lead to increased immigration rather than its containment and control:

(37) . . . Five years from now, 7 or 8 years from now, we will have another illegal alien problem, calling for amnesty, because this does nothing to solve the basic problem . . . it does not close our borders to illegal immigration. It winks at it. . . .

I am reminded further of another instance in more recent history, and in a more grim manner, when we refused to face the reality of the aggression by Hitler's Germany; and a prime minister went to Munich and said he had purchased peace in our time. This bill is another exercise in appeasement of a problem that will not be so appeased.[46]

(38) If you look at the issue of population control, if you look at the fact, and everyone is in agreement that you are going to have between 10 and 20 million people legalized and if only half of those people come forward and take advantage of general amnesty and you multiply that times the chain of seven relatives who will be eligible for entry into this country, then you are looking at between 50 and 100 million new faces that will be added to the population flood to this country.[47]

In statements 37 and 38 illegal immigration is a threat that amnesty will only worsen. In fact, in statement 37, Representative James McClure (R-ID) bluntly invokes a parallel between legalization and the appeasement of Hitler, as if illegal immigration were a coordinated campaign of military aggression and ethnic cleansing that must be stopped.

Some of the other opponents to legalization voiced concerns that the legalization tactic would "send the wrong message" to other countries—a message that the United States "rewards lawbreakers" and grants them the chance to be citizens. For example, one senator gave the following preamble to his statement in *support* of legalization:

(39) I am as uncomfortable as anyone else in the United States with legalizing those who came to the United States illegally. I do not believe in rewarding lawbreakers or ignoring violations of our immigration law. It is my firm conviction that if this legalization is enacted, it will never be repeated. Let those who would seek to take unfair advantage of our generosity and humanity be forewarned. We will not repeat this extraordinary gesture. . . .[48]

Even this advocate of legalization made sure to address the fears of colleagues who thought that once enacted, legalization programs would become the preferred tool for controlling any future illegal immigration. The tone of statement 39 is significant because even the program's advocate affirms that correction of status is a benefit granted begrudgingly. Moreover, the senator warns that legalization is a one-time deal, and that other nations should not mistake this as an invitation to those who might expect to take advantage of American generosity.

A number of senators voiced concern that the legalization measure would send the wrong message about American citizenship:

(40) . . . But when all we do to make a citizen is to say, 'If you have been here illegally for a certain period of time, we will grandfather you in, we will give amnesty,' that does not establish a very high standard for the integrity of this precious right of citizenship.[49]

(41) . . . I sincerely believe that this process will cheapen the value of American citizenship, our most precious right, and this is something to which I cannot be a party.[50]

Statements 40 and 41 question whether the ultimate outcome, the eventual naturalization of those who legalize, sets the wrong tone for citizenship. Legalization, according to this view, would make former lawbreakers eligible for "our most precious right," thereby lowering the bar, or reducing the quality of citizenship. This variation on the undeserving illegal narrative illustrates a general suspicion that new immigrants, when judged as potential citizens, fail to qualify as worthy of this status.[51] Statements like 40 and 41 suggest that even legalization will be insufficient to truly give applicants a clean slate—to the extent that this population is judged to consist of lawbreakers, they will make subpar citizens. Rather than hope that formerly illegal immigrants would take advantage of naturalization, or that they would be fully integrated by taking steps towards full political and social membership, the members of Congress speaking here express distaste that this avenue will be available to former criminals and argue that Congress is lowering the bar and distributing rights to the unworthy.

The Deserving Illegal Counter-Narrative

The deserving illegal counter-narrative addresses the negative depictions of illegal immigrants found in the undeserving illegal narrative. This alternative story about illegal immigrants emerged from congressional discussions surrounding the legalization component of S. 1200. The story was a product of three different types of arguments in favor of legalization: first, that legalization was the only way to deal with a large population of people with significant ties to the United States; second, that legalization was necessary to protect workers and people who were vulnerable to exploitation as a result of their illicit status; and third, that the other alternative, deportation, was inhumane, un-American, and untenable. The deserving illegal narrative is recognizable for its repeated references to the social equity illegal immigrants have accumulated in the United States and to their economic contributions; it also conveys the sense that these are people Americans would want to embrace as members of society. As such, the narrative challenges the negative social construction of the illegal immigrant as a law-breaker and tries to replace it with a nobler construction of illegal immigrants as future, or potential Americans.

One example of such sentiments is evident in the statement below given by Congressman Mazzoli (an original co-sponsor of immigration reform) in the opening remarks for House debate on the final conference report:

(42) Mr. Speaker, we stand on the verge of culminating a task that began many years ago. That task, of course, is to reform our immigration laws —to bring some order and sense to our immigration policy by regaining control of our borders and dealing with the hard reality that many of the finest, most law-abiding residents of the United States are in an undocumented status.[52]

The statement is interesting for its view that illegal immigrants are not only people living among us, but that they are among the "most law-abiding" people despite their illicit status. Such logic suggests that those favoring a legalization program are cognizant that they must overcome all of the rationales for denying this benefit to a group easily described as "lawbreakers."

Thus, in countering the undeserving illegal narrative with a human portrait, supporters of amnesty could recast immigrants in terms of national mythology, representing them as the kind of people who made this country great, the kind of folks we should embrace for what they have to offer. Consider the following three examples drawn from the debate over the S. 1200 conference report:

(43) . . . I also believe legalization is essential in order to regularize that status of those aliens who have built up equities in this country and who have contributed for years toward our economic and social well-being. . . . I know that this was a troubling issue to many of our colleagues on both sides of the aisle, but I can assure you that it is our intention and the conferees intention that legalization be a "one-time" only event and I

wish to emphasize that with a 1982 date, we are talking about aliens who have been in this country almost 5 years—who have roots and families here—and who should be made a part of American society.[53]

(44) . . . Many of these individuals have U.S. citizen children. Many work with U.S. citizens. Many have U.S. citizen friends who, as we often see in the context of private immigration bills, would be appalled to learn that their hardworking friend or neighbor is slated for expulsion from the United States. I therefore do not think it surprising that in a poll conducted by CBS News earlier this year fewer than one-third of the respondents said that the law-abiding, undocumented persons who have lived here several years should be deported from the United States. [54]

(45) . . . The strange thing is, most people are against illegal aliens; most people will tell you to round them all up and send them home; but those same people will say: "By the way, Congressman Lungren, can your immigration subcommittee pass a private bill for this person I know down the street, for the woman who works in my house, for the children who go to school with my children, for the person in the church choir that I sing with; they don't happen to have papers. Will you do something for them?"

That is not schizophrenia; I think it is a recognition [*sic*] that most of the illegal aliens who are here are good people. They are humane people. They have come here to work, and when we know them, we in most cases like them and we will go out for them. But we know we have to do something overall about illegal immigration.[55]

This collection of floor statements advocating legalization depicts illegal immigrants in a manner that humanizes them, emphasizes their roots in American society, and considers the equity they have accumulated and the contributions they have made while residing in the United States. Each statement openly acknowledges prejudices against illegal immigrants, while simultaneously challenging these prejudices with stories of those who are "in the church choir I sing with" (statement 45) "have roots and families here," and "have citizen children" (statements 43–44), or those who "work with citizens" and have "citizen friends" (statement 44) who have gone so far as to write to their representatives requesting private bills to exempt individuals from deportation orders, (statement 45). In statement 45, Republican Representative Dan Lungren (CA) argued that if people were to stop and think about what would happen to the undocumented people in their communities without a legalization program, citizens would be moved to act on their behalf. Representative Lungren questions the depth of the public's concern for immigration control, suggesting that if the public were actually faced with the "round them all up and send them home" scenario, the same public would want private bills exempting individuals in their communities from deportation.

In addition to humanizing undocumented immigrants by making them community members, as well as people who have accumulated social capital, the statements also emphasize the contributions of these immigrants, thereby depicting them as deserving amnesty. Statement 43 asserts that these are aliens "who have contributed for years toward our economic and social well-being," and statement 45 describes the same people as "hardworking" and as working alongside citizens. Statement 45 recalls the "woman who works in my house," "children who go to school with my children," people who "have come here to work." In another example, a congressman directly disputes the notion that illegal immigrants are a burden on society:

(46) . . . A mythology has developed about the harm to our country's economy because of the presence of undocumented workers. The fact is, that with respect to taxation, work and productivity, many of these undocumented workers are contributing a great deal in a great many places to the strength of our economy, not to the detriment of it.[56]

Statement 46 presents a counterfactual view to the prevailing narrative of the burdens of illegal immigration. These people, according to the speaker, are working, productive, and *paying* taxes, not draining them.

In yet another instance, another congressman did draw on the common perception of illegal immigrants as a drain, but then he added a twist:

(47) . . . They do not pay taxes to the United States. They do not have payroll taxes paid for them. In the end, that is draining every year over $100 billion in revenue at the State, local, and Federal level from the tax money which could be used to do other things including reducing the deficit. By making these people come forward out of the shadows, out of that subrosa economy, we are going to help the United States.[57]

Here the argument is that legalization is "going to help the United States" recover "$100 billion" in tax money currently lost in the underground economy of illegal employment. Legalization here is not romanticized; it would make a group of working residents accountable to the IRS and have them pay their fair share.

In addition to casting illegal immigrants in light of their positive characteristics and contributions, the deserving illegal narrative also emerged from arguments made on the floor that emphasized that legalization would provide recourse for a population often exploited and victimized because of their illicit status, as in the examples below:

(48) Today the reality is that 85 percent of many of those who work in agriculture are undocumented aliens. These workers . . . are often abused, live in fear, or exploited and have no rights. That is a bitter reality, but it is a reality.[58]

(49) The choice is a simple one for this House. The choice is protecting an existing system, where we have uncontrolled borders, employers who easily can exploit, workers who can easily be exploited, fear, death, discrimination, random raids, hiding, versus a reform bill that tries to correct those concerns.[59]

The example below comes from Senator Pete Wilson, who would later distinguish himself with a strong stance against illegal immigrants as the governor of California and supporter of the state's Proposition 187:

(50) . . . Today, Mr. President, when undocumented workers work illegally in this country, this sad situation of worker exploitation persists to some minor degree. We really cannot quantify it. The vast majority, I am convinced, of agriculture employers deal fairly with their employees, but it is certainly true that the illegal status of these workers places them in a vulnerable position that subjects them to the possibility at least of cruel exploitation. To be certain, first of all, they are subject to the $1,500 to smuggle them into this country and continue to threaten them with disclosure to the authorities. Similarly, the illegal worker has little in the way of recourse against unscrupulous employers. That has to change. A civilized society cannot tolerate the kind of thinking that has been going on because of this illegal status.[60]

Such statements offer a clear depiction of the various ways in which the existence of an undocumented immigrant is indeed precarious. These statements are striking in the manner that they posit legalization as protecting the illegal population from further victimization. Without scientifically documenting the extent of employer or smuggler abuses, Democrats and Republicans spoke in favor of amnesty for illegal immigrants as the ethical alternative to their exploitation.

Additionally, congressmen favoring legalization argued that such a measure would protect immigrants of Mexican and Central American origin from discrimination:

(51) . . . But the growing numbers of people entering this country illegally, and the growing perception that our Government does not have an effective immigration policy, has led to a rise, in my district, in many parts of Texas, and in many other parts of the country, of hostility and prejudice toward Hispanic Americans. I have witnessed this hostility increase dramatically in the 4 years I have been in Congress. It has been tearing apart my community, and many other communities as well.

If there were a better way to address this problem and reduce these tensions and hostilities, I would champion it. But there is not a better way. If there were, someone would have suggested it by now. And with every week that this problem goes unaddressed, it gets worse and the hostilities and the tensions increase.[61]

(52) I am deeply concerned that if Congress does not meet its responsibility to put our immigration law and policy in order, we will soon see—as we are now witnessing in some areas of the country—increasing resentment against legal immigrants and refugees. I am fearful that unless action is taken to address the undocumented alien problem, the American people will forget their immigrant heritage and restrictionist pressures will grow.[62]

In statements 51 and 52, the illegal status of one group affects even non-immigrant Hispanics, as well as bringing tension into communities and "increasing resentment against legal immigrants and refugees." By this logic, not only would legalization help its target group, but several other groups (legal immigrants, refugees, and Hispanic American citizens) would benefit from this policy. And as statement 52 further suggests, legalization policy would curb the public's restrictionist tendencies.

The final instance of the deserving illegal counter-narrative considers the alternative to legalization—deportation—which the following statements portray as being so unreasonable that it could not be a viable policy option:

(53) The first option, deportation, is really no option at all. First, any effort designed to even attempt to locate, provide hearings to, and then physically deport millions of individuals would cost billions of dollars. To understand just how extraordinarily expensive such an effort would be one must realize that in a typical year INS now is able to deport only about 20,000 individuals at the cost of several million dollars.

Second, and more important, any effort to implement such a massive deportation program would necessarily involve sending out thousands upon thousands of INS investigators to scour the country in search of undocumented aliens. Hundreds of thousands of business premises would be raided. Any individual on the street who "looks or sounds foreign" would be stopped and interrogated. It is inconceivable to me that an investigative effort of this magnitude could be conducted without violating the rights not only of undocumented aliens, but also legal aliens and U.S. citizens as well.

The third reason why deportation is not an option is that, in the case of longtime residents, deportation is unfair, and would be perceived as such by the public. . . .[63]

(54) It became clear to our subcommittee early in the development of a reform bill that the United States had neither the personnel nor the resources—nor probably the national will—to conduct a massive deportation of all persons here without proper papers. For my part, even were there the personnel, resources and will, I do not feel a deportation of every undocumented person would be humane, generous or keeping with the tradition and spirit of our land.[64]

These two excerpts attempt to explain to the House why the deportation of the resident illegal population is simply not a viable policy option. According to Democratic Representative Peter Rodino (NJ), legalization is not only preferable for its humanity, but is also the most efficient option given the INS's notorious lack of funding and resources (statement 54).[65] Another Democratic representative, Romano Mazzoli (KY), hammered this consideration home with the reminder that the INS averages "about

20,000" deportations a year "at the cost of several million dollars" (statement 55). Representative Mazzoli also explained the burdens a deportation policy would place on businesses disrupted by an INS search for undocumented immigrants: "Hundreds of thousands of business premises would be raided." In both statements, the representatives warn of the inevitability of civil and human rights abuses that would accompany a deportation policy. There is the common allusion in both quotations to public resistance to such an unfair policy, which would not reflect national traditions.

This final argument against deportation is interesting given that deportation and repatriation are very much "in the spirit and tradition of our land." In the 1920s and 1930s, many cities with large Mexican populations encouraged Mexican immigrants to return to Mexico voluntarily. The social dislocation and unemployment caused by the Great Depression created a climate of discrimination against Mexican workers who were accused of taking (white) citizen's jobs. The hostile social climate also contributed to the pressures on Mexicans to "repatriate" voluntarily.[66] Moreover, the deportation of Mexican workers and their families has also been federal policy: in 1954 Operation Wetback was the official response to illegal immigration generated by the need for labor during World War II.[67] During this campaign, the Border Patrol deported several hundred thousand people to the interior of Mexico. The round-up also resulted in the deportation of legal residents and U.S. citizens of Hispanic origin, as well as reports of INS abusiveness towards deportees.[68] However, without alluding to the plain fact that the INS has effectively ferreted out illegal immigrants in the past, the speakers of both statements appealed instead to a generous nation—a nation concerned with "the rights not only of undocumented aliens, but also legal aliens and U.S. citizens," and one that avoids discrimination against "any individual on the street who "looks or sounds foreign." This position, in combination with the aforementioned humanizing characterization of illegals as members of communities and as valuable contributors to American society, forged a policy narrative that appealed to the ideal of the United States being a haven for all immigrants. In so doing, though, the narrative discredits a history of immigration policies that have discriminated based on race, ethnicity, and national origin.

To summarize, each example of the deserving illegal narrative portrayed undocumented immigrants as contributing to the society at large and thus as deserving of the opportunity to correct their status and come under the protection of the government. The discourse offered in support of legalization challenged the construction of illegal immigrants as criminals by referring to them instead as law-abiding and hard-working and as members of communities, churches, and schools. Barring their illicit status, these were good immigrants; they were exactly the kind of people this country has long embraced. This counter-narrative did not construct illegal immigrants as criminal aggressors nor as economically disruptive. To the contrary, they were often portrayed as *victims* of crime and workplace abuses. It is essential to note that in many of the statements the undocumented status of this group did not make it criminal; rather, it actually made the group *vulnerable* to crime. Finally, the deserving illegal narrative depicted alternative policy tools—specifically, deportation—as impractical, too costly, and decidedly un-American.

What makes this narrative reconstruction of a criminal group so interesting is that it illustrates how political supporters addressed an issue that was by all accounts controversial and unpopular. Without an opinion poll or public mandate in support of amnesty, members of Congress favoring the approach engaged in questioning the public stance against illegal immigrants, arguing that if the public really understood that a deportation order might affect their friends and neighbors, they would re-evaluate their stance. In short, legalization's advocates in Congress constructed illegal immigrants as deserving the benefit, and then framed the solution as bestowing recognition, re-asserting a legal relationship between the government and unauthorized immigrants, and demanding mutual accountability via the legalization program.

IRCA Narratives and the Social Construction of Target Groups

The analysis of the House and Senate debates produced four major narratives and two corresponding counter-narratives. In each, legislators promoted a particular logic about the goals and potential effects of the bill they debated. A visual review of the narratives and related counter-narratives highlights the extent to which legislative debates serve as a forum in which participants compete to promote or destroy target group constructions in order to build consensus for policy solutions. The tables that follow summarize the relationship between each narrative and the social construction of the target groups as portrayed in these narratives,

TABLE 3.2

IRCA Policy Narratives and the Social Construction of Target Groups

Policy Narrative	Target Group	Narrative Portrayal	Target-Group Construction	Anticipated Policy Tools*	Narrative Policy Solution
Government-Off-Our-Backs	All employers	• Serve public good • Small businesses • Law abiding • Victims of government mandates	Neutral/Positive	Voluntary Positive inducements Self-regulation Resources	• Civil not criminal penalties • Remove sanctions altogether • Facilitate verification, agencies assist employers with compliance
The Family Farmer	Farm employers/perishable crop growers	• Serve public good • Small businesses • Law abiding • Victims of regulations	Positive	Resources	• Government-facilitated guest-worker programs and streamlined H2. • Special legalization incentive for agricultural workers
Anti-discrimination (a)	All employers/farm employers	• Comply with laws • Sanctions force them to discriminate. • Laws unfair to some employers	Positive	Voluntary Positive inducements Self-regulation	• Grant Fourth Amendment Protection • Sanctions should be civil not criminal • Remove all sanctions
Anti-discrimination (b)	Minority & foreign-born job applicants	• Victims of employers • Legal immigrants • U.S. citizens • Victims of government	Positive/Neutral	Voluntary Positive inducements Self-regulation	• Remove employer sanctions • Sanctions should be civil, not criminal penalties • Additional anti-discrimination protections for foreigners
Undeserving Illegal	Illegal immigrants eligible for amnesty	• Lawbreakers • Too many of them • Will eventually be eligible for citizenship	Negative	Punishments	• Do not grant amnesty; it would send the wrong message.

* Based on Schneider and Ingram's social constructions of target populations theory (1993; 1997).

TABLE 3.3
IRCA Policy Counter-Narratives and the Social Construction of Target Groups

Counter-Narrative	Narrative Addressed	Counter-Narrative Target-Group Portrayal	Group's Alternate Social Construction	Anticipated Policy Tools	Narrative Policy Solution
Corrupt Agriculturists	The Family Farmer	• Big business • Special interest • Too powerful • Law-breakers • Uncompromising	Negative	Punitive Coercive	• Sanctions • Remove special protections and special labor provisions
Deserving Illegal	Undeserving Illegal	• Hard working • Law abiding • Community members • Families • Future taxpayers • Future Americans	Positive	Resources	• Legalization

and review the counter-narratives and the alternative social constructions they posited. Each table also compares the type of policy tools that each argument favored with those that Schneider and Ingram anticipate in their social constructions of target populations theory.

Even though the preceding tables focus on the social constructions of the target groups, it is important to note that often the narratives advanced or juxtaposed the social constructions of groups who were not themselves targets of the measures under discussion. For example, in the government-off-our-backs narrative and its corollary, the family farmer narrative, those taking an anti-regulatory stance relied on negative images of big government and portrayed American consumers as injured parties in order to bolster the positive construction of employers (the actual target for sanctions). Those opposing sanctions portrayed employers as serving the public good, providing jobs, and being otherwise law-abiding people. In turn, employer sanctions opponents depicted agricultural employers as shackled by both existing and proposed federal regulations. Opponents of employer sanctions argued that the policy threatened to mire business in paperwork, and the image of the federal government as a bloated bureaucracy heaping regulations and criminal penalties on these honest folk imbues both narratives with a tone of victimization. The only way to deal with the potential disruption to business is to lighten regulations and offer inducements for compliance with them, or to create programs to ease the sting of government oversight.

The rhetoric examined here shows that legislators calculate which images will best support their preferred policy outcomes. These images are selected for their ability to cast groups as either deserving of preferential policy treatment or being unfit for special consideration. In the undeserving illegal narrative, those opposing an amnesty program compared illegal immigrants to legal immigrants in order to highlight the criminality of the former and argue that legalization would unjustly reward lawbreakers. Other versions of the narrative heightened the sense of a looming crisis by suggesting that this population of lawbreakers was too prolific. To embrace the illegal would be to encourage further illegal and legal immigration of the wrong kinds of people, devalue citizenship, and send the message that the United States rewards lawbreakers.

Supporters of legalization employed counterfactual arguments to challenge the lawbreaker image. Speakers utilized imagery typically associated with legal immigrants to re-cast illegal immigrants as rooted in American society, as members of communities, and, despite their status, as otherwise law-abiding. Rather than making a mockery of U.S. immigration laws, these people were the victims of their illicit status: the group was described as vulnerable to workplace abuse and to crime. In the deserving illegal counter-narrative, these were not transient lawbreakers: they were families with children who worked hard and were embedded in our schools, our communities, and our places of work. In short, this counter-narrative constructed this target population in terms more commonly associated with both legal immigrants and U.S. citizens. By representing them in these terms, supporters of legalization offered an alternative image of unauthorized immigrants in which the group was worthy of membership. Such competing social constructions of illegal immigrants are possible because immigrants elicit complex responses from the public. As the poll data presented at the beginning of this chapter demonstrated, perceptions that immigrants take jobs away from U.S. workers or wind up on welfare did not detract from Americans' strong belief that immigrants work hard.

Neutral and Contentious Constructions

While it is evident from the presentation of deliberation that members of Congress largely either sanctified or demonized target groups in these debates, some groups enjoyed neutral rhetorical constructions. For example, in the first version of the government-off-our-backs narrative, speakers argued that the law should not create regulatory burdens for businesses and spoke of the group dispassionately. However, in the version of the narrative dealing with the impacts of sanctions on the agricultural sector, those opposing employer sanctions constructed agriculturists as irreproachable producers of perishable goods that, in turn, benefit all Americans. As such, agricultural employers emerged as victims of Congress's regulatory zeal—an image solidified in the family farmer narrative and, once more, in the anti-discrimination narrative. In those instances, farm supporters pushed amendments that would grant agricultural employers special treatment, such as the H2A and the extension of Fourth Amendment protections to open fields.

Table 3.2 also shows that even seemingly established social constructions can be disputed. Several members of Congress rejected the virtuous and victim constructions of agriculturists, promoting instead an alternative construction that portrayed this powerful contingency as being abusive transgressors of ethical labor practices and exercising a corrupting power on congressional lawmaking. In the corrupt agriculturist counternarrative, farmers were not an interest group, but rather a special interest continually pushing for special favors and beneficial laws, which, because of its power, it often got. Another contentious construction was that of the illegal immigrant.

The existence of neutral group constructions and contested group constructions shows that social constructions do not necessarily pervade every aspect of policymaking. They are, however, most likely to inform those portions of debates in which specific groups are targeted for benefits or burdens (i.e., agricultural employers, illegal immigrants). As a large group is broken down into subgroups that will benefit from exceptions to the rules, social constructions become essential to the justification of policy tools that allow such special exceptions.

Conclusion

In their theory of social constructions of policy target populations, Schneider and Ingram predicted that group image would influence the selection of policy tools; correlatively, policy outcomes would indicate the political power and public image of target populations. What the exploration of IRCA discourse shows, however, is that the process of debate and policy selection in some cases offers an opportunity for legislators to challenge pervasive constructions, which are not in fact fixed or stable at the time of debate. Nor are national myths or symbols exempt from such challenges. To be sure, legislators do selectively employ myth and symbolism as a form of political capital deployed in defense of policy choice. For example, the family farmer narrative is steeped in myth and imagery that has considerable sway in American political culture. But then members of Congress did challenge even this venerable narrative, primarily by invoking the Reagan-era image of the greedy corporate farm, in addition to imagery from the farm-workers movement of brutal working conditions, poor pay, and labor-intensive agriculture. Their doing so demonstrates the crucial role that social constructions play in justifying policy choices.

Social constructions also allow members of Congress to explain why they both single out some groups for favor and argue for the extension of benefits beyond members of a target group. This type of activity occurred with business—a group that Congress targeted broadly for sanctions, but targeted narrowly for a significant benefit, guest-worker visas. Schneider and Ingram recognized that for powerful, positively constructed groups, policy rationales would "feature the group's instrumental links to the achievement of important public purposes."[69] The family farmer narrative fulfills this expectation: supporters of the streamlined guest-worker program (H2-A) reasoned that a provision that benefited a narrow group (farmers, and, even more specifically, perishable fruit growers) was desirable because a better agricultural worker program would benefit countless others (the processing industry, the trucking industry, and, most importantly and broadly, the American consumer). In order to make this argument appealing, its promoters portrayed the farm industry as providing a common good—namely, inexpensive foods consumed by the nation, particularly American families.

This narrative tactic can work in reverse: benefits ascribed to broadly delineated groups can be re-cast as a necessity for a narrowly defined group, which is in turn cast as requiring special protection. In the anti-discrimination narratives, we saw how a concern for civil rights and liberties of minorities justified the anti-discrimination provisions. However, by citing discriminatory application of search-and-seizure provisions in the Fourth Amendment, advocates for agricultural interests were able to extend legal protections to cover farmers as well.

The debate participants relied on images and stories that were logically appealing in order to address questions that have no fixed answers—questions such as what actions serve the greatest good? what is the appropriate relationship between government and business? and which immigrants deserve to share in the American dream? Given the role of target group constructions in rationalizing group benefits and burdens in the IRCA, and given their potential malleability, the question remains whether these same target group constructions would persist through the next round of comprehensive immigration policy reform.

4

Immigrants versus Taxpayers

The 1996 Illegal Immigration Reform and Immigrant Responsibility Act

At 8 p.m. on Tuesday, November 8, voting booths across California shut down, but the 1994 general election would resonate long afterwards. Even after its passage, Proposition 187 would linger in the headlines as both supporters and opponents awaited a final decision from ensuing court challenges to the law.[1] Pete Wilson hung onto the governorship by talking tough about illegal immigrants and hitching his ailing re-election campaign to the popular measure. The California election, while significant, did not occur in a vacuum. California's initiative process provided evidence that illegal immigrants remained an unpopular group of people, and that immigration could serve as a rallying point for voters across party and even class lines. The passage of Proposition 187 would matter nationally not only because California was an electoral-vote-rich state, but also because national opinion polls showed that Americans were concerned about the effects that immigration—all immigration—was having on the country.

In June of 1993, the *New York Times* ran a front-page story that declared that "public reaction against immigration" was "growing . . . at a time when many Americans are out of work."[2] The article quoted a concerned postal worker from Stroudsburg, Pennsylvania, who felt that "our economy is in a bad state and we should take care of our own." Contrasting a June 1993 survey with one taken in 1986 that asked the same questions, the article argued that anti-immigrant sentiment was growing in response to poor economic conditions and "a perception" held by 68 percent of respondents that recent immigrants were primarily illegal. At the same time, this poll reflects the mixed sentiment with which the American public tends to view immigrants themselves: 36 percent of respondents sensed that immigrants "take jobs away from American citizens," while 55 percent viewed immigrants as people who "take jobs Americans

TABLE 4.1
National Attitudes towards Immigrants, 1994

Question*	Very Likely	Somewhat Likely	Not Very Likely	Not at All Likely	Don't Know**	Total %
Will immigrants contribute to the national economy?	8.4	21.4	41.3	21.1	7.7	100
Will immigrants fuel unemployment?	53.9	31.1	7.9	2.3	4.8	100
Will immigrants affect national unity?	33.9	33.7	18.0	7.5	6.9	100

Source: *General Social Survey*, 1972–1996. N = 1,474
* The questions did not distinguish between legal and illegal immigrants.
** The few respondents who did not answer the question were coded as "Don't Know."

don't want," and the same number agreed with the statement that "today's immigrants work harder than people born here." These response rates showed minimal variation from findings for the same line of questioning in 1986.[3]

Nonetheless, scholars studying public opinion on immigration and immigrants have noted that American resistance to immigration surged in the 1990s, and that this resistance corresponded with a growing sense of economic insecurity in the public.[4] In addition, other data suggest that the public was also concerned about the menace to "national unity" that immigration posed. These data come from the 1994 General Social Survey Multiculturalism Module and are presented in Table 4.1. Because the questions on the survey did not ask respondents to distinguish between legal and illegal immigrants, the data reveal the American public's belief that *all* immigration was having negative economic and cultural impacts. As the analysis of congressional debates will show, policymakers promoting immigration restriction appealed to a "public opinion" or "public mandate" to address the immigration problem in its many forms.

Proposition 187 and Federal Policy Design

The new House speaker, Newt Gingrich (R-GA), who presided over the dramatic Republican takeover of the House and Senate in the 1994 midterm elections, made careful note of the strategic importance of the immigration issue in the California election and drew his own lessons for the Republican agenda and future elections.[5] When Lamar Smith (R-TX) introduced H.R. 2202 in 1995, the bill's contents would reflect the influence of 187. In addition to focusing on the lure attributed to public benefits, the bill would also contain provisions that enabled local and state government workers in non-policing entities to report unauthorized immigrants to the Immigration and Naturalization Service (INS).

While a fully restrictive policy might have resonated positively with the public, measures to restructure the legal immigration tiers to de-prioritize family reunification visas did not appear on the final bill. President Clinton, facing re-election in 1996, stated that he favored immigration reform but knew that cuts in the family reunification program would be politically unpopular.[6] The president also made it clear that he would not sign a 187-style bill that kept immigrant children out of schools or that would deny medical care to the ailing.[7] The House nonetheless included a provision in the form of the Gallegly amendment, which allowed states to bar illegal immigrant children from elementary and secondary schools. President Clinton had made it clear in August of 1996 that he would veto a bill containing the amendment, and in October, with the 1996 election closing and the chance of no immigration bill a potential outcome, the House dropped the amendment amidst pressure from Republican Senate leaders.[8]

The policy outcome suggests that viewing the Illegal Immigration Reform and Immigrant Responsibility Act simply as the federal iteration of Proposition 187 overlooks important links between problem definition, target group selection, and policy outcomes, particularly since the reform proposals would expand the population of "problem immigrants" to include both legal and illegal immigrants. That *some* legal immigrant categories went untouched may be a testament to the type of pressure that pro-immigration interests can exert on Congress. However, the law would also restrict some legal immigrants from public benefits, or deny them entry altogether. To accomplish this, Congress would expand and redefine typologies of undeserving immigrants in a way that erased traditional legal distinctions.

The Ideology of Undeserving

The analysis shows that the new policy categories of deserving and undeserving would be cast in ideological terms that pit "taxpayers" against "freeloaders" and, often, the government. This movement had been underway since the 1970s, but reached maturity during the Reagan years according to Thomas Edsall and Mary Edsall:

> The meaning of "taxes" was . . . transformed. No longer the resource with which to create a beneficent federal government, taxes had come for many voters to signify the forcible transfer of hard-earned money away from those who worked, to those who did not. Taxes had come to be seen as the resource financing a liberal federal judiciary, granting expanded rights to criminal defendants, to convicted felons, and, in education and employment, to "less qualified" minorities. Federal taxation had become, in the new coded language of politics, a forced levy underwriting liberal policies that granted enlarged rights to those members of society who excited the most negative feelings in the minds of other, often angry voters.[9]

While immigration reform has typically coincided with economic recession and ensuing insecurity in the public, Kitty Calavita argues that Proposition 187 marked a moment in which immigration too was cast as another redistributive policy that would invoke voter anger. The fact that polls showed voters unimpressed by the initiative's curative potential, but certain that its passage would "send a message to Washington," indicates a politics of anger directed not only towards immigrants, but also towards the state as the arbiter of redistribution.[10] Thus, the IIRAIRA is also a policy expression of this ideological framework.

In many ways, H.R. 2202 would overlap with the 1996 Welfare Reform Act, or PREWORA, which restricted immigrant applications for Supplemental Security Income (SSI), public housing and the newly introduced Temporary Aid to Needy Families (TANF). In addition to these limits, the IIRAIRA reinstated a century-old immigration law that restricted immigrants "likely to become a public charge" and required their families to show proof that they could support immigrant relatives at 125 percent above the federal poverty level. The bill affirmed reigning party belief in fiscal austerity achieved through individual responsibility, and the policy pursued such measures in spite of expert analyses that disputed the premise that immigration produces a net fiscal burden. As the presentation and analysis of the policy deliberation show, rhetorical treatment of immigrants differed from the previous period, and those once construed as new members of the nation would now appear as its greatest menace.

The Narratives of the 1996 Illegal Immigration Reform and Immigrant Responsibility Act

The Zero-Sum Narrative

This narrative emerged from a set of discrete problem statements that linked legal and illegal immigration with a drain on tax money, jobs, services, and classroom space. In floor debates over H.R. 2202, zero-sum discourse was the most common way of framing arguments for limiting welfare, public schooling, and medical care for immigrants. The narrative depicts America as a land of resources, but resources are limited, and those going to immigrants (legal and illegal) are by this logic diverted from American citizens.

The excerpts below come from statements offered in a House debate over the Gallegly amendment, which would have granted states the authority to deny public education to undocumented children.[11] The following example of zero-sum discourse comes from Elton Gallegly's (R-CA) introduction of his amendment for House consideration:

(1) Mr. Chairman, I believe that most of my colleagues here share my view that the Nation's education system is in crisis. Classrooms are overcrowded. Teachers are in many cases overburdened and resources are in short supply. Experts in the field agree that we are barely able to provide a basic education to American students today.

We know that there is a problem, but the body has historically refused to acknowledge the devastating effect of illegal immigration on our education system. This amendment would change that by giving States the option of denying free taxpayer-funded education to those with no legal right to be in this country. Last year, more than 40,000 Pell grants worth a combined $70 million were awarded to illegal immigrants. It is estimated that California alone spends more than $2 billion each year to educate illegal immigrants at the primary, secondary, and post-secondary level. New York spends $634 million; Florida, $424 million; Texas, $419 million.

Mr. Chairman, the list goes on and on, but the dollars and cents are only part of the story. Equally important is the fact that illegal immigrants in our classrooms are having an extremely detrimental effect on the quality of education we are able to provide to the legal residents. When illegal immigrants sit down in public school classrooms, the desk, textbooks, blackboards in effect become stolen property, stolen from the students rightfully entitled to those resources.[12]

Other representatives also made the following statements in support of the Gallegly amendment:

(2) The Supreme Court made the wrong decision 14 years ago. The bottom line is that we are talking about illegal aliens, and they are not entitled to hard-working American taxpayer money when there is not even enough money to go around for the taxpayer.[13]

(3) So here is my proposition. If this amendment goes down, I move that we take the money out of the rest of the budget and we absorb federally the cost of these children. I am going to tell you, you start going out there in a tight budget when we are trying to get to a balanced budget and you start telling your citizens, "I want to take care of illegal immigrants so much that I am going to give up my grant, I am going to give up money coming to my schools, I am going to give up money coming to my colleges, so I can send it."[14]

The Republican representatives quoted in statements 1–3 all charge that illegal immigrant children are being educated in American public schools at a growing cost to citizen taxpayers. As Representative Gallegly declares in the first quotation, and as the other statements reiterate, the nation's public school system is impoverished, and resources conferred upon the children of illegal immigrants are necessarily diverted from school renovation and adequate teaching staff and classroom space for citizen children. These statements are notable as well for another characteristic of the zero-sum narrative, which pits undocumented children against children of taxpayers; the narrative conveys the crisis of resource allocation in terms of who deserves access to the public sector and who does not.

A variation of this resource diversion problem appears in the quotation that follows:

(4) We have heard a lot of talk about compassion here, compassion for children. I would submit to the Members, there is another element of compassion, the senior citizen, the widow who is fighting to hold onto her home, and every year sees her ad valorem taxes go up, and part of that

reason, a significant part, being the cost of education. I would say that this is a matter of compassion, to restore to those who are paying the cost for our failure to enforce our immigration laws the ability to make a decision: Should they or should they not allow those who are illegally in our country to participate in the education system?[15]

According to this statement, the consequences of diverting educational resources to undocumented children are not limited to schools and citizen children; undocumented children are portrayed as thieves, as damaging to taxpayers more broadly, and as threatening needy widows and diligent senior citizen taxpayers. Tax money spent on educating illegal immigrant children is diverted from serving those who are depicted as having paid into the system—older Americans. We can also deduce from Nathan Deal (R-GA, statement 4) that even the sentiment of compassion is a limited resource, as he asks that compassion for children be redirected towards elderly citizen widows.

Children of illegal immigrants were not the only antagonists in the zero-sum story. In the debate record, legal immigrants were also tapping into strained resources upon settling in the United States:

(5)   A record high 20 percent of all legal immigrants now are receiving cash and non-cash welfare benefits. . . .

The chart I refer to now shows that the number of immigrants applying for supplemental security income, which is a form of welfare, has increased 580 percent over 12 years. The cost of immigrants using just this one program plus Medicaid is $14 billion a year.

(6)   It is sometimes said that immigrants pay more in taxes than they get in welfare benefits. However, taxes go for more then [sic] just welfare. They go toward defense, highways, the national debt, and so on. Allocating their taxes to all Government programs, legal immigrants cost taxpayers a net $25 billion a year, according to economist George Borjas. His study also found that unlike a generation ago, today immigrant households are more likely to receive welfare than native households.[16]

(7)   . . . the U.S. welfare system is rapidly becoming a retirement home for the elderly of other countries. In 1994, nearly 738,000 noncitizen residents were receiving aid from the Supplemental Security Income

program known as SSI. This is a 580-percent increase—up from 127,900 in 1982—in just 12 years.

The overwhelming majority of noncitizen SSI recipients are elderly. Most apply for welfare within 5 years of arriving in the United States. By way of comparison, the number of U.S.-born applying for SSI benefits has increased just 49 percent in the same period. Without reform, according to the Wall Street Journal, the total cost of SSI and Medicaid benefits for elderly noncitizen immigrants will amount to more than $328 billion over the next 10 years.[17]

Statements 5 and 6 show the zero-sum logic as applied to welfare usage, as well as how the zero-sum narrative would justify policies that prioritized citizens over non-citizens and measures for distinguishing between potential charges of the state and those more likely to be self-sufficient. The repeated use of the term "non-citizen" is intentional: this type of rhetoric blurs distinctions among various types of legal immigrants as well as distinctions between legal and illegal immigrants; in effect, use of such vague designations as "citizens" and "non-citizens" serves to magnify problems by broadening the problem population, and it affirms that there are qualitative differences between the two groups. In its narrative form, the rhetoric divides worthy citizens from unworthy immigrants, as illustrated in the next statements supporting a revision of the preference structure for legal permanent-resident visas:

(8) . . . America cannot be both the land of opportunity and the land of welfare dependency, and current law encourages many legal immigrants to participate in welfare programs directly or to bring elderly family members to the United States to retire at the taxpayer's expense.

Our immigration system should reward those who bring skills and initiative into this country, but it is not right to penalize our citizens by forcing them to pay benefits to people who have never contributed to the system.[18]

(9) The legal immigration we bring some degree of order to by bringing in accountability. That means when people sponsor other people, immigrants, to come to this country, the sponsor has to give some fiscal accountability. That person cannot just come in and get on welfare and bog our system down to the degree of $28 billion a year which the present legal immigrants are costing the system.[19]

(10) . . . If we don't require sponsors to fulfill their financial obligations, tax-payers will continue to pay $26 billion annually for legal immigration. Sponsors must honor their obligations so legal immigrants may become self-reliant, productive residents of the United States rather than dependents of the welfare state.[20]

These statements offer examples of words, images, and arguments that depict the qualitative deficiencies of immigrants, or "non-citizens." Each of these quotations is notable for the qualitative distinctions the speakers draw between the right and the wrong kind of lawful migrants: good immigrants "bring skill and initiative to this country," and they become "self-reliant, productive residents" (statements 8 and 10) with sponsors who have "accountability" and "honor their obligations" (statement 9) Undesirable immigrants, by contrast, are those who "never contributed to the system," "come in and get on welfare," and become "dependents of the welfare state" (statements 8–10). Whereas the undocumented are broadly painted as undeserving of access to the welfare state because of their illicit status, a distinction between deserving and undeserving legal immigrants also emerges. The distinction is not based on these immigrants' status before the law, but rather on a judgment of their motivations for immigrating.

Each example of the zero-sum narrative above frames immigrant receipt of some public good—tax money, public education—as a public resource diverted from more worthy recipients. Generally, the distinction drawn between "deserving" and "undeserving" underscored the distinction between immigrants and citizens and furthered an ideal of who is assumed to be contributing work and taxes. According to the logic laid out in the narrative, the resolution to the immigration crisis (here framed as a misallocation of resources) plainly lies in the prioritization of citizens above foreigners.

The Pathologies of Federalism Narrative

This narrative is a variation on a theme in conservative ideology that views government as the problem, and in this general respect, it corresponds with the Republican's framework for the "Contract with America." Variations of the narrative surfaced in discussions of H.R. 2202's measures to control costs and expand the powers of local and state police agencies to assist in capturing illegal immigrants. At its core, this is a story about government inefficiency. This inefficiency produces not only un-funded mandates, but also mandates that are not limited to illegal aliens, as one Midwestern Republican representative testified:

(11) We have a very serious issue facing this country with respect to refugees, and I am talking about legal refugees, not illegal refugees. The problem is that the U.S. Government makes a foreign policy decision to allow thousands and thousands and thousands of refugees to come into this country and then it dumps the cost of educating and training and supporting those refugees onto local units of government.[21]

The statement above illustrates the common theme: states are being forced to shoulder the burdens of decisions and failures of federal immigration policy.

Fiscal costs were not the only lament of this narrative. According to another one of its strains, the federal government impeded daily policing at the state and local levels. The Latham-Doolittle amendment directly addressed the issue of conflicting responsibilities between federal and state or local-level policing of illegal immigration. The amendment's provisions encouraged cooperation between local law enforcement agencies and the INS, and were ultimately included in the final IIRAIRA. The following statements from Representative Tom Latham (R-IA) and his colleague Representative Greg Ganske (R-IA) communicate the need for cooperation between federal and state law enforcement agencies because the current system of separate jurisdictions produces a gap in immigration law enforcement:

(12) All we are saying is that the local law enforcement agencies should have an opportunity to work with INS, to be their eyes and ears out in the local communities. These people are on the frontline. These people are the ones who know if someone has violated a deportation order and is in their community under a criminal act by violating that order, and they should, in fact, have the power to detail, arrest, and transport that individual to INS so that they can be deported.

Quite honestly, we have to empower our local law enforcement. We cannot maintain this big control from a Washington base here, and this is what we should be looking forward to, have more people at the local level empowered to protect their communities.[22]

(13) When we discuss the immigration problem plaguing our country, we immediately think of California, Florida, and Texas. What many may not realize is that this crisis also affects America's heartland. It is not just Miami, Los Angeles, and New York, but it is also Des Moines, Perry, and Hawarden. Iowa is currently one of only seven States without an INS office.

. . . Federal immigration officials admit they are swamped and they cannot keep up with the increasing number of undocumented workers in these States. The director of Nebraska-Iowa INS says the number of noncitizens committing crimes is increasing at, quote, "an alarming rate" about 10 percent a year over the last 10 years.

. . . Mr. Chairman, the Latham amendment helps address the problem of the paucity of INS officers by giving local law enforcement officers authority to apprehend illegal aliens when the INS just is not there to do it.[23]

(14) . . . I do not know if my colleague from Texas or California [Reps. Jackson-Lee and Becerra] are aware of things like the San Diego border task force, which is San Diego police officers patrolling the international border and getting in fire fights, gun fights with smugglers and other illegal activity that is related to the alien problem. . . .

In fact, I would ask, Mr. Chairman, that some of these people may be interested in the fact that 2 years ago, while there was flooding along the Tijuana River Valley that citizens were told that their local law enforcement should not intervene and stop illegal aliens from walking through their areas while looting was going on because somehow this might violate the jurisdictional lines between the two. . . .

This is not an issue of the Federal Government encroaching out into the community. . . . We are talking about the fact of doing what we talk about here, allowing the local community to contribute to the federal effort.[24]

The congressmen quoted in statements 12 and 13 communicate a grave dilemma posed by the separation of law enforcement jurisdictions. However, the structure of the federal system is itself not the problem: both statements also tell of criminal activities among the illegal population that go unchecked because of the jurisdictional boundaries. In statement 12, Greg Ganske (R-IA) argues that while illegal immigrants live in America's neighborhoods, they are shielded from deportation or prosecution by the separation between state and federal law enforcement. In statement 14, the federal structure is construed to work against local law enforcement, placing it at odds with the community it serves in San Diego. Additionally, all three statements argue that the federal government is overwhelmed and needs the assistance of local law enforcement to do its job.

Representatives opposing efforts to build links between federal and local authorities argued that a bill that encouraged reporting between local police and other government entities and the INS might ruin relationships between communities and the police, and was a violation of the principles of federalism:

(15) . . . It actually breaks the ground of what we have had in this entire country of jurisdictional responsibility for law enforcement in the hands of our various law enforcement authorities.

You never find the FBI, you never find the border patrol, trying to give someone a speeding ticket. . . . You do not find the California Highway Patrol or any other State's highway patrol trying to enforce national immigration law. And that is because those are separate and distinct activities. [25]

More prevalent than critiques of Latham-Doolittle, however, was the notion that immigration control suffered from jurisdictional divisions among law enforcement agencies.[26]

The Criminal Alien Narrative

This narrative overlaps with the jurisdiction narrative because in both, the villains are immigrants who either are in the country illicitly or are involved in crimes, or both. However, the problem statements associated with the criminal alien narrative follows a different logic from that of the jurisdiction narrative. While the latter narrative arose from sets of statements identifying the separation of law enforcement powers as problematic, the criminal alien narrative emerged from a set of recurring statements linking undocumented immigrants to criminal activity or labeling this group as inherently criminal. What emerges is a narrative construction of an essentially deviant group of people.

The statements below, which generate images of a criminally deviant illegal immigrant population, exemplify the type of rhetoric offered on the floor of the House:

(16) We look at the drugs coming across the flow, and on those drug ride-alongs, 99 percent have involved illegal aliens.

American citizens that are dealing in drugs know that if an illegal is caught, then there is not as much penalty that is going to go to them versus if they are an American citizen.[27]

(17) Mr. Speaker, just to put into perspective the problem we will be considering over the next 2 days let me begin with a few facts.

No. 1: Nationwide more than one-quarter of all Federal prisoners are illegal aliens.

According to the Immigration and Naturalization Service, in 1980, the total foreign-born population in Federal prisons was 1,000 which was less than 4 percent of all inmates. In 1995, the foreign-born population in Federal prisons was 27,938, which constitutes 20 percent of all inmates. The result is an enormous extra expense to be picked up by the Federal taxpayers.[28]

(18) . . . We went into the place [an apartment complex housing suspected illegal immigrants], and I mean it was so bad, the conditions, that it was unbelievable; I mean the filth, the debris, and I could see needles where druggers were using it. We would see a mattress where prostitutes were using it, and in the corner was a teddy bear, and yet we could not go in. There were violations, and it seemed like there were more rules to keep us from resolving the problem.[29]

The statements above illustrate the causal relationship that members of Congress drew between illegal immigrants and criminal behavior. In the first quotation (16), illegal immigrants are involved in drug-trafficking and drug-dealing. In statement 17, the crimes are not identified, but the imagery of prisons whose inmates are one-fourth illegal immigrants sends a message about the proportions of the illegal immigration crisis while at the same time placing a significant portion of these people in the federal prison system. Finally, while the first two examples clearly delineate the criminal nature of the illegal population, statement 18, by contrast, does not claim that the immigrants are criminals, but rather that the areas in which they reside are crime-ridden; crime coexists with this population. We do not know whether the "prostitutes" or "druggers" are themselves illegal or even immigrants, but this criminal climate is intertwined with the illegal dwellers.

While criminal activity reappeared as a theme throughout the transcripts, speakers relied upon another important problem statement: the criminality of persons who have entered U.S. territory without inspection. Members of Congress speaking in support of H.R. 2202 repeatedly reminded their colleagues that illegal immigrants are criminals by definition. The following excerpts illustrate this practice:

(19) . . . The issue here is that an illegal alien, healthy, sick, or injured, is still an illegal alien. Anyone present in the United States illegally is a lawbreaker, and should expect to suffer the consequences if caught.[30]

(20) . . . [T]his is a system that is working backwards. We spend millions and millions of dollars in border patrol and INS and signs at the border saying "Do not come across." It is illegal to cross into this country illegally. It is illegal.[31]

Some statements were less explicit in relating illegal immigrants to crime, but they still effectively linked the undocumented population to criminal activity. The Tate amendment, which was included in the final draft of the bill, punished illegal immigrants by denying them the chance to reapply for legal entry. Below is an excerpt from Representative David Dreier's introduction of the final version of the bill to the full House:

(21) Mr. Speaker, the gentleman from Washington (Mr. Tate) and the gentlewoman from California (Mrs. Seastrand) will offer a commonsense amendment to clarify that if someone violates American laws and enters the country illegally, then they will no longer be eligible to later become a legal immigrant. Legal immigration should be reserved for those who respect our laws.[32]

In keeping with the sense that this is a population of lawbreakers, the law would produce a criminal mark for those crossing the border illicitly.

In the discussions about portions of H.R. 2202 limiting benefits access to illegal immigrants and their children, an additional crime was linked to illegal immigrants—welfare fraud. The Fourteenth Amendment of the U.S. Constitution grants birthright citizenship to children born of illegal immigrant parents. Because these children are citizens, they are entitled to AFDC, but because agencies cannot issue checks directly to the children, their parents (who may be undocumented) receive the disbursements.

Though the speaker reiterates that public benefits are a magnet for illegal immigration, in this case the magnet also leads criminals to commit more crime. Thus, the situation resulting from providing for the poor citizen children of undocumented parents is welfare fraud:

(22) . . . So you are in a situation that when you say you are going to give illegal aliens public assistance funds for their children, you are de facto either giving them money to support themselves in violation of the welfare law, or you are condoning the fact that they are working in violation of the law. They are not declaring income, which is a violation of their welfare status for their child. So what we have here is a catch-22 in an absurd situation.[33]

An analogous problem statement is that illegal immigrants come to the United States to give birth to citizens so that they can consume their child's benefits:

(23) I think we have all seen situations in which we have heard the traditional description of bootstrapping your way into a benefit. This is booty-strapping. This is a situation in which, by virtue of the act of illegal entry on the part of a parent, the birth of the child gives the right to benefits from the taxpayers' coffers.[34]

The rationale of this excerpt is that welfare must be denied to U.S. citizen children in order to return the rule of law to the country. Thus, while the Fourteenth Amendment grants these children the rights of full U.S. citizenship, their parents are defined not as parents of citizens, but as perpetual offenders transgressing immigration laws and defrauding federal and state governments.

The Lawless Border Narrative

The hearings on the implementation of Operation Gatekeeper, the border deterrence measures that the IIRAIRA would expand, produced much of the rhetoric about the lawless border. This story line is linked to the criminal alien narrative because as the means for illegal immigration (criminals), the border is also a breeding ground for smugglers, drugs, violence, and generalized chaos, as the following excerpted testimonials illustrate:

(24) I think that all three Congressmen [at this hearing] know what the scenario was back then [before Gatekeeper]. We were overrun, completely and totally. Our apprehension rates were running anywhere from 2,500 to 3,000 on a daily basis. People were camping on the United States side. There was no delineation of the border. There wasn't a fence; there were remnants of fences. People were all over the place. I had a terrific challenge, in my mind, as to how I am going to control this portion of the border; this is literally incredible. . . . It was completely out of control. . . .[35]

The statement above by Gus de la Vina, then a regional head of the INS, speaks to the necessity of fortifying and delineating the border and of bringing order to the region by physically segregating the two sides. The chaos language appears in phrases like "we were overrun" and "people were all over the place," and imagery of a dilapidated place in which "remnants of fences" are the only separators between the orderly United States and the disorderly population threatening to overtake the country is also apparent.

In the testimonials and ensuing discussions, the U.S.-Mexico border was described as a "hot-spot," a war zone with casualties, and a region where territory must be controlled with firepower, deterrence measures, and barricades. The following exchange between Brian Bilbray (R-CA), whose district in San Diego County was the site of Gatekeeper, and the head of the National Border Patrol Council illustrates this type of rhetoric:

(25) Mr. Bilbray: Could you control the border in the sector [San Diego] sector with twice the forces now?

Mr. Bonner (President of National Border Patrol Council): I don't think you could. Smuggling is organized crime, both the smuggling of people and drugs. You have certain parts of turf of that are staked out by these criminals. You don't just move from Tijuana over to Mexicali, for example without getting your kneecaps blown off. . . .

Mr. Bilbray: Mr. Bonner, let me just tell you, as somebody who has had to pull illegal aliens drowning out of his pool at 3 a.m., somebody who has regrettably had to recover bodies with a 9-year-old son in tow, something I don't think any child should have to live through, there are those of us who have seen our neighborhoods turning into a battleground. . . .[36]

According to Representative Bilbray, the chaos of the border spreads into communities so that "our neighborhoods are turning into a battleground." It follows, then, that having identified the border as the problem, policy-makers would see fortressing as the solution:

(26) We have $5 million in, and that is now passed and this will be signed by the President, and the defense bill for National Guardsmen to build a steel fence in East County.

But we are going to have to have out there 400 or 500 or 600 Border Patrol agents basically for deploying on the line . . . and if we can't make the academy turn out people at a high enough rate, only able to buildup at a couple hundred to 1,000 a year, we are going to have to do what we do in time of war. That means blow the academy open, enlarge it drastically, maybe borrow military facilities and roll through maybe 15,000, 20,000 Border Patrol agents. . . .

But I think what we're coming to realize now is there is no substitute for having a border. That means having a fence, roads for lateral movement, lights, lights so you can work this thing at night, and people.[37]

In statement 25, the border appears as a breeding ground for criminals, criminal behavior, contraband, and cadavers. To regain control of the crisis depicted, legislators present called for military-style deployment, which, as a Republican congressman explains in statement 26, is what "we do in time of war," not just of the Border Patrol, but also of the National Guard.

In these statements, the border is described as the source of illegal immigration. In this respect, the lawless border narrative is notable for its de-contextualization of illegal immigration as a phenomenon—it is not the product of another nation, or the result of social and economic structures, or a cyclical movement of populations from both sides that has existed historically in the region. Rather, the region, the actual boundary between the United States, and Mexico is identified as the problem source, and the cure for illegal immigration rests in the enforcement of that line.

The Government-Off-Our-Backs Narrative

This narrative, notably, appeared in the IRCA debates a decade earlier. Once again, the story portrays immigration control efforts (regulations embodied by the federal government) as imposing heavy or even unnecessary burdens on particular groups of people, namely employers. The narrative characterizes employers as virtual underdogs who diligently comply with the IRCA's requisites for hiring in good faith, yet find themselves either ensnared in the inefficient federal bureaucracy or reaping punishments for their adherence to the law. While the IRCA debates over the immigrant labor force in agriculture introduced this narrative, its 1995–1996 version spoke generally of the burdens that government imposed on all employers—not just agriculturists.

The storyline appeared in portions of the *Congressional Record* dealing with efforts to improve employer sanctions and verify worker eligibility. Analyses of the INS's implementation of employer sanctions from previous years revealed that both weak enforcement and poor resources led to the persistence of illegal hiring. The *Record* shows that some members of Congress had assimilated this information and demanded more funding for sanctions enforcement. However, many more legislators made an argument whose logic pinned the failure of sanctions on the onerous regulations and misdirected crackdowns on employers, instead of on shortfalls in policy implementation. The narrative sets the federal government against employers, portraying the government as punishing the wrong people.

Legislators deployed this narrative in an appeal to streamline the worker eligibility procedures. In this narrative, federal efforts to crack down on undocumented immigrants mire employers in paperwork and policing. The narrative characterizes employers as responsible individuals doing their best to comply with excessive federal laws. The solution is for the government to ease the burden on employers and to encourage compliance by facilitating it:

(27) I've talked to people that have literally been fined $50,000 for forgetting to cross the Ts and dot the Is and you didn't fill out square C, that's another $3,000. And for these people, it's a nightmare. Now, if you compare that to a system where you could dial in a social security number and get a response and get a verification number, you write that down on your notebook and you hire the person that's in question, then you go on about your business, and if somebody questions you later, all you have to do is show that you did the verification call.[38]

(28) In short, the ultimate big brother is Congress saying they know better than employers how to run their businesses. Let us trust business

owners to decide what is best for them. The quick check system is a convenience many want, and that is why the National Federation of Independent Business does not oppose this quick check verification system.[39]

(29) . . . In reality, we all know that the I-9 process already exists out there that the employers must use with potential employees. But right now we put these employers in a catch box. As my colleagues know, if they ask too many questions of a potential applicant for a job, they question the documents as to whether they are counterfeit, they can be sued by these applicants. But on the other hand, if they do not ask enough questions and they hire an illegal, then the INS can come in and fine them.

So we are putting these employers in difficult situations, which this process, by use of the 1-800 number on a voluntary basis, will help alleviate. It will be a defense to those employers. . . .[40]

All three statements depict businesses that are faced with onerous compliance requirements. In the first, there are the heavy fines levied for inattention to small details; in the second, Congress meddles in the functioning of business; and in the third, regulations result in a "damned if they do, damned if they don't" scenario for employers. Statements 27 and 29 depict a system whose design causes employers to violate the law. Each speaker favors a system that is easier for employers to use.

Interestingly, the argument that government should not burden business also provided ammunition for members of Congress wishing to strike the national expansion of a worker eligibility hotline:

(30) Mr. Chairman, this system is to be added on top of the burdensome I-9 document review requirements that started us down the road, down the path of making employers into Federal agents. Congress was assured in 1986 that that program would, quote, "terminate the problem." Well, it has not. Remarkably, that program's very failure is advanced as a justification for proceeding further down that path.[41]

(31) Whether we like it or not, this is an unfunded mandate, an increased paperwork burden on American business. Phone-in verification is an addition to the I-9, not a substitute. Employers must keep this additional information in order to prove they obey the law.[42]

As both statements illustrate, those who opposed the hotline's expansion pointed to existing verification procedures (the I-9 form) and cautioned against adding additional procedures for employers.

A similar logic of lifting the burdens of employment eligibility from the shoulders of businesses also appeared among supporters of extended and/or streamlined guest-worker programs.[43] In this case, not only are requirements for guest workers difficult to comply with, H.R. 2202 might leave some sectors without the labor needed to run them:

(32) Mr. Chairman, my district consists of approximately 18,000 farms. Most of these farms engage in the production of cucumbers, sweet potatoes, tobacco, and peanuts, very labor-intensive work. Roughly 80 percent of the produce in my district is harvested by seasonal migrant workers. Throughout our Nation, as in North Carolina, seasonal workers have helped labor-intensive farm commodities to become the fastest growing sector of the U.S. agricultural world.

However, farmers in the South are having a very difficult time finding people to do farm work. If it was not for the migrant workers, our farmers would not be able to harvest their crops. We need to guarantee our farmers an ample supply of legal workers. . . .

Congress is trying to control illegal immigration, not destroy the work force of the American farmer. Please support the Pombo Amendment.[44]

(33) Many fruit and vegetable growers assert that the big problem with the H-2A program is that the Department of Labor administers in bad faith, intending to make it unworkable and unattractive to growers. . . .

Growers also complain that it takes too long to get workers under the current H-2A program. They must file applications at least 60 days before the date of employment. My amendment slashes this period by 33 percent and creates a 40-day application period. It will ensure growers the workers they need when they need them.

. . . Mr. Chairman, I agree with the gentleman 100 percent that U.S. workers should have the priority in every instance. But the fact of the matter is that while we still require them to actively recruit and we should require them to actively recruit U.S. workers, it has to be done in such a fashion that once that recruitment period is over, there is a reasonable amount of time to get the paperwork processed and get workers there when they have actively recruited and have not been able to get those workers.

My amendment simply requires that they have a little more time, 20 more days, to get that paperwork processed and get the workers there. We have had many instances, in fact some of the people on the other side of the last amendment spoke about the fact that they go through the process, by the time all the work is done they are halfway though the harvest season and they do not get the opportunity to get the workers when they need them.[45]

The speakers in statements 32 and 33 emphasize that the H-2A program is not working for growers because the Department of Labor "administers in bad faith," and the program is inefficient in getting workers in time to harvest crops for farmers who fill out worker requests. The first speaker cautions Congress "not destroy the workforce of the American farmer" by reforming immigration laws without streamlining H-2A. The second statement pleads with Congress to make H-2A attractive to growers by giving them more time to file forms and by cutting down on how long it takes the Department of Labor to fill harvest needs. While the Pombo-Chambliss reforms did not pass, the Goodlatte amendment did, increasing the cap on guest worker admissions from 17,000 to 100,000 and streamlining the H-2A application procedures.[46]

The Cure-Is-Worse-than-the-Disease Counter-Narrative

As is customary in debates, those who did not agree with the proposed policy solutions had opportunities to voice their opposition. However, in contrast to the IRCA debates, which revealed a point-counterpoint pattern in the policy narratives, in the case of the IIRAIRA debates, only one true counter-narrative emerged, in discussions of the Gallegly Amendment, and the public charge provisions for legal immigration (Title V, subtitles B and C).

This storyline disputed the merits of the bill, warning that if H.R. 2202 (or specific components of it) passed, a variety of foreseeable problems would result, problems perhaps worse than the ones facing the legislators at present. This is actually a common rhetorical device referred to as a "parade of horribles," which, as its title and the following examples illustrate, employs hypothetical and hyperbolic situations, often playing upon common fears in an effort to dissuade an audience from a particular action or from accepting a particular idea. The Gallegly amendment debates, for example, gave rise to a consistently grim scenario regarding the effects of its passage and states being able to deny illegal immigrant children the right to an education:

(34) . . . supporters of this proposal often mention the cost to our school systems, and of course, they, are substantial. But the societal costs, Mr. Chairman, of allowing States to deny public education to children are even greater. Such a policy would contribute to crime, to illiteracy, to ignorance, to discrimination. It would clearly run counter to the long-term interests of American communities and American society. Denying an education to any child, I think is unwise and inhumane.[47]

(35) . . . The first best preferred outcome is, of course, that those who came here illegally be returned to the country of their origin with their children, and that would be constitutional to do because the children are under the custody of the parent. But we do not have the resources to do that. This bill does not give us the resources to do that. We are not hiring INS agents to expel every illegal family that is here.

So, Mr. Chairman, I put to my colleagues the essential tradeoff. Is it better to have such children in school, or kept out of school at the risk that their parents would be turned in to the Immigration and Naturalization Service? Are there gangs in Los Angeles waiting to recruit such children? Are there gangs in San Jose willing to recruit such children? Are there gangs in San Francisco and every major city of my State of California? Of course there are. If these children are here, we must educate them rather than have them be recruited, if those are our options.[48]

(36) . . . We have no right to point fingers at children and block their entrance to the schoolhouse. All we will succeed in doing is stigmatizing children and encouraging negative behavior. . . .[49]

(37) . . . At a time when juvenile violence is on the rise, this amendment would deprive a large group of children in our communities of the only thing that can keep them out of trouble, and that is an education. . . . Children thrown on the streets by this amendment will not simply

disappear. They will be left with nothing to do during school hours, tempting them to pursue a host of non-educational activities. One can only imagine the possibilities. . . .[50]

(38) Mr. Chairman, not coming from a State that has a serious immigration problem, I have tried to listen and learn about this issue. . . . But let us all understand something. The question here is not whether people can come into this country. . . . The question is, while we are finding [illegal immigrants] and while the deportation process is moving forward should their children be on the streets unsupervised or in the schools? I think the vast majority of American people would say, "Well, they should be in the schools. They should not be out running loose as gangs unsupervised on the streets."[51]

(39) . . . These children will not leave the United States simply because they are not in school. They will be, as all of our speakers pointed out, on the streets, joining gangs, left at home alone, for there is a price to be paid in terms of community health and community well-being, not to mention the harm to the children themselves.[52]

Statements 34–39 show little variation in the case they make against denying education to undocumented children, and this case follows a distinctive narrative pattern: these children should not be denied schooling, but if the Gallegly amendment were to pass, children would end up on the streets, in gangs, and create a long-term problem for society.

This narrative is the counter to the zero-sum storyline. It explains why it is preferable for states to provide space in classrooms for illegal children; it provides its own resolution (keep these kids in school); and it offers a plausible if hypothetical scenario (juvenile crime), should states bar them from schools. And while only six examples appear above, nearly all of those who spoke against Gallegly reiterated this logic.

In a similar manner, the cure-is-worse-than-the disease narrative disputed the bill's section 607 provisions to stop AFDC and Food Stamp disbursements to illegal immigrants collecting payments on behalf of their citizen children:

(40) This section of the bill makes it virtually impossible for many American children to receive public benefits. It creates a two-tier caste system where U.S.-born children of immigrants are treated differently from the

children of U.S. citizens. This ignores the premise of equal protection, a blatant violation of these children's constitutional rights.

This provision affects far more than just the children of undocumented parents. It also affects the U.S.-born children of legal permanent residents. These are American children of parents who work hard and pay taxes, who start businesses and create jobs. Under these provisions, they too would be unable to file for benefits on behalf of their U.S. citizen children.

If these provisions are not removed, Congress will create a costly and overburdened administrative system. Our children will be forced to choose between a bureaucratic nightmare or relying on the kindness of strangers. This surely is a recipe for disaster.[53]

(41) Mr. Chairman, our duty as Members of the House of Representatives is to uphold and defend the Constitution of the United States. Sometimes this is not popular. If it were popular, we would not have to take an oath to uphold and defend the Constitution of the United States. . . .

It is not popular to stand up and say anything good in favor of the children of those who have come here illegally. But it matters as an issue of law and our Constitution that such children born here are American citizens. There is no debate on this issue. There is no dispute on this between both sides. Both sides have agreed these are American citizens.

Now, what do you do with the child who is an American citizen? The child cannot receive benefits except through the parent. There is no other way. You do not give benefits directly to children.

Accordingly, the bill as presently presented and without the amendment of the gentlewoman from New York would constitute a violation of the 14th amendment. It would deny to some citizens, on the basis of nothing they have done wrong, benefits to which other citizens are entitled.

Mr. Chairman, it is unconstitutional; we must vote against this policy and for this amendment.[54]

(42) Mr. Chairman, I would just like to follow up on the points made by the two gentlemen from San Diego [Mr. Cunningham and Mr. Bilbray] . . . the notion that undocumented aliens, illegal aliens, are not here in this country working, is a fiction, because employer sanctions in their present state without verification is a fiction. So the notion that everyone who is here undocumented has children of AFDC is nonsense, pure

nonsense. The GAO reported back in 1992 that 2 percent of the funds are going to the children of undocumented aliens, 2 percent of the funds. That puts it in perspective.

Remember what the gentleman from California (Mr. Campbell) said. If you want to get to this issue, propose a constitutional amendment to change the 14th amendment. Do not create a big government, cumbersome, guardian process to deny U.S. citizens their rights. Change the Constitution which makes them citizens. I will fight it with every ounce of my energy, but that is the honest way to go.[55]

The Republican and Democratic congressmen quoted in statements 40 and 41, respectively, argue that H.R. 2202 is bad public policy because section 607 violates the Constitution and would create a "bureaucratic nightmare." As statement 41 further asserts, 607 is a solution out of proportion to the size of the problem. The resolution to this variant of the cure-is-worse-than-the-disease counter-narrative would be for Congress to strike 607 altogether and/or pursue the issue as a constitutional amendment instead.

Another variation of the counter-narrative challenged H.R. 2202's components by arguing that they would lead to discrimination against groups or individuals. Debates over the Latham-Doolittle amendment, which gave local law enforcement the authority to assist the INS and Department of Justice in locating, apprehending, and detaining illegal immigrants, provide examples of the discrimination counter-narrative:

(43) . . . I think this amendment may have good intentions, but it certainly is paved wrongly and the road goes in the completely wrong direction. This is not the direction we should send local law enforcement, to make them the entrappers of individuals who may look different or speak a different language. . . .

In particular, our large cities, like a Houston that has a multicultural community, it is important that those communities who speak a different language realize that when the police come, they are there to enforce the universal laws and prevent crime against those citizens, and anyone who is doing a crime will be arrested.[56]

(44) . . . If I can just cite for my colleagues' consideration at some point the reports by the Commission on Civil Rights, which has said that in the past there have been occasions when some very aggressive, zealous

local law enforcement officials have actually detained people because of their foreign-looking appearance or because of their racial or ethnic appearance.

We have had instances where local law enforcement officials, believing they have the authority, have taken some of these measures without that authority and in fact caused the violation of certain rights that individuals have in maintaining their own privacy and being free of government intrusion, especially if they have committed no wrong. Just because one may look foreign does not mean one should be apprehended or stopped. . . .[57]

The representatives quoted in statements 43 and 44 both raise the issue of potential for discrimination should local law enforcement incur the authority to assist the INS. Texas Democrat Sheila Jackson-Lee (statement 43) argued that Latham-Doolittle might erode relationships between local police and immigrant communities, while Representative Xavier Becerra (D-CA, statement 44) cited precedents of policing abuses against racial and ethnic minorities to suggest that an expansion of authority might encourage additional abuses by local officials.

A final variant of the cure-is-worse-than-the-disease counter-narrative emerged as the House debated better ways to verify worker eligibility and improve the social security card so that it would be harder to counterfeit. Both policy cures would lead to violations of citizen privacy and push the federal government into the role of "Big Brother." Examples from the debate over extending the 1-800 employer verification hotline appear below:

(45) OK, [the 1-800 pilot program extension] is the famous camel's nose under the tent amendment. This is the one where it starts off real nice. Not to worry, folks. It is OK. Trust us. We will make it a pilot project. Will that make it OK? We will make it a temporary project. We will make it voluntary. We will do it just like we did the Japanese internment program when we said we are going to find out who the Japanese are that need to be rounded up. And how did they do that so quickly? They used the census data. Government trusters, that is where that came from. So congratulations, voluntary, temporary program for employment verification.[58]

(46) . . . To have the Federal Government of the United States be a last word on whether someone works today or whether someone does not

is particularly odious. It is anathema to the reason most of us came here. To have the Federal Government of the United States say, "You may work today because we have decided that you're here legally, and we're going to trust that all the records are right, that we're going to go ahead and say that there's no glitch in it," and all in an effort to make the I-9 form, odious by itself, work better is wrong-headed as well as being merely wrong. . . .[59]

(47) . . . I ask my colleagues here today to listen and to listen closely as I relate a personal story about the dark side of employment verification, because no matter how well-intentioned this system appears, the consequences can be ominous.

I raised my kids in France for a few years while I served as the U.S. Ambassador to UNESCO in Paris. One day my son was coming home from school alone. He was apprehended by the French police and asked to produce his national identity card. He did not have it with him. He was detained, arrested, and taken to jail. I had to go take him out, simply because he did not have a card. He did not look French.

Are we ready, as a bastion of freedom and democracy, to subject the citizens of this country to the same type of insidious mistakes? If we do not pass the Chabot-Conyers amendment to strike, I think we will be doing that. . . .

Mr. Chairman, do not be deluded. This employment verification is only the first step. As the gentleman from Michigan (Mr. Conyers) has said, this is the nose under the tent towards a national identification card, a first step towards the loss of our freedom. Remember this, only a small percentage of employers knowingly hire undocumented workers. . . .[60]

Statements 45–47 invoke slippery-slope logic: do not create an employer verification hotline because it will entice the federal government to trample citizens' privacy. The pilot program is a "nose under the tent" that the House should defeat lest it prod the nation towards police state tactics. Such tactics are exemplified in references to the World War II internment of Japanese, and the anecdote that Esteban Torres (D-CA) delivered (statement 47) in which French officials apprehended a child who was not carrying any documentation. The consequences, should the national voluntary hotline pass, would be dire, and the only way to avoid the slippery slope is for legislators to vote to strike it.[61]

Summary: H.R. 2202, Policy Narratives, and Social Constructions

The five narratives that pervaded congressional discourse about H.R. 2202 framed each problem for a specific type of policy solution. Table 4.2 compares the type of policy tools that Anne Schneider and Helen Ingram's social constructions of target populations theory anticipates for each target group's construction to the policy tools legislators selected to resolve immigration issues. Table 4.2 shows that, as was the case for the IRCA, so for the IIRAIRA, actual immigration policy tools corresponded closely with the tools that Schneider and Ingram's theory would predict, given the social constructions of the target groups. For negatively constructed groups (illegal immigrants, legal immigrants, and children of illegal immigrants) some of the policy tools were designed to coerce specific behaviors, such as individual or family-level fiscal responsibility. Other tools such as incarceration, identification requirements, and threat of deportation were of the punitive type that is attached to truly negatively constructed groups (in this case, "criminal aliens"). By contrast, the "good guys" here, the INS/Border Patrol and employers, enjoyed inducements and resources.

Again, the narratives also juxtaposed multiple group constructions. For example, in the zero-sum narrative, the negative social construction of immigrants as freeloaders was contrasted with frequent references to "taxpayers" and "citizens." In these debates, "citizens" could legitimately claim public benefits by birthright, and "taxpayers," who were construed as hard-working and deserving of the public benefits they presumably subsidize, were conflated with "citizens." This type of juxtaposition was evident as well in the pathologies of federalism narrative, where the positive construction of state and local officials played against the illegal immigrants who were repeatedly portrayed as criminals. Even though the resolution of this narrative lay in targeting states and localities for federal assistance, the political cachet of the narrative rests on the deviant construction of illegal aliens—a construction further fortified by the criminal alien narrative.

What is perhaps most remarkable about the 1994–1996 period when contrasted with the debates in the 1980s is that there were few challenges of the target populations' constructions. The debate and hearing transcripts revealed only one true counter-narrative whose various expressions shared the thematic thread of H.R. 2202 being worse than the troubles it would address. Other objections to the policy took the form of

TABLE 4.2

IIRAIRA Policy Narratives and the Social Constructions of Target Groups

Policy Narrative	Target Group	Narrative Portrayal	Social Construction	Anticipated Policy Tools*	Actual Policy Tools
Zero Sum	Legal and illegal immigrants, children of illegal, immigrants	• Freeloaders • On welfare • Non-contributors • Absorbing citizens' benefits	Negative	Punitive Coercive	• Restrict access to SSI, housing, TANF, Food Stamps** • Enforce public charge laws
Pathologies of Federalism	States and localities	• On the front lines • Diligent • Frustrated by federal laws • Burdened with crime and illegal immigrants	Positive	Voluntary Positive inducements	• Facilitate information sharing among jurisdictions. • Block grants to states absorbing costs of immigration populations.
Criminal Alien	Illegal immigrants	• Lawbreakers	Negative	Punitive Coercive	• Incarceration • Identification • Deportation
Lawless Border	The INS/Border Patrol	• Overwhelmed • Under siege	Positive	Resources	• Barrier construction • Expansion of patrol border & pilot programs
Government-Off-Our-Backs	Employers	• Trustworthy • Diligent • Law abiding	Positive	Voluntary Positive inducements Self-regulation	• Streamlined I-9 • Streamlined H-2A • Verification hotline • Burden of proof shift to plaintiffs: proof of employer's "intent to discriminate."

* Based on Schneider and Ingram's social construction of target population theory (1993; 1997).

** Although the Gallegly amendment would have denied access to schools, and although it enjoyed consideration on the floor, it did not pass.

critiques, or rebuttals about particular measures that had nothing to unify them other than their shared objection to the policy. The problem with critiques is that they offer policymakers nothing to act upon or, worse yet, suggest that any activity is pointless. This latter suggestion appeared in the debates over border enforcement; most of these critiques simply stated that border deterrence measures would not work, intimating that enforcement, in essence, was futile.

To evaluate the success of the one counter-narrative that did emerge, we can consider whether or not it achieved an alternative portrayal of its target group. Recall that IRCA counter-narratives about agriculture and illegal immigrants employed counterfactual arguments to dispute the family farmer and undeserving illegal narratives. Agricultural employers were not only victims, but also victimizers who preyed on an unprotected workforce. Illegal immigrants were not only freeloaders or criminals, but also members of the community, families, and taxpayers. Table 4.3 revisits the IIRAIRA narratives and compares the social constructions of groups appearing in them to how the counter-narrative characterized the same

TABLE 4.3

IIAIRA Policy Counter-Narratives and the Social Construction of Target Groups

Group	Narrative Portrayal	Counter-Narrative Portrayal	Social Construction
Legal Immigrants	Freeloaders On welfare Don't contribute	None	Negative
States and Localities	On the front lines Diligent Frustrated by federal laws Shoulder the burdens of law enforcement and illegal immigrants	Law enforcement is discriminatory	Mixed
Illegal Immigrants	Criminals	Criminals	Negative
Children of Illegal Immigrants	Absorb public dollars that should go to American citizen children	Innocent Protected by Constitution Potential delinquents	Mixed
Employers	Trustworthy Diligent Law abiding	None	Positive
Federal Government*	Inefficient Punishes the wrong people (employers)	Big Brother Insidious	Negative

* Not an IIRAIRA target group, but a group that was contrasted with target groups and whose construction, therefore, remained elemental to the policy stories used to justify the IIRAIRA's components.

group (where applicable). In the primary example of the cure-is-worse-than-the-disease counter-narrative, members of Congress who opposed the denial of education, medical care, and welfare payments to children of illegal immigrants pointed to the crises the nation would face if the law barred children from the social safety net. While this substantially contested the zero sum narrative, the counter-narrative did not alleviate the negative social construction of these children. In fact, the power of the challenging story rests in a particular rhetorical form, the parade of horribles. As such, the counter-narrative portrayed these children uniformly as little criminals, or as potential gangsters requiring schooling to curb their tendency towards delinquency. In this noteworthy respect, these children of immigrants did not dodge the criminal alien stigma even though their right to an education remained protected by the Supreme Court.

Narrative Constructions and Alternative Stories in the IIRAIRA

When Anne Schneider and Helen Ingram expanded their theory of social constructions and policy design to account for policy change, they noted that "changed social construction[s] of deservedness can precipitate change in policy and, alternatively, public policy can alter construction."[62] In light of the shift from the IRCA to the IIRAIRA, their statement, on both accounts, does not hold true in the case of illegal immigrants. Many of those legal immigrants targeted under IIRAIRA's benefits restrictions had been brought under the protection of the state through the IRCA's legalization programs. Immigrants' newly acquired legal status should, in theory, have exempted them from being cast as undeserving. Yet as the narrative analysis of the 1996 IIRAIRA demonstrated, legal status no longer served to shield them from negative constructions, particularly when the new policy climate expanded the population of undeserving by rhetorically lumping immigrants with other groups in society characterized as freeloaders and lawbreakers.

The stated purpose of the IIRAIRA was to deter illegal immigration and control the quality of legal immigration by limiting those who could not provide for themselves or their families. This would serve the broader goal of restoring fiscal order to overspent budgets, although the bill did little to directly address the primary complaint of states, which was the maldistribution of tax dollars. While the goal of the policy was to remove people from publicly funded rolls, a lesser-known fact is that Congress voted in 1998 and 2002 to gradually reinstate immigrant access to federal aid programs.[63] Much of this was done quietly, with some pressure from immigrant advocacy groups, and was accomplished through provisions tucked away in other bills that had nothing to do with immigration. In fact, the senior presidential advisor at the time, Karl Rove, joked that the president would sign the 2002 Farm Security and Rural Reinvestment Act, which reinstated Food Stamps for certain immigrants and minor children, "by candlelight."[64]

The interplay of these policy events—the national political spectacle of bashing immigrants, followed by an unpublicized, calm legislative acknowledgement of a policy mistake or overreach—confirms that legislative policymaking is not a neutral ground for equally armed groups to barter for preferential policy. Elected officials have a disproportionate ability to amplify target-group constructions. These developments in the aftermath of the IIRAIRA indicate a power bias that Peter Bachrach and Morton Baratz once identified as the ability to control the terms of debate.[65] Benefits reinstatement, which occurred without a corresponding public gesture designed to mute the negative politicking of the past, hardly constitutes a political correction in favor of immigrants and their advocates. Instead, the reinstatement conferred benefits on immigrants without conferring the broader American populace with the message that perhaps the IIRAIRA was a policy gone too far.

The comparison between IRCA and IIRAIRA suggests that much can be gleaned from studying both the curative and communicative features of policy. The failure of the IIRAIRA to bring fiscal discipline to immigration-driven problems did not come from its lack of enforcement or under-funding; the policy failed because solving fiscal problems was simply not its ultimate purpose. The utility of the IIRAIRA lay in the theater of government activity: the IIRAIRA putatively pursued fiscal discipline, but played upon bias against immigrants and others deemed lazy or motivated by a life lived at taxpayer expense, in order to build consensus and provide reassurance in the face of a perceived crisis. In this regard, the IIRAIRA is the product of symbolic politics in the sense that Murray Edelman described.[66] However, the IIRAIRA also stands as an example of degenerative politics, in which political consensus is pursued through the denigration of others, and relies primarily on the rationales conjured through target-group constructions.[67]

Immigration policy history could be written as a history of scapegoat politics, as different periods have witnessed popular consensus forged from the scorn with which different groups were regarded. Yet this history must also be considered against policy efforts that do not pursue these tactics in order to better begin to understand why some groups manage to escape their negative constructions, while others face greater difficulties in doing so. Contrasting the IRCA's sanction and legalization debates with the discussions in the 104th Congress which expanded the scope of troublesome immigrants demonstrates that some groups suffer from entrenched negative constructions that neither time nor a single policy is apt to dismantle. That the negative construction of unauthorized immigrants is so deeply entrenched that a large-scale regularization program would not rectify the social perceptions of this group suggests why later efforts to build congressional coalitions to pass legalization programs would face major impediments to success. The cross-period comparison also shows that as the ideology of balanced budget conservatism took root, immigration issues would be recast according to its logic. As immigrants were defined as freeloaders, they joined a broader population of undeserving people seen as not pulling their weight.

It is important to understand, however, that the image of the freeloader immigrant is a product not only of what he or she is seen to take, his or her motives, or even how he or she behaves, but also of *who* the immigrant is. To understand why immigration politics is prone to degenerative policymaking requires an exploration of how assumptions about class, gender, and national origin combine with discussions of status to delineate which people are the most problematic for the nation.

5

Problem Mexicans

Race, Nationalism, and Their Limits in Contemporary Immigration Policy

As elected officials, members of Congress are conscious of the values and traditions of the public they serve, as well as of the society of which they themselves are a product. While it is no longer politically acceptable for immigration policies to single out groups for exclusion based on race or national origin, legislators continue to distinguish between the "right" and "wrong" kinds of immigrants, accomplishing these distinctions through rhetorical devices that forge distinctions between "us" and "them." This may on its face seem unremarkable since, at its essence, immigration policy is set up to administer the relationship between foreigners and the state. However, discourse that conveys who the problem foreigners are assists in assuring the public that government has narrowed the field and identified target groups needing control and restriction. Whether the policies discussed accomplish their stated goals is immaterial: the public spectacle of immigration control suggests that government attends to sources of economic insecurity and social instability. And yet, the process must be viewed as more than theater, because the emotive appeal rests in the actual accomplishment of social divisions that distribute or deny real benefits to groups and individuals.[1]

The previous chapters focused on the instrumental nature of social constructions—the representation of target populations in the service of policy choice and policy justification. What follows is a deeper investigation of the language employed to distinguish immigrants for the purposes of public assurance that policies are just and fair in their allocation of benefits and burdens. While it may seem that discourse about immigrants in both policy periods employed "neutral" or descriptive terms (illegal, legal, criminal, guest-worker, etc.), it is easy to uncover the many ways in which these constructions are not neutral at all. The language of deserving and undeserving captures a host of other social divisions, and it does not simply mark people in terms of their roles as policy target populations, but judges them in terms of their potential to be considered present or future members of the polity. In an era in which overt racism and nativism are discredited as "extreme" and not reflective of the political mainstream, special attention must be paid to ways in which elected officials signal who can and cannot claim to be American.

Race and Its Limits in Official Discourse

In their attempt to discuss the major political divisions that mark congressional policymaking on immigration, James Gimpel and James Edwards have posited that immigration politics reflect an ideological schism between Democrats and Republicans over redistributive policies.[2] Congressional efforts to restrict immigration, according to Gimpel and Edwards, do not reflect racism, and their analysis of public opinion and interviews with members of Congress do not give primacy to race in explaining policy preferences in the public or in legislative outcomes. Instead, they surmise that political divisions on immigration policy simply mirror ideological divisions over the role of the state in redistributive social policy. However, research on welfare policy and state-level tax revolts beginning in the 1970s suggests that ideological divisions over the role of government in redistributive policy have a racial component to them.[3] The partisan divide Gimpel and Edwards demonstrate to have overtaken immigration debates can be considered part of a discourse of deserving and undeserving—a shared understanding in both the public and among political elites of *who* are the recipients of redistributive policies.[4] In the United States, race plays a role in solidifying popular conceptions of who deserves and who does not deserve public benefits, and that is why race cannot be sidelined.

The discourse of elite racism requires specific attention because it involves a language often obscured by a seemingly neutral rhetoric of fairness, rule of law, and tax redistribution. Such redistributive discourse is a relatively thin mask for a "coded language" of racism.[5] Teun van Dijk, who has conducted extensive analyses of media, textbook, and parliamentary debates in the United States and Western Europe, argues that elected officials do not need to make overt references to specific groups in promoting policies that restrict immigrants or undo civil rights policies; instead, they can rely on certain forms of hyperbole, figures of speech, metaphors, and euphemism that clearly communicate bias in a manner understood by the collective audience:

> All these meanings derive from socially shared representations about minorities and immigrants, and are not merely the unique, contextually specific constructions of an individual speaker. And since many recipients share these representations, such discourse will also be eminently recognisable. . . .[6]

We can expect this type of masked, or coded, talk from politicians precisely because they do not wish to be construed as xenophobic or racist, and yet, because these speech patterns are stereotypical (so much so that in van Dijk's analysis, they did not change much from country to country, despite expected cultural and linguistic variations), it is fairly easy to identify racially-infused speech.

Racialized discourse is that which attaches specific characteristics as well as value judgments to a group based on its physical attributes or national origin, and van Dijk offers a useful typology of rhetorical strategies common to parliamentary debates in which immigrants and other minorities are "characterized as at least problematic, if not threatening."[7] For example, while "positive self-presentation" is a form of nationalist rhetoric designed to extol the worthy traditions of self-described democratic, generous, and tolerant nations, this rhetoric will often precede appeals for immigration restriction.[8] In the American Congress, I found that this rhetoric takes a particular form in which representatives often refer to their own immigrant ancestry as a reflection of the positive attributes of the nation. The following examples came from a 1996 debate over the Chrysler amendment to H.R. 2202, which struck down limits that the bill originally placed on family reunification and employment visas and lowered the cap on refugee admissions:

(1) . . . America is a nation of immigrants. My grandfather came to America from Norway when he was 16 years old. Like most immigrants, he sought a better life for himself and his family. . . . There is a problem with illegal immigration in our country. We need to take strict steps to reduce and eliminate illegal immigration. But let's not destroy what has contributed to America's greatness for past centuries.[9]

(2)   Just stop and think of where your ancestors came from. Why did they join the cosmic race here? It was for the same reasons that we enjoy being Americans. It is the land of opportunity and the home of the brave, and we enjoy a degree of personal liberty that is unprecedented.[10]

The Chrysler amendment's passage was a defeat for immigration restriction; that Representatives Torklidsen (R-MA) and Crane (R-IL) would deploy their personal stories in support of maintaining family and labor migration lends some credence to the notion that positive immigration stories like theirs are at least a useful rhetorical strategy in justifying expansive immigration policies. Gary Freeman's typology of immigration politics in liberal democracies emphasized that in such systems, immigration mythology serves as a potent ideological constraint to those who would wish to push for more restrictive admissions.[11] However, Freeman's characterization of these stories as constituting a structural bias against restrictionism does not endure a more careful reading of American immigration mythology and its various political uses.

To illustrate, reconsider statements 1 and 2 in conjunction with the statements below:

(3)   We are a country of immigrants. Our ancestors came here for the promise of a better life and a better place to raise their families. They wanted the American dream. This bill does not deny this dream to anyone. Contrary to what has been said about this bill, it maintains America's historic generosity toward legal immigration and places a priority on uniting families.

   Our current system of legal immigration is clearly flawed. . . . People should not be fooled into believing the rhetoric that only illegal immigration needs reform. . . . until we reform legal immigration, we will continue to face the same problems.[12]

(4)   . . . I rise today as the daughter of immigrants . . . like most Americans . . . I believe that legal immigration is the lifeblood of this country, enriching our Nation economically and culturally. We should, of course, be open to reasonable reforms in our legal immigration policy. . . .[13]

(5)   Mr. Speaker, my heritage is German, Irish, Polish, and even a little Bohemian, and my children are all of that plus Norwegian, and I appreciate America as a Melting pot. . . .[14]

Each of the representatives quoted in statements 3–5 used their personal immigration history and "America-as-land-of-immigrants" tales in prelude to explanations for why some immigrants required restriction. In statement 3, Barbara Vucanovich (R-NV), who supported caps on legal immigration as well as the IIRAIRA's other measures designed to curb legal and illegal immigration, draws exactly this distinction: present immigration (legal and illegal) is problematic, and reform of the system appears necessary to maintain the better life and dreams that immigrants of the past pursued. Likewise, Jane Harman (D-CA) in statement 4 rose as the "daughter of immigrants" to support "reasonable reforms in legal immigration." These stories of immigrant ancestry ensure that the comparisons between desirable and undesirable immigrants are not simply divisions between legal and unauthorized. Given the racial breakdown of the U.S. Congress (still a majority white), and given the predominantly European ancestry of the past immigration to which the officials allude, these are stories that divide good, appropriate, legal, from bad, threatening, illegal immigration precisely along racial lines. European immigrants pursued the mythical American dream; their sons and daughters assimilated and made good—even became members of Congress. Contrast the language of historical immigration—"lifeblood," "American dream," "enriching," "what has made America great for the past centuries" (statements, 1, 3, and 4)—with the terms these officials use to describe current immigrants—"illegal," "problems" (statement 1). Immigration mythology does not simply serve as a constraint on restrictionism, it is used for the very opposite purpose—to rationalize restrictionism. Immigration myths, as stories of nationhood and identity, are malleable when deployed for the purposes of defining who constitutes the American people.

In the American legislative context, pro-immigration discourse that rationalizes restriction follows the form that van Dijk identified as the language of positive self-presentation. Such language is often deployed either in advance of restrictionist appeals or to justify policies that accomplish this.[15] While some of the speakers quoted above (like Representatives Torklidsen and Harman) voted to maintain higher caps on legal immigration, all the statements came from individuals who voted for the 1996 IIRAIRA. As previous chapters explained, the law had a significant impact on the legal immigrant population in residence, as well as on the families of those sponsoring immigrants for legal entry. Representative Harman, a Democrat from California, was one of the bill's original co-sponsors.

A second type of rhetoric that van Dijk observed is "negative other-presentation," which, as seen above, is often prefaced with the rhetoric of positive self-presentation. Some of this rhetoric is flagrant, "us versus them" language that offers images and stories of invasion and threat:

(6) The night before last, or rather, Monday night, I went down to the California-Mexico border. . . . Now, down there at that border I saw American territory controlled by people who are not Americans, standing there, 1,000 of them. One of them turned around, he did not know there was a Congressman there, he probably would have laughed if he did. He just thought I was one of the border guards again. He turned around and dropped his pants and gave us the international—to use the western acronym, a B.A. . . . It kind of symbolized for me the whole situation there. They are controlling American territory.[16]

(7) Mexico is a resource-rich country . . . Yet Mexico has adopted a type of Socialist experimentation—including so-called land reforms—which has brought the country to its current straits.[17]

(8) . . . I voted against NAFTA because I did not want to send American jobs to Mexico. . . . But the only thing worse than NAFTA is bringing in a bunch of Mexicans to take American jobs. Now that is what this is all about. If you are for your folks, vote against it. If you are for those folks, vote for the Pombo amendment.[18]

Statements 6–8 all employ hyperbole to heighten the sense of threat. In statement 6, Representative Robert Dornan (R-CA) tells a tale of hundreds of "people who are not Americans," but who are "controlling American territory." Not only are "they" occupying America, but "they" behave crudely; not only are "they" simply disregarding territorial sovereignty, but "they" are disrespecting it. The congressman presents his anecdote as emblematic of "the whole situation there." In statement 6, an excerpt from an extensive speech, Senator Jesse Helms (R-NC) focuses on the threat of of socialism. Here, context is important: in 1986, the Republican Reagan administration and its policies towards Latin America were framed in terms of Soviet encroachment and control in the region. By remarking on Mexico's "Socialist experimentation" with land reforms (most of which occurred under Lázaro Cardenas in the 1930s, though the Mexican government has since had to contend with conflicts over land tenure in rural areas), the senator suggests that Mexico is also part of a broader, and growing, regional problem of Soviet corruption at a time when the containment of socialism and communism was utmost on the administration's agenda. In the final example (statement 8), a representative from Mississippi frames the threat as one of American job losses. His choice of phrasing displays a disgust not commonly seen in official rhetoric, no matter how restrictionist the speaker. The congressman's statement sets up the division in terms of nationality: a vote on legislation is set up as being either for Americans or for "those folks," whom he has identified as "a bunch of Mexicans."

The negative presentation of immigrants appeared in discussions of the economic and cultural burdens of immigration. The zero-sum narrative discussed in Chapter 4 contained many references to immigrants as burdensome and not contributing to society. The issue is not whether immigrants actually produce economic burdens, since evidence suggests that in the short term, the undocumented population can add substantial costs to the municipalities and states that host them.[19] What makes this rhetoric problematic is that it is an incomplete presentation of the conditions that policy is supposed to address. The flipside to the discussion of net fiscal costs of immigration (also bolstered by economic analyses) is that businesses receive a boon; furthermore, there is evidence that federal coffers receive a boon, and analyses suggest that in the long run, localities with immigrants enjoy economic growth and diversification.[20] The examples above are not of talk about troubling *conditions* so much as they are of talk about troubling *people* who have been portrayed as society's detractors. In the IIRAIRA debates, burdens were discussed without reference to tax contributions of even legal immigrants. Often when contributions were discussed, these were not attributed to current immigrants, but rather to immigrant ancestors, as statements 1–5 illustrate.

Another form of negative other-presentation involved expressions of moral judgments about the activities and motivations of immigrants. This dynamic was apparent in the deserving illegal narrative: migration for the purpose of maintaining family, or the performance of "hard work," was equated with values indicative of the pursuit of the American Dream, specifically, upward mobility and personal responsibility. This contrasts with rhetoric that cast other immigrants as being motivated by receiving welfare checks, securing birthright citizenship for their children (to secure benefits for themselves), and having their children attend public schools. Many of these images appeared in the zero-sum and criminal alien narratives discussed in previous chapters, but to illustrate further, consider the following statements about the burdens that illegal immigration places on the school system:

(9) . . . But I also look at Brownsville, TX, which is having severe economic problems, and I watch it adding one new school room every other week. One of the main problems is illegal alien children who have to be taught in that school. That is the additional burden that is happening to us.[21]

(10) . . . there was a woman from the interior of Mexico who had actually taken the time to write three letters to the school district to make sure that her children could get a public education in the United States even if they were illegal. She could not believe it, so she waited three times to get an answer back that says, "If I bring my children here, from Mexico, do I have to show they're legally here?" And they said, "No, you have no problem at all getting them educated in this country." I think that is the message we must stop sending.[22]

(11) Let me make a proposition to the Members of the Congress. Let us take American taxpayer dollars and send it [*sic*] to Mexico or to any other country and educate their children. Those that have chosen to stay in their country and to abide by our border laws, they probably have a better right to our taxpayer dollars to educate their children than those that break our laws to bring their children here and get an education at taxpayer expense.[23]

Each of these statements, drawn from both the IRCA and IIRAIRA debates, does not simply describe conditions; each is an example of value judgment. While work and social mobility appear as legitimate reasons for immigration (even illegal immigration, in that illegal immigrants are described as being motivated by available American jobs), education of the children who may accompany laborers is not. Statements 9 and 10 are both accounts of Mexican immigrants whose undocumented children are schooled at taxpayer expense. Again, highlighting this aspect of these accounts is not to deny existing evidence of costs to school districts in which illegal immigrant children cluster. However, since these legislators are not promoting laws that would redistribute federal dollars to cover such costs, much of this rhetoric simply offers opinions and judgments that accomplish little more than maligning Mexican immigrants. One might just as easily imagine that these immigrants are ensuring social mobility and the

American Dream for the second generation by enrolling their children in schools. One might even remark at the perseverance and initiative displayed by the Mexican mother profiled in statement 10 who made certain her children could, in fact, participate in schooling despite their status. Instead, the parents of undocumented children appear driven by selfishness, and their children are depicted as being undeserving of education.

These discussions also contrasted sharply with the construction of immigrant children in the IRCA debates. During the legalization discussions, children were discussed as proof that immigrants were enmeshed in U.S. neighborhoods and interacting with citizens. Children were not a vehicle to a life of welfare dependency, but construed instead as proof of immigrant integration. During the IRCA debates, the nuclear family symbolized stability and integration. As a rhetorical tool, the otherwise law-abiding, family-oriented illegal immigrant countered the image of the criminal, border-jumping male. During the IRCA debates, the image of the immigrant family was non-threatening, and employed to soften pre-existing assumptions about who immigrates illegally and why.

Stigmatizing Mexican Immigration

Since the 1965 Immigration and Nationality Act removed race and nationality as factors for excluding immigrants, the political focus on legal status has obscured how racial ideologies still permeate the crafting of immigration policies. We understand the racial fears encoded in policy, and yet the discussion of race can appear incongruent when matched against policies that deviate from restrictionism. Clearly, if our foreign admissions continue to hail primarily from Latin America and Asia, it would appear that true racists may rant all they want, but rule of law and a commitment to Civil Rights ideals reign supreme in the end. And yet, racialized images are clearly engaged in distinguishing the deserving from the undeserving. The use of racialized language and images as markers of disentitlement assures the populace that policies are just in denying access to some people.

Thus far in this study, I have provided numerous examples in which elected officials named Mexicans specifically in their negative portrayals of immigrants, but this level of specificity was not always necessary. The unspecified "illegals" appearing in the undeserving illegal, zero-sum, criminal alien, and lawless border narratives were understood to be the Mexican migrants who cross the border in violation of the law and with the intent or likelihood of violating further laws. This criminality, when combined with attributes of laziness, welfare usage, and female childbearing, forges an image of the Mexican illegal that is race-based in that it attaches this set of politically and socially defined attributes to a group on the basis of both their nationality and their identifiable presence in the United States.

Moreover, the definition of *who* is illegal is affirmed by the absence of other images of unauthorized immigrants from the debates, such as the university students who decide to stay in the United States past the expiration of their temporary permits or the tourists who violate the terms of their visas. While the evidence in both the 1981 and 1994 task force reports stated that temporary visa overstays produced up to 40 percent of the resident undocumented population, students and tourists were not mentioned, much less demonized, by congressional reformers. Such omission is possible because neither students nor tourists fit the profile of who is "illegal" in the United States. Congressional discourse implies that illegal immigrants are Mexicans, and thus without attributing negative constructions directly to Mexican immigrants, Mexican immigrants are conflated with the criminal and undeserving attributes that members of Congress employed in support of restriction measures.

During the IIRAIRA debates, both the zero-sum and criminal alien narratives involved negative depictions of Mexican and/or Latin American hordes (arriving via Mexico). For example, in Chapter 4, statement 1, classrooms in California were "overcrowded," teachers were "overburdened," and illegal immigrants were "stealing" from American students. In statements 5–10 of Chapter 4, members of Congress from Florida, Texas, New York, and California spoke of the situation both nationally as well as in their own states in which welfare and Medicaid faced bankruptcy from immigrant overuse. While none of these representatives spoke directly of immigration from Mexico or Latin America, each representative hails from a state in which legal immigration from Latin America is the largest legal (and illegal) source of immigration. Thus without overtly mentioning those immigrants, they convey which immigrants are the problem.

While the immigrant laborer enjoyed a neutral construction in the government-off-our-backs narrative (again, a narrative in which employers, not immigrants would be the direct targets for beneficial policy), the immigrant laborer was absent from all of the other narratives. The zero-sum and criminal alien narratives implored lawmakers to protect U.S. jobs and social services from the poverty and chaos emanating from across the southern border. The fact that these immigrants are often recruited for labor (or from 1994–1996 would consist of people who had undergone legalization) is notable if only for its absence.

The dearth of a positive counter-portrayal of the immigrant laborer (documented or otherwise) only reinforces the negative portrayal of the immigrant freeloader. It is one thing to portray Mexican immigrants as necessary for agricultural production; it is another to depict these immigrants as being necessary to the very functioning of the economic order. As much of this labor is Mexican, the implication for the group is that its contributions as laborers would be minimized in the IIRAIRA debates, and that its image as consisting of criminals and welfare defrauders would obscure considerations of their actual legal status and work contributions. In the absence of a countervailing construction, it has been easier for law-makers to justify closing the door to those they have both overtly and implicitly defined as the wrong kinds of immigrants.

Race Neutrality in Target-Group Constructions

While racial images permeated discussions of undeserving immigrants, the debate analysis reveals that race can disappear from immigration rhetoric under certain circumstances. In the deserving illegal narrative, other markers such as "legal" "hard-working," "law-abiding," "seeking opportunity," "tax-paying" and "necessary" were attached to immigrant subjects. Immigrants were also portrayed race-neutrally when they were the *indirect* targets of immigration reforms. In those instances in which businesses would be the recipients of immigrant labor, immigrant constructions were neutral, stripped of any race- or nation-specific language. For example, both the IRCA and the IIRAIRA included debates over amendments for guest worker programs. While illegal immigrants during both policy debates were the subjects of narratives that portrayed them negatively (the undeserving illegal and criminal alien narratives), when the policies targeted these immigrants indirectly, they were characterized in a neutral, even abstract manner as simply elements needed for the ultimate success of that sector. Take, for example, statements 8 through 11 in Chapter 3, in which senators from western, agriculture-heavy states like California and Washington pleaded for an agricultural guest-worker program. Farmers would be the direct targets of a guest-worker program, and even though they argued that guest workers are a necessity for farm production, the workers themselves were virtually absent from statements that instead focused on the farms and farmers and their products. During the IIRAIRA discussions about streamlining employer verification, workers did appear in discussions dealing with the burdens that the I-9 processing placed on employers (see Chapter 4, statements 32 and 33). Again, though, workers in these instances were neutrally constructed; no references to their race or nationality appeared in these arguments for streamlining guest-worker applications. In short, when agriculturists would be the targets of policy benefits (guest-worker assurances and procedural streamlining), the immigrant labor force was constructed race-neutrally.

Mexican migration has long filled U.S. labor needs, and this fact acts as a constraint on this groups' racialized construction in specific contexts. Although a neutral portrayal does not disparage immigrant labor, it is nonetheless problematic because it does not place immigrants from Mexico at the scene of production. Thus, the productivity of Mexican laborers, and the centrality of this population to the viability of agriculture and other sectors of the American economy do not serve to counter to the undeserving illegal and criminal alien narratives—narratives that not only attach disparaging qualities to Mexicans, but do so without being challenged.

The Mark of the Border

One of the places in which language linked a specific group of people to the immigration crisis was in allusions to the U.S.-Mexico border. In fact, "the border" appeared often as a euphemism for Mexicans. When speakers referred to the border without specification, no one ever asked, "Which one?" It was understood, even when not specified, that the U.S.-Canadian border was *not* the problem. In fact, the northern border only appeared once in the 1994–1996 debates—debates in which the physical establishment and maintenance of the land borders supplied one of the linchpins for policy efforts. In the sole instance that the Canadian border was the subject of discussion in the 1990s, a congressman from Michigan wanted to see more checkpoints along the northern border to *facilitate* crossings and ease shopping excursions for his constituents. Even though the IIRAIRA also targeted the U.S.-Canada border for increased surveillance for suspected terrorists, there was none of the "hot-spot" or siege language for the northern border that appeared in discussion about the southern.[24]

The southern border, by contrast, appeared simultaneously as a menace, as the source of illegal immigration, and as the site of the impending deterioration of the American nation:

(12) . . . We have more law enforcement in the Capitol Police at any one time than we have on our entire southwest border. Mr. Chairman, this amendment [to increase INS enforcement] is essential for our national health and our survival as a nation we know now. Our borders are out of control. . . . They are leaking like a sieve. . . .[25]

(13) . . . I am reminded a bit of how the French . . . constructed an invincible line called the Maginot Line, and it was to withhold any German attack. The Germans flanked the Maginot Line and of course rendered the defense useless. We build triple fences, our Maginot Line against immigration. . . . We ourselves are going to allow the transport of unskilled workers up from Mexico around the fences and on to farms where they can wander off and become a continuing part of the illegal immigration problem this country has had an experience with.[26]

(14) . . . Soviet expansionism in Central America is causing havoc in Guatemala, Honduras, El Salvador, and Costa Rica. Nicaragua is a Soviet base. The fires are burning in Central America and could ignite a volcanic eruption in Mexico. . . . [T]he situation in Central America and the Caribbean . . . is very grave. The convulsions wracking Central America today may well propel an explosion of "feet people" fleeing the chaos and illegally entering these United States.[27]

In statement 12, the southwest border is "out of control" and "leaking like a sieve" from lack of enforcement. Statement 13 draws a parallel between the IIRAIRA's border fortification efforts and the defensive posture of France during World War I. Statement 14 offers a parade of horribles: Senator Helms is actually speaking against the IRCA's legalization measures, but he is conjuring images of hypothetical crises that may flow from the legislation. Here Mexico, and not just the border, is vulnerable to the conflagrations that were visible in Central America during the 1980s.

The vision of the lawless U.S.-Mexico border evident in the IIRAIRA debates and in the statements above is the same that has long appeared in popular Anglo-American conceptions of this region:

> . . . during the age of Prohibition in the United States, cities such as Ciudad Juarez and Tijuana had achieved fame as playgrounds for pleasure-seeking Americans. Throngs of visitors crossed into Mexico to drink, gamble, and partake of other nighttime recreation. . . . The stereotype of Mexican border towns as Sodoms and Gomorrahs was added to the already long list of negative images of Mexico. In the American mind the border came to represent a divide between progress and backwardness, between good and evil.[28]

Thus, layered on top of the income disparity is a conception of the border as a place breeding a distinctive morality. This treatment of the border has less to do with poverty than it does with views of the border as a place of depravity. The border is viewed as a place of chaos and lawlessness, political instability and corruption, and the "criminal alien" narrative meshes well with such standing biases against the border region.

The border marks more than territory, however. Urban sociologist Mike Davis has conceptualized the southern border as a layered entity serving different functions. The "first border" is the internationally recognized boundary, while the "second border"—signaled by the interior checkpoints located fifty or so miles from the boundary—serves primarily to assure locals in otherwise far-flung places that Washington, D.C., remains a physical presence capable of exerting control from a distance. Finally, the "third border" marks Latinos, whether citizen or immigrant:

> But the border doesn't end at San Clemente. Indeed, as any ten-year-old in East L.A., or Philly's El Norte knows, borders tend to follow working-class Latinos wherever they live . . . In suburban Los Angeles, New Jersey and Chicago, the interface between Anglo majorities and growing blue-collar Latino populations is regulated by what can only be typed a "third border." Whereas the second border [the INS checkpoints in the interior of the United States] nominally reinforces the international border, the third border polices daily intercourse between two citizen communities.[29]

In the highly formal discourse of Congress, the border divides more than two countries; it symbolizes a relationship between the sending and receiving nations that involves the additional layer of colonialist attitudes of superiority towards Mexico and Mexicans. These attitudes prevailed in discussions about policing both the region and the Mexican immigrant population. "The border," along with the various meanings and imagery that the region carries, is a mark that the Mexican-origin population must bear—and one that European immigrants and their grandchildren do not.

The Vital Border?

The emphasis on the southern border and repeated references to the region's many problems is understandable, given the economic disparity between the United States and Mexico—a disparity that simply does not exist between the United States and Canada. While the 2000 Census ranked Canada fifteenth among the top twenty nations supplying the U.S. with unauthorized immigrants, the truth is that Mexico does supply the majority.[30] However, while not commonly done, it is possible to discuss the border without reference to threat, invasion, or economic or moral decay.

Although the narrative in which first-world order and industrialism meet in a violent clash with third-world desperation was a recurring feature of the IRCA debates, other images did emerge in the 1980s that provided an alternative vision of the border as a place of potential for both nations:

(15) I am also convinced that we should open up trade with Mexico, so that goods and services can come across the border instead of people, so that people on both sides of the border can get a job, earn a living, feed their children and stay at home. I, for one, am willing to enter into a trade agreement with Mexico to give them some initial advantages, to get that trade going, recognizing that ultimately trade is a two-way street, and they have to open up their markets as well.[31]

(16) . . . the bill contains an amendment that I have offered that authorizes the President of the United States to negotiate with Mexico a free trade zone. . . . We have such an agreement with Israel, and are presently negotiating one with Canada.[32]

In statement 15 a Republican Texas senator, Phil Gramm, acknowledges the reality that the border's problems of low wages and unemployment are regional and not exclusive to Mexico. In statement 16, a Democratic senator from California places Mexico on par with the industrialized nations of Israel and Canada. In 1992, the North American Free Trade Agreement (NAFTA) also posited a less desperate contrast between the two nations, portraying them as economically interdependent and with borderlands exemplifying economic dynamism.[33] However, this recognition of international or regional interdependency was largely absent from the IIRAIRA debates.

Likewise, the recognition that the border is a space hosting cultural fusion rather than a dividing line between different cultures appeared only once:

(17) I believe that we do have a problem in this country with our inability to control illegal immigration, but I am convinced that it is not as big a problem as many would have us believe. I grew up and have lived virtually my entire life near our border with Mexico. In southern Arizona, we have created a thriving society that has integrated two cultures and two peoples. While we do have our tensions and problems, we are working together to make our part of the country a better place.[34]

This vision, however, was not shared in Congress. Instead, congressional talk about the southern border was overwhelmingly about a line dividing two distinct nations, moralities, and peoples. One side of that line represented rule of law, and the other represented disorder, irresponsibility, and immorality (drugs, prostitution, human trafficking, assault, and robbery). The only things guarding the lawful from the lawless were the fences. This is yet another case in which an imbalanced portrayal not only skews understanding of the immigration problem, but also narrows the field of potential solutions that might be pursued. Migration would be a non-starter in NAFTA discussions, as though the integration of communication, travel, and trade could exist without people.[35]

The Uses of Race and National Origin in Immigration Discourse

Immigration laws define a broad class of people, "immigrants," and then redefine the component parts to justify differentiated policy treatments. In this process, race signals people who are undeserving. The racialized imagery of immigration restriction assuages: it communicates that the freeloaders, the threats, the people unwilling to conform to standards and values prized in the polity are being denied entry or access on arrival. The race-neutral image of "hard-working" modern immigrants aligns with the myth of European immigration, and justifies legislative measures that secure foreign labor and advances business needs.

The uses of race for policy purposes pose a particular dilemma for immigration policymaking. As distressing as the appearance of racialized constructions appear when they are employed to stigmatize people and groups, the immigration case complicates judgments that can be drawn about whether policy discourse should pursue or avoid distinctions drawn among immigrants of different national or regional origins. In the case of the Mexican-origin population, the use of nation-specific language that accentuates the negative is as politically problematic as nation-neutral imagery that does not accentuate the specific relationship of this population to the United States. There is a limit to the comparisons that can be drawn between European immigrants of the first and second waves specifically because the relationship of the United States, Mexico, and the population of Mexican origin is unique. Narratives that obscure this uniqueness in favor of accounts that make this population "just like" other immigrant groups, in turn, constrain our ability as a nation to contend with the good and the bad of this exceptional relationship with Mexico. More broadly, constructing all new immigrants in terms of past immigrants is problematic in that it does not feature them in present times, and currently contributing. Meanwhile, as the narrative analysis of the IIRAIRA debates has shown, the positive construction that compares these immigrants to past (white) European immigrants can easily collapse as soon as contemporary immigrants are portrayed as not measuring up.

There is also another, practical problem with the racialized policy discourse presented here: the current era of immigration is characterized by a diversity of national origins previously unseen in the United States. While immigrants originating from Mexico comprise the largest share, the next largest populations hail from China, the Philippines, and India.[36] These immigrant populations are also affected by comprehensive immigration policy reforms, but their presence in the United States and their policy concerns are masked by discourse that racializes immigration legislation as policy concerned only with Mexican immigration.

Gender, Family, and the Internal Threat of Mexican Immigration

While race and nativism are often viewed as ever-present markers for exclusion in U.S. immigration policy, race did not form the only axis of division in the immigration policy debates. Immigrants were regularly judged
against their fulfillment of traditional or stereotypical gender roles, and
"deserving" immigrants fulfilled these roles. While such depictions can
assist in the appeal for women as worthy immigrants, to the extent that
such depictions obscure women's actual experience as immigrants, they
undermine the creation of images that might anchor these women more
firmly as essential members of the polity.

Women proved a special predicament for immigration control. In fact,
women did not need to be in the United States for their fertility to be
discussed as a justification for immigration reforms, as the following excerpts from a Senate debate about the IRCA illustrate:

(18) Let me just give one illustration. I mention Mexico not because Mexico
provides the only problems, but I think we have to recognize that the
main problems are from Mexico . . . Let me just give one illustration of
why this is such a tremendous problem.

Mexico today has a population of 70 million people. If, by the end
of this century, Mexico reaches a status where one female produces
one female—I am not trying to be sexist, but that is the way demog-
raphers talk about zero population growth—Mexico will taper off with
a population of 175 million people. If that does not happen until the
year 2020, Mexico will have a population of 270 million people eventually. If we think we have illegal immigration problems today, my friends
can look down the road a piece and the problems are just going to be
horrendous.[37]

(19) A friend from Mexico says it has a population of 82 million with one of
the highest birth rates in the world. You have a country there that has
economic instability and serious problems, and that could have serious
political instability. If that happened we would have 20 million more
over that border in a hurry. There is no way in the world we could han-
dle it without adequate immigration laws.[38]

(20) We have 2 million illegal immigrants, more or less, coming in every
year, in addition to the 6 or 12 million that we have now. If you look

at the demographic statistics, things are going to get much worse, not better. . . .[39]

In these discussions, birthrates are not being discussed in a neutral manner. The senators employ birthrate statistics to stir the imagination of their colleagues and goad them into action. Moreover, these statistics are not being deployed as factual support; they are marshaled to augment fear. Different numbers appear in these statements for Mexico's population count (70 million, 82 million), and yet each of these different counts serves as the basis for calculation of further (hypothetical) statistics. In these calculations, potential illegal immigrants are born en masse, at alarming rates, and women are the site of this reproductive boom. While the Democratic senator in statement 18 disavows sexism and claims neutrality in his use of scientific terminology, "zero population growth," this term technically refers to equilibrium having been reached between birth rates and death rates. As such, it requires that the equilibrium occur in the population of both women and men.

Dorothy Roberts has written about current efforts to limit unauthorized immigrants from giving birth on U.S. soil and has suggested that discussions of revising the Fourteenth Amendment to restrict birthright citizenship are modern-day reflections of past eugenic efforts "directed at the children of racially undesirable immigrants."[40] It is certainly true that race is present in these discussions, and most clearly so when the border becomes the delineator between proper and improperly acquired citizenship. However, it is also necessary to consider the specific ways in which legislative discourse reveals a specific bias against immigrant women, dictating appropriate roles for female migrants and employing moral judgment in discussing both the actions and motives of these women.

For women immigrants, those who showed agency in migration were often judged as "undeserving" for displaying questionable motives in migrating. In statement 10, a woman from Mexico was portrayed as being lured to the United States by the desire to have her illegal children educated here at taxpayer expense. Her story was presented as emblematic of "the message we need to stop sending." The practice of birthright citizenship was also portrayed as a magnet for women motivated by the benefits attached to their child's citizenship:

(21) I understand the attraction of this country. We are a wealth-generating society and a free society. . . . I look at a situation where in Matamoros a

woman goes into labor and they put her in a car and rush her across the border to have her child born in the United States. I understand that. If I were a Mexican citizen and my wife was in labor, I would want her child born in this country too.

But . . . I look at a country with a 2,000-mile common border. I look at an industrialized nation that has a Third World country next door to it, and I know what that means to us.[41]

(22) . . . This is booty-strapping. This is a situation in which, by virtue of the act of illegal entry on the part of a parent, the birth of the child gives the right to benefits from the taxpayers' coffers.[42]

In both statements, these new citizens are not only burdensome, but when their mother's motives are judged as "wrong," these children are presented as lesser citizens in light of the motives of their mothers. These arguments shift the location of the immigrant invasion from the border to a threat from within the nation itself as illegal women gave birth to "children" (and notably, not "citizens") in U.S. hospitals.

Phyllis Pease Chock, who has analyzed appearances of gendered discourse in congressional immigration hearings, noted that immigrant women represent a special dilemma for immigration control as "neither surveillance by the Border Patrol nor labor discipline appeared to be able to offer satisfactory means of controlling this unruly fecundity."[43] Moreover, women and their children (existing or yet unborn) are commonly viewed as dependents of their male counterparts. While legislators and experts in the hearings spoke of men as laborers, women and children were discussed solely as dependents. Chock concluded that "These assumptions implied that women and children may less assuredly be immigrants and citizens in their own right, and that their status as immigrant or citizen is dependent on their husband/father's status."[44]

The gendered constructions of not only who migrates but why they migrate that Chock found throughout congressional testimony in the 1970s and early 1980s remained a feature of immigration debates of the mid-1980s and 1990s. During the IIRAIRA debates, women appeared without men—specifically fathers—when they were discussed as having "anchor babies," and were, in turn, judged as immoral migrants motivated by public education or benefits for themselves or their children. Conversely, the immigrant woman who was part of a nuclear family appeared in rhetoric presenting these women's migration for the sake of family reunification as an act of virtue:

(23) . . . I would like to place, Mr. Chairman, a personal face on this whole question of legal immigration.

. . . Claudia Gonzales left her family in Houston as a teenager to care for her grandparents in Mexico. She rejoined her family in Houston at age 23 where she has begun a new job and is attending school. . . . Claudia's father said, who has lived here since 1967: I have worked hard here and pay taxes. What am I going to say to my son 21 and my daughter who is 23?

Mr. Chairman, that is the real face of legal immigrants, hard-working taxpayers. . . . Now we have a situation where parents and children cannot be united.[45]

This is a statement from one of the more outspoken advocates for immigrants during the 1996 debates, Representative Sheila Jackson-Lee (D-TX). Yet this statement plays upon stereotypes about female immigrants: Claudia travels both to Mexico and the United States as the member of a nuclear family (in Houston) and caregiver to extended family (in Mexico). While Claudia is described as having a job, the congresswoman's appeal for Claudia to remain in the United States is justified by way of her father's working hard and paying taxes, as well as Claudia's status as his child (even though she is 23 and legally an adult). This example, which came from an official advocating more liberal immigration policies, shows the difficulty facing female immigrants as they or their advocates pursue their claims on the polity. Neither the women's capacity to reproduce labor power, nor their own participation in the labor force emerged in the debates as a contribution to the nation during either policy period. In fact this statement is one of the few times in the IRCA or IIRAIRA discussions in which a woman immigrant was portrayed as working. Instead, the female immigrant's fertility and dependency (on welfare, on men) were more common in the debates.

Such assumptions about the motivations of female immigrants run contrary to evidence showing that the immigrant labor force has become increasingly feminized since the 1960s and even more so since the implementation of the IRCA. This is true even for the Mexican immigrant population, which had until the post-IRCA period been predominantly male.[46] Moreover, while it is often assumed that women migrants are compelled by family reunification, researchers in the field cannot discount economics as a motivation, particularly when research shows that a majority of immigrant women participate in the labor force once they are in the United States.[47] Pierrette Hondagneu-Sotelo's study of domestic workers offers accounts of Latin American women who leave their families behind to become primary or dual-income earners.[48] Nonetheless, in official discourse, women immigrants are dependent migrants: they depend on welfare, and on families, on husbands, when they are acknowledged at all.

The difficult political position of women immigrants is aggravated since the very images that classify immigrants as deserving are the same ones that can subvert these women's claim to contribution and belonging. As the concept of "citizen" is increasingly defined as "productive," "working," and "tax-paying," women immigrants are denied the foundation in which to anchor their claims of membership, or bolster the claims of their children, when they are absent from these images.

Legal Status and Its Limits: The Devaluation of Birthright Citizenship

Even though the IIRAIRA itself never went as far as to restrict birthright citizenship, this feature of American citizenship came under attack during the policy debates. Furthermore, lawmakers repeatedly appealed to their colleagues to distinguish between citizen children and those of immigrants in crafting policy. This occurred, for example, in the debates over the Gallegly amendment, which sought to bar undocumented children from school. A review of the discussion excerpted in statements 1–4 in Chapter 4 shows that the actual status of the children discussed was sidelined and the resulting constructions characterized immigrants as undermining the nation by adding their poor dependents (also rhetorically denuded of legal status) to the welfare rolls. In fact, because proponents of the amendment were often vague in addressing the legal status of the children in question, their colleagues often had to remind speakers that some children of illegal immigrants are citizens of the United States. Sometimes those speaking referred to "children of illegal immigrants" when the context of the statement elucidated that they were actually referring to children who were themselves undocumented. In reality, as the Commission on Immigration Reform noted, it is not uncommon that families have members with different statuses, but the extent of this phenomenon is difficult to ascertain because of the general difficulties in obtaining data on the resident illegal population in the United States.

In addition to sending messages about which immigrant groups the state was willing to take in as members, Congress reconstructed the meaning of American citizenship between the passage of the IRCA and the IIRAIRA. While immigrants during both periods were scrutinized in terms of their potential for membership, each policy presented an ideal of citizenship that was distinctive. Thus, although three qualities of citizens did remain constant during both sets of debates—namely, paying taxes, following the law, and being engaged in hard work—other qualities differed across the two periods. The legalization debates in the mid-1980s gave rise to a conception of citizenship that not only involved hard-work, self-improvement, and self-sufficiency, but also recognized work with a communal purpose and that such work was integral to the functioning of the economy and the society. Correspondingly, family, community participation, and rootedness in neighborhoods and communities were also seen as important qualities. This view of the integrationist aspects of immigrants in the nation was supplemented with a view of their individual investment in the United States, which included their working hard, enrolling their children enrolled in American schools, and behaving lawfully. In short, these were people who had earned a right to legalization and who would eventually earn the right to naturalize if they so chose. Finally, the deserving illegal and portions of the anti-discrimination" narrative dealing with legal immigrants and naturalized citizens defined membership as incurring the protection of the state.

In 1995–1996, however, the model of citizenship that emerged was different. First, in the portions of the criminal alien narrative that dealt with illegal immigrants bootstrapping benefits from citizen children, the discourse questioned the practice and validity of birthright citizenship. Much of the congressional discourse questioned the motivations of many legal immigrants as well. The IIRAIRA ensured that only citizens would have access to much of the social safety net. However, by constructing immigrants as undeserving, legislators also questioned these immigrants' worthiness as permanent members and potential citizens. Deservedness did not relate to legal status, as the negative construction of citizen children of illegal immigrants demonstrated. Rather, entitlement equated to tax-paying, and the focus on rights to public benefits linked the meaning of citizenship to benefits access.

This juxtaposition of immigrants against a citizenship standard (a standard which was, in turn, reaffirmed by immigration control policies) forms yet another variable facet of immigrant target-group construction. This is in part due to the initial non-citizen status of all immigrants, which limits their protection as denizens of the state. However, while each policy marked immigrant target groups as deserving or undeserving, each policy also produced a different model of citizenship. The model implied in the 1986 policy is notable for its emphasis on social ties and a reciprocal relationship between those who contribute to the society and the government that offers its protection to individuals in recognition of these contributions. In 1996, citizenship is plainly about benefits entitlement and the notion that individuals deserve to take out of the government what they are presumed to put in. The constitution of citizenship in 1996 is purely economic, and discussion of what makes a good or bad member revolved around assumptions about who is or is not working hard and paying taxes. Even as pro-agriculture representatives fought for more and easier access to farm workers, no story emerged that depicted these immigrants as both legal and hard working. Nor did refugees emerge as a distinct class of immigrants who, by definition and law, are entitled to public assistance. In 1996, immigrant work apparently lacked the social value or contribution that would make this population deserving of federal protections. Thus, not only did much of the rhetoric demonize immigrants, but the IIRAIRA discourse also reduced citizenship to economic citizenship—a construct in which the contract between people and government concentrates on non-immigrant work, on paying taxes, and on self-sufficiency.

The shifting grounds on which these images of the citizen potential of immigrants were based may seem evidence of symbolic politicking given that the Fourteenth Amendment has not been changed and that efforts to rescind birthright citizenship have not resulted in measures to do so. However, these efforts to devalue the birthright citizenship of children of immigrants and to restructure membership in fiscal terms serve to undermine the very nature of American democratic citizenship, which envisions the relationship between individual and nation as voluntary and consensual, and not an inheritance, a privilege of class, or a function of dues-paying.

Fiscal Citizenship and the Immigrant Freeloader

At their most fundamental level, discussions about immigration reform in the 1980s and 1990s were discussions about the membership of and the expectations from the immigrant population. The outcome from the IRCA may suggest a more generous definition of what membership means in that advocates of legalization reached beyond legal status to identify work, community, and family as signifiers of community belonging. However, both the IRCA and the IIRAIRA debates echo deeper strains and conflicts over the political economy of federal programs and racial divisions. These conflicts reach beyond immigration restriction to ideological and social divisions that have been brewing in U.S. party politics since the Civil Rights revolution and the development of associated federal programs that are presumed to be paid for by white middle- and working-class citizens, but that service Hispanic and African Americans who are generally presumed not to contribute to their fiscal maintenance. The interplay of these themes has been well-documented elsewhere,[49] but I would add that the inclusion of immigration policy in this discourse of deserving and undeserving Americans is a logical capstone for this trend, even if the IRCA experience suggests that it is not an inevitable one. By divesting immigrants of their actual status and image as laborers, legislators who supported IIRAIRA not only devalued their contributions in a rhetorical sense, but also declared that even legal immigrants are not potential citizens: citizens pay taxes, after all, and immigrants, according to 104th Congress, do not.

During both policy periods, references to "the American people" and "citizens" meant those people to whom the government owes first fiscal consideration, as in the following plea from Republican Congressman Dana Rohrabacher (CA):

(24) Whose children do we care about? Why are we here? Who are we representing? We are supposed to care about the people of the United States of America. All of these children are wonderful children who have been brought here by illegal aliens. We care about them. But we have to care about our own kids first. . . .[50]

Most commonly, "citizen" was used interchangeably with "taxpayer" with little regard for the fact that legal immigrants, who have Social Security cards, also pay income taxes, and that those who own property contribute property taxes. Unauthorized immigrants residing in the United States purchase goods and services from stores that do not ask for one's legal status before money exchanges hands. Like the rest of the consumer population, therefore, illegal immigrants pay sales taxes. In the immigrant destination states of California and Nevada, for example, sales tax can be quite high (more than eight cents to every dollar, whether for toilet paper or a pair of jeans). In most states, sales taxes generate a large segment of state budgets.

But the notion of illegals "not paying taxes" does not hold at the federal level either. In fact, the proliferation of false green cards and Social Security cards used by illegal immigrants is believed to be the source of nearly seven billion dollars in subsidy to Social Security coffers that may never be claimed by illegal immigrant workers who paid into the system.[51] Many have paid into the system legally as well by using the Internal Revenue Service's "tax ID"—a number the service began generating in 1996 for those who do not hold a social security number.[52]

To the degree that immigrants' claims to birthright citizenship for their children, Social Security, and public education have been restricted or even questioned, the final message is that these cannot be citizens in this new fiscal sense. To the extent that these are not the European immigrants of the first and second waves, public officials have marginalized their contributions as well. Finally, when elected officials cast immigrants from Mexico and Latin America as the purveyors of overpowering fertility, criminality, and moral decay, these immigrants and their children are not portrayed as forming a part of either the history or the future of the United States. Instead, this population appears a problem population.

Conclusion

Power and Image in Immigration Policymaking

We typically study public policy as a mechanism for problem-solving and expect that research, deliberation, and rationality are applied to solving social problems. Likewise, when public policies fail, analysts quickly attribute these failures to factors such as budget inadequacies, illogical mandates, poor administration, and unanticipated consequences. However, if we consider immigration policy not simply as problem-solving mechanism but as an opportunity to structure and manage claims on the state, we can more easily understand why these policies appear on their surface to be contradictory or designed to fail.

The conflict over immigration is not about differences in research, pilot program evaluations, or task force recommendations. Rather the conflict is at its core about a politics of reassurance. Debates over contemporary immigration policy comprise Murray Edelman's concept of "political spectacle," or the use of events, crises and social problems to threaten, reassure, and ultimately, create consensus regarding a contentious issue. Nor is the politics of reassurance a smokescreen, or diversion: its expressions are fundamentally instrumental, enabling government to channel real benefits to or force real burdens upon certain groups of people.

The deliberative process reveals the critical role that values can play in policy design, especially when officials classify some groups and actions as necessary for the public good. With the issue of immigration control running contrary to traditional partisan divisions and incorporating numerous conflicting interests, legislators rely heavily on established immigration myths and carefully crafted story-telling to generate consensus on appropriate action. Official discourse pays regular homage to immigration as our national story—our civic myth—but immigration policy language reveals that ambivalence about immigration is our less celebrated national phenomenon. Nonetheless, this ambivalence sits quite comfortably alongside our nation-of-immigrants mystique, and both are ready and available for deployment during immigration reform discussions.

The IRCA debates showed members of the legislature competing over the political construction of the illegal immigrant population. A decade later, the IIRAIRA debates showed minimal struggle over the decidedly criminal construction of illegal immigrants or the construal of immigrants as freeloaders. The language officials employed to justify the passage of the 1996 IIRAIRA combined the contemporary ideology of balanced budget conservatism and the divisions forged between deserving and undeserving members with ascriptive traditions that linked Mexicans to undesirable attributes. Not only did deviant constructions of the unauthorized correspond with punitive policy measures, but these constructions also accentuated a list of qualities and behaviors that marked immigrants more broadly as unworthy of consideration for social membership. Immigrants' roles as laborers, or even as reproducers of the labor force, virtually disappeared from congressional discourse in the 1990s. The immigrant family was portrayed as another invasion of the nation, as individuals brought their unproductive dependents into the nation: pregnant wives, children, and elder family members would end up on welfare or take up space in schools, hospitals, and communities. This image of the immigrant freeloader obscured the various legal statuses of the subject groups. For example, from 1994 to 1996 both congressional rhetoric and policy promoted a construction of legal immigrants that looked much like that of the undocumented. Virtually none of the characteristics that would commonly mark legal immigrants as deserving emerged in the IIRAIRA discussions. However, while legal immigrants were negatively portrayed in the IIRAIRA debates, they were never fully ascribed the criminal essence which marks the illegal immigrant.

A Point of Contrast: The Not-So-Negative Construction of Employers

There was also a shift in the negative construction of U.S. employers during the periods examined here. While in the 1984–1986 period there appeared a negative image of agricultural employers that highlighted the worker and workplace abuses associated with this industry, by 1996 the association of employers with criminal or abusive behaviors was virtually non-existent, even though by this time it was illegal to hire unauthorized workers. Instead, by 1996, employers appeared as victims of government regulations, drowning in paperwork, and fearful of punishment, even though evidence showed that sanctions were weakly enforced.

Negative stories about employers appearing in the 1980s focused on their disproportionate influence in Congress and charged them with not using the system fairly. But negative image, in combination with employers' portrayal during both periods as regulatory victims, hardly matches the overall rhetorical indictment that many in Congress showered on illegal immigrants. One reason for this indictment is, of course, that this group has violated immigration law. However, while congressional lawmakers would prohibit employers from hiring unauthorized workers—and even though the law would criminalize the activity for repeat offenders—lawmakers did not construct employers as deviants.

That business interests benefiting from both legal and illicit immigration flows would escape characterization as lawbreakers is a function of the special role that business occupies in American politics. Charles Lindblom once argued that the privileged position of business in policymaking is fundamental to the functioning of a pluralist democracy; this intimate relationship ensures that regulations on enterprise are weakly enforced or riddled with loopholes.[1] Guest-worker programs, legalization designed specifically for agricultural workers, the reduction of paperwork and red tape for employers, and the expansion of the Fourth Amendment to cover open fields and ranches from the searches of INS inspectors, together provide evidence of the privileged position that the farming industry enjoys in immigration lawmaking. Congress did charge agriculture statutorily with regulatory burdens in employer sanctions and worker eligibility requirements, but Congress imposed these regulations on *all* employers. By contrast, agriculturists—even more specifically, perishable fruit growers—were singled out for special benefits.

An interest-group-driven explanation of policy outcomes would predict a well-organized, politically powerful group like agriculture to receive benefits. Agriculture is often the example offered in American political textbook explanations of iron triangles, and the privileged position of this industry ensures that it will enjoy particularized benefits through immigration legislation. The power of agricultural interests has been central to explaining why agriculture escaped hiring regulations for so long, and why, once blame and punishment were enacted, they were rarely implemented. However, agriculture enjoys more than the power that comes from organization, money, and access to the legislative process; this sector of the economy also enjoys a positive social construction. It is not that the power of agriculture allows this target group to escape punishment; rather, the competing positive construction based on myths of the family farmer as producer of common goods widely enjoyed by Americans allows this target group to escape criminalization. In the end, without a criminal construction, it is difficult for legislators, even policy implementers, to defend policing, fines, jail time, and other coercive policy tools associated with curbing criminal behavior. Even when they operate in overt violation of established laws, employers do not bear the stigma of criminality that marks the illegal immigrant.

Target-Group Constructions: Another Face of Power

We generally think of interest-group power and contextual opportunities as translating into policy designs that benefit certain groups, and these explanations have dominated how we typically explain immigration policy design.[2] Alternatively, the loss of benefits should represent a loss of group strength or advocacy, or a change in contextual factors that disadvantage a previously influential group. Yet, this analysis presented a case in which an unpopular and relatively politically weak group (illegal immigrants) gained a significant benefit (legalization), only to see the gradual gains that could accompany legal status diminished quite soon after this victory. This development suggests some limitations to a path-dependent view of policy outcomes; the cross-period comparison of immigrant group constructions demonstrated that rationales depicting groups as deserving benefits would not be bankable in the next policy period.

The discourse analysis of measures targeting agricultural employers reaches beyond traditional pressure group and contextual factors that we anticipate will produce policy shifts, or at least explain the narrow distribution of benefits to target groups. Most people are aware when Congress undertakes immigration reform, however, the public is not as likely to understand that immigration restriction does not include labor immigration to specific sectors of the economy. Nor could we fault the public—it is illogical given the stated goals of the policies and the grandstanding of the IIRAIRA's supporters. Employers continue to elude blame for illegal immigration or abstract, out-of-control immigration, even as this blame persists in being attached to immigrants.

Another axiom of policy change is that institutional change—for example, in party control of an administration or of Congress, or of the federal courts—can open avenues to political influence for some groups while closing the door to others.[3] However, the debate analyses presented here suggest a significant caveat: some groups are simply more subject to the effects of partisan change in Congress than are others. Partisan control of Congress can affect how amenable the legislature is to certain policy narratives. For example, a Republican-controlled Congress is more likely to generally discredit narratives calling for stricter regulations for businesses than a Democratic-controlled Congress. At the same time, the rationales, symbolism, and mythology employed in these debates exist independently of the two parties, and have existed long before either the IRCA or the IIRAIRA. The construction of some immigrants as morally, socially, and economically marginal allows restriction policy to coexist with imported labor in legislation touted as restrictive. While truly powerful groups do not always get what they want from government, they certainly do not suffer substantive setbacks on benefits previously secured, regardless of which party is in power.

Given that the social construction of immigrants was unstable during the period of reforms studied here, we might ask why it is that some constructions appear to carry more weight or are more likely to shape the tone of debate than are others. Part of the answer lies in the very nature of American immigrant mythology. The construction of the poor, but hard-working and upwardly mobile proto-citizen is intrinsically unstable. Images of toiling, deserving immigrants easily collapse when economic times are difficult; images of the immigrant contributor are easily contradicted by images of impoverished newcomers and desperate border-crossers who have just embarked on the multi-generational process of social mobility. The proto-citizen construction likewise collapses too easily along fault lines of race, gender, class, and legal status, as some types of work are valued while others remain invisible or unacknowledged in accounts of American immigrant history and nation-building.

However, another part of the answer lies in the social context in which policymaking occurs. Because legislators negotiate these laws amidst economic downturn, heightened media coverage, debate by policy researchers, and, of course, public opinion polling, we expect members of Congress to be sensitive to the social context as they draft policies. As a result, lawmakers will offer problem definitions and justifications for their solutions in ways that will ring true among their voting constituencies, and that will respond to changes in contextual circumstances.[4] This is so even in circumstances like the 1986 IRCA in which Congress passed a legalization component that ran counter to the majority public opinion. Although legalization was a policy solution that was initially designed to pay for itself and not impose direct costs on the citizen public, this policy solution required a broader justification of the target group as deserving of the legalization benefit.

While this analysis did not focus explicitly on the political parties as variables explaining policy change, it does recognize that party plays a role insofar as parties and the ideologies they represent create forums that are either more or less amenable to certain problem definitions and policy narratives. Just as social constructions must resonate within the social context, these constructions must have political resonance, too. As we saw, the source of the problem of illegal immigration did not change between 1986 and 1996. Rather, as Congress shifted from Democratic control to Republican control (1994), we saw a change in how the problems and solutions were defined. The Democratic Party was in control during the IRCA debates, and while immigration reform was controversial and the policy tools contentious, narratives and counter-narratives developed for each side of the issues, giving the appearance of full debate. On the other hand, from 1994 on, Republican control of Congress created a context in which a complete redefinition of the immigration problem as an issue of fiscal discipline became viable. Suddenly, all immigrants became a problem, and those (of either party) who disagreed with the policy narratives and negative immigrant constructions were hard-pressed to mount a counter-narrative in an ideologically infertile political context.

Illegal immigrants, by definition have a tenuous relationship with the government, which derives from their illicit mode of entry, and, as a result, these immigrants are the group most easily demonized for policy purposes. In the 1980s, supporters of legalization provided a rhetorical reconstruction of illegal immigrants as embedded, permanent members of the American social fabric. This construction was deployed by a contingent of congressmen and women who skillfully challenged the undeserving illegal narrative. However, even with elected officials as advocates, unauthorized immigrants continued to be construed as criminals, and this construction leaves them especially vulnerable to the manipulation of political elites who may be more interested in laying blame than addressing immigration and related social issues.

Immigration as Political Spectacle: The Policy Predicament

In *Immigrant America: A Portrait*, sociologists Alejandro Portes and Ruben Rumbaut documented the extraordinary diversity of today's immigrants in terms of nation of origin, educational attainment, and labor force participation, noting that this heterogeneity in immigrant stocks is unparalleled in U.S. history.[5] New immigrant groups, the evidence suggests, will not follow a singular path to assimilation, nor will they live a uniform immigrant experience.[6] However, this diversity was largely absent from the public face of policy deliberation in the periods studied here. When immigrants were identified by nation, overwhelmingly the nation mentioned was Mexico. While Mexico ranks first among source nations for legal and unofficial immigration, Mexican immigration is only part of the story.

Although India, the Philippines, and China would follow Mexico as top source countries of legal admissions from 1995 to 2006,[7] contemporary immigration discourse concentrates on the southern border, on Mexican illegal immigration, and on amorphous immigrant dependents that have been racialized as Mexican. Others who also have a stake in national policies are invisible from public deliberation. Thus, while immigrants from Asian source nations face long waiting periods of five or more years for reunification with spouses and seek opportunities to regularize their status, they disappear from policy discussions that have turned family reunification into an avenue for state dependency and that have put a Latino face on legalization measures and guest-worker visas. These non-Mexican immigrants, in turn, face the choice of aligning themselves with a politically maligned group or pursuing claims on an individual or small collective basis. Even then, these immigrants still suffer the maligning anti-immigrant sentiment that comes from an officially sanctioned characterization of immigrants as freeloaders.

Immigration policy has been and will likely continue to be a highly contested issue area in which conflicting desires produce contradictory policy measures. However, the lesson of the IRCA is that negative politicking is not an inevitable outcome of anti-immigrant contexts. Congressional policymakers can and do buck popular opinion, and social constructions are just as powerful in redistributing benefits to unpopular groups as they are in justifying the policies that punish them. That Congress was willing at one time to bestow the opportunity for regularization of status for illegals, and therefore pull even this marginalized group under the protection of the state, shows that elected officials are not always seduced by scapegoat politics. Most significantly, however, the return to a punitive policy approach shortly after the IRCA is troubling in that it represents the collapse of a new government/client relationship forged through legalization.

The American public is not the only constituency with a stake in immigration control. For, not only do these policies assign rights and legal standing to potential immigrants and resident aliens; these policies, like other social policies, also convey lessons to their clients about where they stand in relation to the government and the society they inhabit. Policy designs that penalize and stigmatize groups can effectively bloc avenues to self-empowerment for those who depend on the government for protection. For those immigrants who seek permanence and protection of their stake in the United States, it is likely that their political advancement and participation will be stymied if political activity persistently entails challenging a negative construction.

Epilogue

As I complete this book, the nation is once again embroiled in a bitter debate over immigration control, how best to accomplish it, and what course to pursue in dealing with the resident unauthorized population, whose size is currently estimated to lie somewhere between 10 and 12 million people. Each chamber of Congress has pursued solutions (either singly or in combination) that follow four general formats: criminalization of the act of illegal immigration and unauthorized presence in the United States; extension and expansion of southern border control efforts, including limited or no due-process procedures for those people apprehended there; expansive guest-worker programs; and a broad-scale legalization program. Supporters of each option have publicly defended their preferred solutions with stories with antecedents that have appeared in policy debates past. These stories continue to enjoy resonance today because they are built upon narratives and social constructions that are so firmly entrenched in the policy culture that even such important contextual changes as new administrations, shifts in party ideology and legislative control, and other key events, cannot dismantle them.

The latest round of immigration reform efforts has occurred amidst several historic changes in the political and policy dynamics of both the United States and Mexico. First was the November 2000 election of Texas governor George W. Bush to the presidency. As the Republican presidential candidate, Bush had worked to pull the Republican Party back from the anti-immigration message that it had pursued nationally in the 1990s, as well as in the West and South. Having accumulated support from Latino voters in his state (he even increased his share of the traditionally Democrat-leaning Latino vote from 28 percent in 1994 to 49 percent for his 1998 re-election), as well serving as a border state governor, Bush had the credentials to steer the national party in a different direction. During his campaign, Governor Bush established that he was interested in pursuing a large-scale guest-worker program and offering work eligibility to immigrants already working in the United States unofficially.

A second key development was the historic December 2000 Mexican general election that broke seventy-one years of the Institutional Revolutionary Party's control of the presidency. Mexico's new National Action Party president, Vicente Fox, instantly pursued a policy agenda in which migration and U.S.-Mexico relations were foremost. President Bush met several times with Vicente Fox to informally discuss the issue and invited the Mexican president to make his case before the U.S. Congress during his official state visit in September 2–8, 2001.[1] However, any potential U.S.-Mexico binational approach to stem Mexico's out-migration and authorize the Mexican labor force in the United States was snuffed mere days later as attacks on the United States by al-Qaeda terrorists on September 11, 2001, redirected the national agenda. Among the many vulnerabilities exposed by the attack was the government's inability to identify and track dangerous immigrants. Consequently, the attack heightened official and public concerns over an immigration system that, in retrospect, appeared to facilitate the maneuverings and planning of al-Qaeda operatives both within and without the United States. The attack also heightened public and official concerns about border security. Congress dismantled the INS and reassigned its administrative and enforcement responsibilities to the Departments of State and Justice, respectively, while, in turn, these departments were grouped under the new Department of Homeland Security.

Doing a Job the Government Won't Do

The fight over federal responsibility has gathered steam since the 1990s, when California emerged as a model for states and localities wishing to assert that a conflict of interest exists on immigration issues. This conflict was defined in fiscal terms in California, and the enforcement of measures intended to bring fiscal discipline would come to rely on citizen policing. In this respect, the state of California essentially approved the activities of border vigilantes and the citizens of the "Light Up the Border" campaign in doing what the federal government would not. Although Proposition 187 did not pass court scrutiny, the ideological wheels were in motion. Soon afterwards, in 2004, Arizona anti-immigration activists offered a 187-style ballot measure, Proposition 200. To them, the lesson of the failure of 187 was that denial of public schooling to undocumented children was a poison pill. Therefore, citizens of Arizona passed Proposition 200, which barred illegal immigrants from receiving public benefits but left children in schools.

Likewise, Arizona would become the scene of a new citizen-manned border control campaign, the Minuteman Project. The Minuteman Project, co-headed by Californian anti-immigrant activists Chris Simcox and James Gilchrist, commenced with the group's arrival in Tombstone, Arizona, on April 1, 2005. They recruited over one thousand civilians to mend fences and assist the Border Patrol in spotting and apprehending suspected illegal immigrants.[2] The group, which Gilchrist claimed was partly comprised of "retired trained combat soldiers," arrived as an armed band to the march in Tombstone, and from there, marchers would fan out and position themselves every quarter mile along a twenty-mile section of the U.S.-Mexico border. President Bush referred to the civilian patrols as "vigilantes," and the U.S. Department of Homeland Security assigned over five hundred additional Border Patrol agents to Arizona, where they would contend with individuals from the civilian gang accidentally tripping movement sensors.[3]

Far from being a small-scale demonstration in a remote segment of Arizona known mostly for its claim to Wild West folklore, the event attracted the attention of the federal governments in Mexico City and Washington, D.C. The Minuteman Project's leadership announced their mission and plans well in advance, and thus, prior to the project's launch, the government of Mexico issued a diplomatic note requesting that American officials ensure that immigrant's rights would be respected.[4] On March 29, Mexico's Foreign Relations Department announced that its consulates in Arizona would file criminal complaints against illegal detentions of its citizens by Minutemen, and warned that Mexico would consider civil action against individual Minutemen if necessary.[5] President Fox increased Mexico's military presence along the border, claiming the deployment would ensure the protection of the rights of Mexican citizens.

The project also attracted the attention of all major network and cable news organizations, as pro-immigrant protesters from Arizona and California and Chicano activists, the Brown Berets, as well as anti-immigration protesters arrived to Arizona in response to the Minutemen's presence. The project would receive the endorsement of CNN's Lou Dobbs, who, on his evening program described President Fox and President Bush's description of the group as vigilantes as "unfortunate," and instead hailed the Minutemen as "a terrific group of concerned, caring Americans."[6] While

U.S. officials reported a slowing of illicit crossings in the Minutemen's targeted sector, they credited the drop in traffic to the Mexican military.[7] Nonetheless, Simcox announced in May of 2005 that the group would deploy along the U.S.-Canada border.[8] The group translated their media attention into a cross-country tour, and other chapters of the organization opened up around the United States.[9] In the Virginia chapter, members photographed congregations of day laborers and potential employers and threatened to mail the photographs to federal authorities.

Activist reaction against immigration has not been the only reply to a perception that the government does not control immigration effectively. A flurry of state and local legislation following the path set by California and Arizona suggests that immigration remains a major front in the battle between federal versus state and local jurisdiction. In early 2006, the Georgia statehouse moved to restrict immigrant access to public services, but a court declared the law unconstitutional. A Proposition 200–style measure was removed from the Colorado 2006 ballot when a court review found that the measure violated the state's electoral rules by addressing multiple issues.[10] Arizona's voters, meanwhile, overwhelmingly passed three additional propositions in 2006 that denied bail to illegal immigrants, denied them awards of punitive damages, and outlawed receipt of state subsidies. The likelihood of court review, restraining orders, and even overturn of such laws has not served to deter states and municipalities seeking to assert their interests in immigration policymaking: by the time heavy campaigning would begin for the 2006 midterm election cycle, state and local governments had passed seventy-seven directives on illegal immigration, while hundreds more awaited final decisions in their respective institutions of origin.[11]

Among these laws is the Illegal Immigration Relief Act passed in July of 2006 in Hazleton, Pennsylvania. The city ordinance requires landlords to evict illegal immigrants and any businesses that have hired illegal immigrants to fire them. The law also forbids the city of Hazelton to produce information in any language other than English, and it bars city employees from communicating in a language other than English. The ordinance also requires that residents of Hazleton acquire a residency card. While many in the town are pleased, others sense the law unfairly targets the influx of Latino immigrants to the former steel town. According to reports from Hazelton, although it is unclear when or how the law will be enforced, there is a climate of fear among the legal, illegal, and citizen Latino population. As immigrants fear being seen in public, Latino-owned businesses, many of which had revitalized the town's business district, have had to close in the face of disappearing clientele.[12] And fear persists among the town's Latino population even though a judge halted enforcement of the ordinance, and the Pennsylvania chapter of the American Civil Liberties Union, in conjunction with the Puerto Rican Legal Education Fund has filed a lawsuit against it, claiming that the law interferes with federal jurisdiction over immigration and that its English-only provision violates the First Amendment.[13]

Criminals or Working Tax-Payers?

It is amidst these events that bills increasing border barricades and security and legislation that would reify the criminal status of unauthorized immigrants emerged. House Resolution 4437, passed on December 16, 2005, would have made living in the United States illegally a criminal offense resulting in a one-year jail term and would have required all people caught crossing the U.S. border illegally to be detained. Additional criminal penalties would apply to people found assisting illegal immigrants. Section 1002 of the bill called for the building of hundreds of miles of fences along the U.S.-Mexico border, and Section 1003 charged the Department of Homeland Security with conducting a study to determine the necessity and feasibility of constructing a "state-of-the-art barrier system along the northern international land and maritime border of the United States."[14] Prior to passing 4437, the House even toyed with an amendment that would have revoked birthright citizenship, but fearing that the bill would stand no chance of passing the Senate, the House leadership did not allow a vote on the proposal.

In April of 2006, the Senate offered its own proposal for comprehensive reform that included a guest-worker program and a large-scale program for legalization, tightening up employer accountability and, of course, increased border security. The political debate that resulted revolved around whether illegal immigrants should be punished in the terms outlined in the House bill, or offered the opportunity to legalize or participate in the workforce through new, legitimate but temporary channels, as recommended by the Senate. Although the post-2001 party and public environment seemed to favor bills pursuing border security, policing, immigrant detention, and removal, appeals for legalization rested on storylines tested during the 1980s and on social constructions of immigrants as hard-working, family people.

A brief sampling of public stances that key leaders in the immigration debates issued, illustrates how the landscape of congressional immigration politics in 2006 retains many of the contours seen in the 1980s and 1990s. The first discussion excerpt, from Senator Richard Durbin (IL), the Democratic Party Whip, was offered in support of the Senate's version of reform:

> . . . The people who are undocumented are a major part of America's economy, 29 percent of our agricultural work force in . . . Congressman Sensenbrenner's state. . . . They've become an integral part of our economy, an important part. And what I believe we need to do is to really stop the illegal flow and create a legal flow of immigration, people whom we can identify. We'll know their names, where they live, where they work. That'll make us a more secure nation.[15]

Senator Durbin offered the familiar construction of illegal immigrants as "hard workers," but also pitched legalization as a necessity for national security. As the Senator explained, the rationale is that identifying who is here and locating them within the nation will be better insurance than not knowing who lives among us.

This security framing of the legalization issue originated in January of 2004, when President Bush (who still enjoyed high approval ratings based on his handling of the war on terror and the Iraq and Afghanistan wars) announced that he would pursue a large-scale guest-worker program. With the presidential election approaching, immigration would prove a sticky topic for Republicans, who were sharply divided between pro-business interests that favored the President's guest-worker option and those that wanted to see the government take either a tougher or more restrictive stance on immigration. President Bush, who faced no Republican challenger in his bid for re-election, viewed the proposal as an opportunity to reach beyond his traditional constituency early in the election cycle. Republican strategists had learned from the 2000 election that the president would need to reach beyond his base to secure his re-election, and the guest-worker proposal offered a chance to lure to Latino voters, who were emerging as an important swing group in Nevada, New Mexico, and Arizona, among other states. The president also retreated from talk of a large-scale legalization in order to dampen critics of this unpopular approach on the Right.[16] When examinations of the plan by the senate judiciary subcommittee on immigration raised concerns about what the president's plan meant for border security, particularly in light of past failures of immigration agencies to keep terrorists out, the administration and campaign officials began to frame the guest-worker program as an enhancement to national security. According to a Bush campaign worker quoted in the conservative *Washington Times,*

> . . . so I think at the end of the day this immigration announcement was every bit as much a homeland security announcement, because of the extra measures to tighten the borders. . . . By getting a large number of temporary workers into a program, we have a better idea of who is coming and going in the United States of America.[17]

Using similar language in a 2006 televised address to the nation, President Bush appealed to the public to support congressional efforts to reconcile the two bills, and keep both a guest-worker and legalization option:

> Illegal immigration puts pressure on public schools and hospitals, strains state and local budgets, and brings crime to our communities. These are real problems, yet we must remember that the vast majority of illegal immigrants are decent people who work hard, support their families, practice their faith, and lead responsible lives. They are a part of American life—but they are beyond the reach and protection of American law.[18]

Note the President's appeal turns on the construction of illegal immigrants as hard-working family people. As was the case for Senator Durbin's statement in favor of legalization, the President's argument for legalization also reflects the impact of September 11th and security concerns on the immigration debate. However, while recalling the IRCA legalization rationales, the legalization-as-security-measure defense could also be read as a variation of the argument made in the 1980s, in which legalization would bring accountability to the problem of those unaccounted for, and allow the government to secure taxes.

In another example from the 2006 campaign for reform, James Sensenbrenner (R-WI), sponsor and champion of the punitive H.R. 4437, attacked the Senate bill's inclusion of a legalization program. Sensenbrenner likened the Senate plan to purchasing citizenship for $2,000—the fee that

the Senate suggested in addition to the payment of back taxes for applicants for legalization:

> . . . Now, American citizenship should not be for sale. And what the Sen-
> ate bill [1033] does is it says if they pay those $2,000 fines, they can end
> up being a citizen. I think American citizenship is priceless, and it ought
> to be done the legal way just like my ancestors did. . . .[19]

His stance appears ironic given his position during the IIRAIRA debates
in which he and his colleagues argued that citizenship was purchasable in
principle—that rights of citizenship are secured through the activity of
tax-paying.

At the end of his statement, Representative Sensenbrenner, in keeping
with a theme that I have argued is a hallmark of contemporary immigration rhetoric, referenced to his own (white, European) ancestors, and past
immigration more generally, as emblematic of the rule of law that ought
to govern immigration. However, the distinction between legal and illegal
did not exist for the nation's European ancestors: absent a border patrol at
maritime ports of entry, and during a time of lax enforcement and minimal land migration, immigrants from Europe simply arrived. Yet this notion of legality attributed to past immigration is treated as a historical fact
and perpetuated in official discourse—as well as being appropriated by
those who see the distinction between past and present-day immigration
as defining "right" and "wrong" immigration.

Ultimately, 2006 would end without comprehensive immigration reform. The single measure that both chambers could agree on, building a
seven-hundred-mile fence along the southern border with Mexico, along
with a mandate for a study of building a fence along the U.S.-Canada border, was signed into law by President Bush two weeks before the 2006
midterm elections. Comprehensive efforts to address immigration issues
awaited the outcome of an election in which the war in Iraq was the policy issue that far outweighed other concerns on American minds. Upon
capturing Congress in the 2006 election, Democrats announced that
immigration reform would be a priority, and they envisioned progress
would be made in this one policy area in which they and President Bush
shared common goals. However, little else was heard for several months
until members of a bipartisan group of twelve senators announced that
they had been secretly meeting with Homeland Security Director Michael
Chertoff to draft a bipartisan immigration bill. The result was legislation

that would restructure legal immigration preferences via a points system that favors skilled workers over family-sponsored immigrants, and that offers a guest-worker program along with a large-scale legalization program. The proposed bill also included over $4 billion to fund border security efforts.[20] Legalization would cost applicants $5,000, and would have required payment of back taxes, had this provision not been removed by the president.[21]

The bill was offered with limited opportunity for debate, or addition of amendments. While the hope was that the bill would satisfy enough people to pass through the Senate and be re-written in the House (which had promised to follow the former's lead on the issue), the bill suffered in attempting to please too many constituencies. Pro-immigrant interests that previously aligned, such as the high-tech lobby and ethnic groups, were divided over the new points system. Although the program's emphasis on skills seemed to benefit high-tech businesses, new hiring regulations and the removal of current allowances for employers to sponsor specific workers displeased the lobby.[22] The bill's guest-worker provisions threatened to divide labor unions on the Left, and the legalization, guest-worker, and family reunification provisions divided ethnic lobbies, particularly certain non-Hispanic advocates who would not benefit from changes.[23] On the Right, the bill was criticized for undermining border security and doing nothing to stem the overall number of immigrants.[24] While the president pleaded for Congress to reach an agreement and pass immigration reform, his administration's mishandling of both international and domestic crises, his low approval ratings among his Republican base, and his loss of political capital within his own party have all greatly diminished his ability to lead on immigration issues. Nor did legalization enjoy popularity as a plan for dealing with the resident unauthorized population.[25]

The Senate bill also incurred the wrath of those who see legalization programs as rewarding lawbreakers. In a display of principled consistency, representative Elton Gallegly (R-CA) offered the following critique of the Senate bill in the *Los Angeles Times*:

> If we grant this amnesty, we only encourage yet even more illegal immigration. . . . Only one lawbreaker has to return to apply for permanent residency for a family of lawbreakers.[26]

On June 28, 2007, the bill failed a crucial vote to close debate and move forward. With the 2008 presidential campaign looming, it appears unlikely that the 110th Congress will pursue comprehensive reform again. It may be that the era of comprehensive bills is past, and it may make more sense to separate the immigration issue into its component parts, with Congress passing individual items such as the specialized agricultural guest-worker program, AgJobs, and the DREAM Act (which offers legalization and naturalization paths for undocumented students entering college or the military). If this is the case, 2009 may produce a legalization program that looks like the 2000 LIFE Act, which was a legalization program far more limited in scope and reach than the IRCA's amnesty program.[27] The limited approach to immigration reforms might provide solutions without the spectacle of degenerative politics that have accompanied recent sweeping reform efforts.

Immigration and the Real Test of Latino Political Power

The 2000 Census indicated that the U.S. Latino population has grown by 60 percent (to 35.3 million people) since the 1990 Census and that the vast majority of these (21 million) are of Mexican origin. While many have argued that a legalization program and the creation of a special visa program for guest workers would play much more positively among Latino voters, immigration remains a relatively low issue priority among voting Latinos, who rank the War in Iraq, the economy, and healthcare more highly.[28] Yet, like it or not, the immigration issue will continue to define the American Latino population. While this population may not be able to choose which particular aspect of the larger issue defines it, Latinos may have a role in the contest to define the terms of the debate and the constructions officials use to discuss immigrants. The contest will involve Latinos, immigrant or not, because it is clear that anti-immigration ideologies easily trade critical distinctions in favor of caricature and facile claims.

The political importance of Latinos could be defined as turnout at the ballot box, but the political power of Latinos will be measured by the group's ability to secure substantive and enduring victories at the policy table. Image remains elemental to such power. Image determines not only who is only viewed as a criminal, but also who is treated as a criminal (treatment that still eludes employers hiring in violation of existing laws). Image determines whose claims are perceived as rightful, and who is viewed as a deserving member with rights of privileges and claims to all aspects of the state. Image also determines whose contributions are considered in both the history and future of the nation. The difference between political importance and power has everything to do with the ability to control public image. Immigrants, it appears, are aware of this.

The immigration debates of 2005–2006 occurred against the backdrop of multiple protests against H.R. 4437, which were attended by thousands across the United States. Beginning on February 25, 2006, in California, the protests quickly gathered in size and momentum as immigrants and their supporters in Los Angeles, Houston, Denver, Chicago, Atlanta, and mid-sized cities throughout the Midwest like Milwaukee and Detroit marched en masse throughout March and April, culminating in a May 1 "Day without an Immigrant" rally that was billed as a work-stoppage designed to call attention to the crucial role that immigrants maintain in the economy.

The number and size of these protests surprised many observers, including me. The outbreak of protests suggested that immigrants were not waiting for members of Congress to speak on their behalf, and were instead trying to fight their persistent characterization as criminals. Protesters' signs and chants declared, "WE ARE NOT CRIMINALS" in a direct challenge to H.R. 4437's measures that would make felons of millions of people residing in the United States.[29] In case there is any question of who feels targeted by the flurry of technically neutral immigration reform activities at the state and federal levels, the flags carried by protesters (and criticized by pundits), along with camera footage of the protestors, confirm that Latino immigrants have heard the message loudly and clearly. Whether this momentum can be channeled into policies that, in turn, solidify their social construction as embedded in the economy and the nation remains to be seen.

Notes

NOTES TO THE INTRODUCTION

1. Michael J. Shapiro, "Winning the West, Unwelcoming the Immigrant: Alternative Stories of 'America,'" in *Tales of the State: Narrative in Contemporary U.S. Politics and Public Policy*, ed. S. Schram and A. Neisser (New York: Rowman and Littlefield, 1997).

2. Roberto Suro, "States Take Immigration Woes to Capitol with Pleas for Relief; Lawmakers Offer Governors Everything but Money," *Washington Post*, June 25, 1994.

3. Paul Feldman, "62% Would Bar Services to Illegal Immigrants," *Los Angeles Times*, September 14, 1994.

4. "Immigrant Laws Dubious," *Pittsburgh Post Gazette*, August 20, 2006; Patrik Jonsson, "Federal Court Eyes Local Crackdown of Illegal Migrants," *Christian Science Monitor*, March 15, 2007; Kim Cobb, "Oklahoma Bill Casts One of the Widest Nets," *Houston Chronicle*, April 23, 2007.

5. Murray Edelman, *The Symbolic Uses of Politics* (Urbana: University of Illinois Press, 1974).

6. Anne Schneider and Helen Ingram, "Social Construction of Target Populations: Implications for Politics and Policy," *American Political Science Review* 87, no. 2 (1993); Anne Schneider and Helen Ingram, *Policy Design for Democracy* (Lawrence: University of Kansas Press, 1997); Anne Schneider and Helen Ingram, eds., *Deserving and Entitled: Social Constructions and Public Policy* (Albany: State University of New York Press, 2005).

NOTES TO CHAPTER 1

1. Schneider and Ingram, "Social Construction of Target Populations."

2. On immigration and its effects on the conception of "the people," see Michael Walzer, *What It Means to Be an American* (New York: Marsilio, 1992); Robert A. Dahl, *On Democracy* (New Haven, CT: Yale University Press, 1998); Bonnie Honig, *Democracy and the Foreigner* (Princeton, NJ: Princeton University Press, 2001); Rogers Smith, *Civic Ideals* (New Haven, CT: Yale University Press, 1998). On the potential of immigration to undermine civic cohesion and cultural identity,

see Samuel P. Huntington, "The Hispanic Challenge," *Foreign Policy* (March/April 2004); Samuel P. Huntington, *Who Are We? The Challenges to America's National Identity*, paperback ed. (New York: Simon & Schuster, 2005). On the specific challenges to nations posed by the phenomenon of large-scale, unauthorized immigration, see Peter Schuck and Rogers Smith, *Citizenship without Consent* (New Haven, CT: Yale University Press, 1985), William Rogers Brubaker, ed., *Immigration and the Politics of Citizenship in Europe and North America* (Washington, DC: University Press of America, 1989).

3. On security imperatives, see, for example, Peter Andreas, *Border Games: Policing the U.S.-Mexico Border Divide* (Ithaca, NY: Cornell University Press, 2000); Christopher Rudolph, "Security and the Political Economy of International Migration," *American Political Science Review* 97, no. 4 (2003). For the political-economic perspective, see James Hollifield, *Immigrants, Markets, and States: The Political Economy of Postwar Europe* (Cambridge, MA: Harvard University Press, 1992).

4. Vernon Briggs, *Mass Immigration and the National Interest* (Armonk, NY: M.E. Sharpe, 1984); Saskia Sassen, "America's Immigration 'Problem,'" *World Policy Journal* 6, no. 4 (1989).

5. Philip L. Martin, "Good Intentions Gone Awry: IRCA and U.S. Agriculture," *Annals of the American Academy of Social and Political Science* 98, no. 1 (1994); Philip L. Martin and J. Edward Taylor, "Immigration Reform and Farm Labor Contracting in California," in *The Paper Curtain: Employer Sanctions Implementation, Impact and Reform*, ed. Michael Fix (Santa Monica, CA, Washington DC: RAND and Urban Institute, 1991).

6. James Gimpel and James Edwards, *The Congressional Politics of Immigration Reform* (New York: Longman, 1998), 241–43; William Branigin, "Immigration Employment Provisions Dropped; Sen. Simpson Blasts Business Community in Attempt to Keep Overhaul Bill Intact," *Washington Post*, March 8, 1996; Carolyn Wong, *Lobbying for Inclusion: Rights Politics and the Making of Immigration Policy* (Stanford, CA: Stanford University Press, 2006), 101–5.

7. Kitty Calavita, "Employer Sanctions Violations: Toward a Dialectical Model of White-Collar Crime," *Law and Society Review* 24, no. 4 (1990); Robert Bach, "Mexican Immigration and the American State," *International Migration Review* 12, no. 4 (1978).

8. Daniel Tichenor, *Dividing Lines: The Politics of Immigration Control in America* (Princeton, NJ: Princeton University Press, 2002), 267–74; Wong, *Lobbying for Inclusion*. According to Tichenor, these groups have always existed, but the Civil Rights revolution, as well as changes in the composition of the electorate and representation, have created a context that has privileged these groups and amplified their political power.

9. Gimpel and Edwards, *The Congressional Politics of Immigration Reform*; Edwin Harwood, "American Public Opinion and U.S. Immigration Policy," *Annals of*

the American Academy of Political and Social Science 487 (1986). Likewise, Gary Freeman offers a clientele model of policymaking in which the two interests that benefit most from immigration—ethnic groups and business—have largely captured the process. While the policies benefit the few, the costs are diffused among the many, and the public, which often disagrees with expansionist policies, suffers from disorganization. Gary P. Freeman, "Modes of Immigration Politics in Liberal Democratic States," *International Migration Review* 29, no. 4 (1995).

10. Branigin, "Immigration Employment Provisions Dropped; Sen. Simpson Blasts Business Community in Attempt to Keep Overhaul Bill Intact."

11. Gimpel and Edwards, *The Congressional Politics of Immigration Reform*, 48–49.

12. Wong, *Lobbying for Inclusion*.

13. Curt Anderson, "Senate OKs Reinstating Food Stamps; Bill Restores '96 Cutbacks," *Chicago Sun-Times*, May 13, 1998. Traditionally, legal immigrants holding official refugee status have been eligible for government benefits like food stamps and housing assistance. This access reflects the special, often emergency circumstances in which refugees are admitted to the United States.

14. "USDA Announces Restoration of Food Stamp Eligibility for Qualified Legal Immigrant Children," States News Service, October 1, 2003; Anderson, "Senate OKs Reinstating Food Stamps; Bill Restores '96 Cutbacks."

15. Frank R. Baumgartner and Bryan D. Jones, *Agendas and Instability in American Politics* (Chicago: University of Chicago Press, 1993).

16. Thomas Byrne Edsall and Mary D. Edsall, *Chain Reaction: The Impact of Race, Rights and Taxes on American Politics* (New York: Norton, 1991), 129–39; David O. Sears and Jack Citrin, *Tax Revolt: Something for Nothing in California* (Cambridge, MA: Harvard University Press, 1982).

17. Title IV of the Personal Responsibility and Work Opportunity Reconciliation Act of 1996 (PREWORA) barred legal aliens from receiving SSI and Food Stamps unless they had worked in the United States for ten years. Legal immigrants entering the country after 1996 would be ineligible to receive any social services (except for emergency medical care) for their first five years in the country, and their sponsors would have to provide an affidavit of financial support (the "deeming" requirement) for those first five years. The determination of alien qualification for many means-tested programs, such as TANF (Temporary Aid to Needy Families, or the block grant program that replaced the AFDC) and Medicaid, was a decision that the new law left to the states.

18. Tichenor, *Dividing Lines*. Tichenor, a historical institutionalist, sees policy change as a function of four processes that explain why restrictionist immigration policies emerge during some periods, while other periods witness expansive or liberal immigration policies. For him, the answer lies in interlocking processes of 1) institutional change, which provides new actors new windows of opportunity to try new policy approaches, 2) changing coalitions, 3) the changing role

of experts in crafting policy, and 4) international considerations and imperatives that can vary from one policy period to the next.

19. Ibid., 285–88.

20. Baumgartner and Jones, *Agendas and Instability*.

21. John Higham, *Strangers in the Land: Patterns of American Nativism 1860–1925* (New York: Atheneum, 1969); Desmond King, *Making Americans: Immigration, Race, and the Origins of the Diverse Democracy* (Cambridge, MA: Harvard University Press, 2000); Erika Lee, *At America's Gate: Chinese Immigration during the Exclusion Era, 1882–1943* (Chapel Hill: University of North Carolina Press, 2003); Mae Ngai, "The Architecture of Race in American Immigration Law: A Reexamination of the Immigration Act of 1924," *Journal of American History* 86, no. 1 (1999); Mae Ngai, *Impossible Subjects: Illegal Immigrants and the Making of Modern America* (Princeton, NJ: Princeton University Press, 2004); James A. Tyner, "The Geopolitics of Eugenics and the Exclusion of Philippine Immigrants from the United States," *Geographical Review* 89, no. 1 (1999).

22. Edward George Hartmann, *The Movement to Americanize the Immigrant* (New York: Columbia University Press, 1948).

23. Tyner, "The Geopolitics of Eugenics,"; Mae Ngai, "The Strange Career of the Illegal Alien: Immigration Restriction and Deportation Policy in the United States, 1921–1965," *Law and History Review* 21, no. 1 (2003); Ngai, *Impossible Subjects*. Chapter 3 of Ngai's *Impossible Subjects* provides an excellent account of Filipino immigration, settlement in the United States, and policy that then encouraged the repatriation of Filipinos after the 1934 Tydings-McDuffie Act made the Philippines a commonwealth of the United States and set a gratuitously low immigration quota of fifty. While Ngai documents the failure of repatriation to rid the country of the "Filipino problem" (as the majority of Filipinos refused to partake in the program), she argues that "the cultural impact of the project—and the broader movement for decolonization and exclusion within which it was embedded—was more far-reaching" (126).

24. Lee, *At America's Gate*.

25. Ibid., 33–35.

26. Ibid., 33.

27. See, for example, Joe R. Feagin, "Old Poison in New Bottles: The Deep Roots of Modern Nativism," in *Immigrants Out! The New Nativism and the Anti-Immigrant Impulse in the United States*, ed. Juan Perea (New York: New York University Press, 1997); Dorothy E. Roberts, "Who May Give Birth to Citizens? Reproduction, Eugenics, and Immigration," in *Immigrants Out! The New Nativism and the Anti-Immigrant Impulse in the United States*, ed. Juan Perea (New York: New York University Press, 1997); Shapiro, "Winning the West, Unwelcoming the Immigrant."

28. Feagin, "Old Poison in New Bottles," in Juan Perea, ed., *Immigrants Out! The New Nativism and the Anti-Immigrant Impulse in the United States* (New York:

New York University Press, 1997); Kevin R. Johnson, *The "Huddled Masses" Myth: Immigration and Civil Rights* (Philadelphia: Temple University Press, 2004).

29. Johnson, *The "Huddled Masses" Myth*, 93–106.

30. Ngai, "The Architecture of Race in American Immigration Law"; King, *Making Americans*; Lee, *At America's Gate*. All employ racial formation in their own discussions of past immigration policies.

31. Michael Omi and Howard Winant, *Racial Formation in the United States from the 1960s to the 1990s* (New York: Routledge, 1994). It is presumed that whites are always at the top and blacks remain at the bottom, while other groups then are either absorbed as "honorary" whites, or otherwise denigrated to occupying lower points in the social strata as "black" or, at least, "not white."

32. Ibid., 95–112.

33. King, *Making Americans*, 243–46.

34. Nancy F. Rytina, "U.S. Legal Permanent Residents: 2004" (U.S. Department of Homeland Security, Office of Immigration Statistics, 2005).

35. King, *Making Americans*. See also Rogers Smith, "Beyond Tocqueville, Myrdal and Hartz: The Multiple Traditions in America," *American Political Science Review* 87 (1993); Smith, *Civic Ideals*.

36. Ibid., 195.

37. Kitty Calavita, "Immigration, Law, and Marginalization in a Global Economy: Notes from Spain," *Law and Society Review* 32, no. 3 (1998); Loic Wacquant, "The Penalization of Poverty and the Rise of Neo-Liberalism," *European Journal on Criminal Policy and Research* 9 (2001); Kitty Calavita, "The New Politics of Immigration: 'Balanced-Budget Conservatism' and the Symbolism of Proposition 187," *Social Problems* 43, no. 3 (1996); Gregory A. Huber and Thomas J. Espenshade, "Neo-Isolationism, Balanced-Budget Conservatism, and the Fiscal Impacts of Immigrants," *International Migration Review* 31, no. 4 (1997).

38. Calavita, "Immigration, Law and Marginalization."

39. Susan Bibler Coutin and Phyllis Pease Chock, "'Your Friend the Illegal': Definition and Paradox in Newspaper Accounts of U.S. Immigration Reform," *Identities: Global Studies in Culture and Power* 2, nos. 1–2 (1995).

40. Jacqueline Maria Hagan, *Deciding to Be Legal: A Maya Community in Houston* (Philadelphia: Temple University Press, 1995), 99, 108–25.

41. Mara S. Sidney, *Unfair Housing: How National Policy Shapes Community Action* (Lawrence: University Press of Kansas, 2003); Mara S. Sidney, "Contested Images of Race and Place: The Politics of Housing Discrimination," in *Deserving and Entitled: Social Constructions and Public Policy*, ed. Anne Schneider and Helen Ingram (Albany: State University of New York Press, 2005).

42. See also Sanford Schram, "Putting a Black Face on Welfare: The Good and the Bad," in *Deserving and Entitled: Social Constructions and Public Policy*, ed. A. Schneider and H. Ingram (Albany: State University of New York Press, 2005).

43. Peter Bachrach and Morton S. Baratz, "Two Faces of Power," *The American Political Science Review* 56, no. 4 (1962).

44. Douglas Arnold, *The Logic of Congressional Action* (New Haven, CT: Yale University Press, 1990), 22–35.

45. Schneider and Ingram, *Policy Design for Democracy*, 111–12.

46. Edelman, *The Symbolic Uses of Politics*, 6.

47. Schneider and Ingram, "Social Construction of Target Populations," 334.

48. Ibid., 339–40; Schneider and Ingram, *Policy Design for Democracy*, 132–35.

49. Shapiro, "Winning the West, Unwelcoming the Immigrant," 17.

50. Higham, *Strangers in the Land*, 11.

51. Ibid., 106.

52. Ngai, "The Architecture of Race in American Immigration Law."

53. Ngai, "The Strange Career of the Illegal Alien"; Ngai, *Impossible Subjects*, 127–66.

54. Ngai, "The Architecture of Race in American Immigration Law."

55. Lina Newton, "'It's Not a Question of Being Anti-Immigration': Categories of Deservedness in Immigration Policymaking," in *Deserving and Entitled: Social Constructions and Public Policy*, ed. Anne Schneider and Helen Ingram (Albany: State University of New York Press, 2005).

56. Calavita, "The New Politics of Immigration"; Leo Chavez, *Covering Immigration: Popular Images and the Politics of the Nation* (Berkeley: University of California Press, 2002); Jack Citrin et al., "Public Opinion toward Immigration Reform: The Role of Economic Motivations," *Journal of Politics* 59, no. 3 (1997); Thomas J. Espenshade and Katherine Hempstead, "Contemporary American Attitudes toward U.S. Immigration," *International Migration Review* 30, no. 2 (1996); Joseph Nevins, *Operation Gatekeeper: The Rise of the "Illegal Alien" and the Making of the U.S.-Mexico Boundary* (New York: Routledge, 2002); Huber and Espenshade, "Neo-Isolationism, Balanced-Budget Conservatism, and the Fiscal Impacts of Immigrants."

57. Schneider and Ingram, eds., *Deserving and Entitled*, 1–28; Martin Gilens, *Why Americans Hate Welfare: Race, Media, and the Politics of Antipoverty Policy* (Chicago: University of Chicago Press, 1999).

58. Robert A. Dahl, *Who Governs? Democracy and Power in an American City* (New Haven, CT: Yale University Press, 1961).

59. A clear mark of "foreigner" or "immigrant" is language; it is not coincidental that the English-Only movement (now renamed "Official English") took root in the early 1980s during a time of increased immigration from Latin America, Asia, and the Caribbean. On Asian immigrant and ethnic group language use, discrimination, and legal challenges, see Angelo Ancheta, *Race, Rights and the Asian American Experience* (New Brunswick, NJ: Rutgers University Press, 1995), 104–26. For a discussion of Spanish language use, and maintenance beyond the first generation, see Richard Alba, "Immigration and the American Realities

of Assimilation and Multiculturalism," *Sociological Forum* 14, no. 1 (1999). On Spanish language as a social stigma from without and within Latino communities, see Lisa Garcia Bedolla, *Fluid Borders: Latino Power, Identity and Politics in Los Angeles* (Berkeley: University of California Press, 2003), 61–99. Although the racial experiences of Afro-Caribbean immigrants are bound together with African Americans in the United States, Haitian Creole serves to distinguish Haitians from other West Indian immigrants, and the language is often rejected in favor of English to mitigate racial, ethnic, and class discrimination. See, for example, Alex Stepick, *Pride against Prejudice: Haitians in the United States*, ed. Nancy Foner, New Immigrants Series (Needham Heights, MA: Allyn and Bacon, 1998), 80–84. Language has also been demonstrated to produce significant interactive effects with race. For example, English language fluency is an important determinant of economic success of Afro-Caribbean immigrants, who are often hailed as a "black success" story. Afro-Caribbean males who do not speak English are even more economically marginalized than their African American counterparts. Suzanne Model, "Caribbean Immigrants: A Black Success Story?" *International Migration Review* 25, no. 2 (1991).

60. Ancheta, *Race, Rights and the Asian American Experience*, 62–81; Claire Jean Kim, "The Racial Triangulation of Asian Americans," *Politics and Society* 27, no. 1 (1999); Ngai, *Impossible Subjects*, 37–50 and 177–201; Ngai, "The Architecture of Race in American Immigration Law"; Tyner, "The Geopolitics of Eugenics."

61. David Gutiérrez, *Walls and Mirrors: Mexican Americans and Mexican Immigration* (Berkeley: University of California Press, 1995), 28–38.

62. In 1845, just before the war, the United States annexed a newly independent Texas. At the end of the war, and with the Gadsden Purchase of 1853, the Mexican territories of Alta California, Nuevo Mexico, and parts of Sonora were ceded to the United States for $15 million. All told, 50 percent of Mexican territory would become the U.S. states of California, Nevada, Utah, Colorado, New Mexico, Arizona, and Texas. These territories also included what is at present southern Wyoming, part of the Oklahoma panhandle, and the southwestern corner of Kansas. Matt S. Meier and Feliciano Ribera provide an in-depth account of the land grabs and armed skirmishes that would result in the U.S.-Mexico war as well as maps detailing the resulting territorial changes In *Mexican Americans/American Mexicans: From Conquistadors to Chicanos*, revised ed. (New York: Hill and Wang, 1993), ch. 2–4.

63. Meier and Ribera, *Mexican Americans/American Mexicans*, 67–69.

64. Gutiérrez, *Walls and Mirrors*, 18.

65. Meier and Ribera, *Mexican Americans/American Mexicans*, 69–86. See also Tomas Almaguer, *Racial Fault Lines: the Historical Origins of White Supremacy in California* (Berkeley: University of California Press, 1994), 75–104, which offers case accounts of land loss and appropriation in California, to argue that the new class hierarchies produced by capitalist agriculture redefined Mexicans and

Japanese as "laborers." In California, what Almaguer describes as the proletarianization of Mexicans (and to an extent, Japanese) is how these groups come to be defined as "nonwhite."

66. Gutiérrez, *Walls and Mirrors*, 37.

67. Huntington, "The Hispanic Challenge."

68. Ibid., 36.

69. See for example, Richard Alba, "Mexican Americans and the American Dream," *PS: Political Science and Politics* 4, no. 2 (2006); Frank Bean, Susan K. Brown, and Ruben G. Rumbaut, "Mexican Immigrant Political and Economic Incorporation," *PS: Political Science and Politics* 4, no. 2 (2006); Luis R. Fraga and Gary M. Segura, "Culture Clash? Contesting Notions of American Identity and the Effects of Latin American Immigration," *PS: Political Science and Politics* 4, no. 2 (2006). Responses to Huntington's article appear on Foreign Policy's website, www.foreignpolicy.com/story/cms.php?story_id=2530.

70. Peter Brimelow, *Alien Nation: Common Sense about America's Immigration Disaster* (New York: Random House, 1995).

71. David Montejano, "Who Is Samuel P. Huntington? Patriotic Reading for Anglo Protestants Who Live in Fear of the Reconquista," http://www.texasobserver .org.

72. Cited in Kitty Calavita, "California's 'Employer Sanctions': The Case of the Disappearing Law" (Center for U.S.-Mexican Studies, University of California, San Diego, 1982), 13.

73. David E. Lorey, *The U.S.-Mexico Border in the 20th Century* (Wilmington, DE: Scholarly Resource Inc., Imprints, 1999), 69–70.

74. The program was a negotiated agreement with Mexico, in which the former would provide contract workers to U.S. farmers, and in exchange, the United States would grant full labor and wage protections available to U.S. workers to the guest workers. The reality was that the INS aided farmers in circumventing policy stipulations, including legal protections, which, at the time were virtually nonexistent even for U.S. workers. For a more extensive discussion of the pathologies of the Bracero program, see Kitty Calavita's *Inside the State*.

75. Gutiérrez, *Walls and Mirrors*, 163–65; Ngai, "The Strange Career of the Illegal Alien."

76. Brubaker, ed., *Immigration and the Politics of Citizenship in Europe and North America*.

77. Leo R. Chavez, "The Power of the Imagined Community: The Settlement of Undocumented Mexicans and Central Americans in the United States," *American Anthropologist*, no. 96 (1994); Hagan, *Deciding to Be Legal*.

78. Michael Walzer, *Spheres of Justice: A Defense of Pluralism and Equality* (New York: Basic Books, 1983).

79. The H2 Program is the largest, channeling labor (largely Mexican) into the agricultural sector. H2 visas tend to last several months at most.

80. Tyche Hendricks, "Bush Guest Worker Plan Recalls Bracero Program," *San Francisco Chronicle*, January 16, 2004. At the time of writing, the program did not replicate the contract labor system of the Bracero program in recognition of the latter's facilitating abuse. Guest workers in the Bush program would be freer agents, but the wage reduction component was used in the Bracero program as well. This feature resulted in tens of thousands of workers being defrauded of their wages, according to Kitty Calavita, *Inside the State: The Bracero Program, Immigration and the I.N.S.* (New York: Routledge, 1992). In 2006, President Bush himself would insist that the program include a "pathway to citizenship" instead of forced return. This stance conflicted with that of House (and some Senate) Republicans, as well as prevailing public opinion.

81. Seth Stern, "An Uneasy Deal with an Illegal Workforce," *CQ Weekly*, March 14, 2005, 624.

82. In a Pew Hispanic Center report, Jeffrey Passel and Roberto Suro presented an analysis of Census and Current Population Survey Data that showed unauthorized immigration surpassing legal entries in 2003 and 2004 Jeffrey S. Passel and Roberto Suro, "Rise, Peak, and Decline: Trends in U.S. Immigration 1992–2004" (Washington, DC: Pew Hispanic Center, 2005).

83. Ellwyn R. Stoddard, "A Conceptual Analysis of the 'Alien Invasion': Institutionalized Support of Illegal Mexican Aliens in the U.S.," *International Migration Review* 10, no. 2 (1976); Ngai, "The Strange Career of the Illegal Alien."

84. Nevins, *Operation Gatekeeper*, 24–37.

85. Jorge Bustamante, "The 'Wetback' as Deviant," *American Journal of Sociology* 77, no. 4 (1971): 708.

86. Ibid., 715.

87. Ngai, *Impossible Subjects*, 68.

88. Ngai, "The Strange Career of the Illegal Alien"; Ngai, *Impossible Subjects*, 62–75.

89. Ngai, "The Strange Career of the Illegal Alien," 72.

90. Nestor P. Rodriguez, "The Social Construction of the U.S.-Mexico Border," in *Immigrants Out! The New Nativism and the Anti-Immigrant Impulse in the United States*, ed. Juan Perea (New York: New York University Press, 1997), 213.

91. Timothy C. Brown, "The Fourth Member of NAFTA: The U.S.-Mexico Border," *Annals of the American Academy of Political and Social Science* 550 (1997).

92. Oscar J. Martinez, *Border People: Life and Society in the U.S.-Mexico Borderlands* (Tucson: University of Arizona Press, 1994), 21–22.

93. Omi and Winant, *Racial Formation*.

94. Johnson, *The "Huddled Masses" Myth*; Ancheta, *Race, Rights and the Asian American Experience*.

95. Calavita, "Immigration, Law and Marginalization," 560.

96. Edelman, *The Symbolic Uses of Politics*, 172.

97. David O. Sears, Carl P. Hensler, and Leslie K. Speer, "Whites' Opposition to 'Busing': Self-interest or Symbolic Politics?" *American Political Science Review* 73, no. 2 (1979); Raymond Tatalovich, *Nativism Reborn? The Official English Language Movement and the American States* (Lexington: University Press of Kentucky, 1995); Edsall and Edsall, *Chain Reaction*; Sears and Citrin, *Tax Revolt*.

98. Teun A. van Dijk, "Principles of Critical Discourse Analysis," *Discourse and Society* 4, no. 2 (1993).

99. Tatalovich, *Nativism Reborn?* As of November 2006, twenty-five states have "English-Only" or "Official English" laws.

100. California Secretary of State, "Statement of Vote November 8, 1994 General Elections," (Sacramento, CA: Office of the California Secretary of State, Elections Division, 1994); Bruce M. Cain and Karin McDonald, "Nativism, Partisanship and Immigration: An Analysis of Prop 187" (paper presented at the annual meeting of the American Political Science Association, San Francisco, CA, 1996).

101. Citrin et al., "Public Opinion toward Immigration Reform: the Role of Economic Motivations."

102. Peter deLeon, "Social Construction for Public Policy," *Public Administration Review* 65, no. 5 (2005): 635; Schneider and Ingram, "Social Construction of Target Populations," 334; Teun A. van Dijk, "On the Analysis of Parliamentary Debates on Immigration," in *The Semiotics of Racism: Approaches to Critical Discourse Analysis*, ed. M. Reisigl and R. Wodak (Vienna: Passagen Verlag, 2000), 88.

103. See Robert Lieberman's critique of social constructions theory in "Social Construction (Continued)," *American Political Science Review* 89, no. 2 (1995).

104. Andrea L. Campbell, *How Policies Make Citizens: Senior Political Activism and the American Welfare State* (Princeton, NJ: Princeton University Press, 2003); Sidney, "Contested Images of Race and Place"; Sidney, *Unfair Housing*; Suzanne Mettler, *Dividing Citizens: Gender and Federalism in New Deal Policymaking* (Ithaca, NY: Cornell University Press, 1998); Ange-Marie Hancock, *The Politics of Disgust: The Public Identity of the Welfare Queen* (New York: New York University Press, 2004).

105. Helen Ingram and Anne Schneider, "The Choice of Target Populations," *Administration and Society* 23, no. 3 (1991): 333–56.

106. Van Dijk, "On the Analysis of Parliamentary Debates on Immigration."

107. Edelman, *The Symbolic Uses of Politics*; Murray Edelman, *Constructing the Political Spectacle* (Chicago: University of Chicago Press, 1988).

108. Emery Roe, *Narrative Policy Analysis: Theory and Practice* (Durham, NC: Duke University Press, 1994); Emery Roe, "Narrative Analysis for the Policy Analyst: A Case Study of the 1980–1982 Medfly Controversy in California," *Journal of Policy Analysis and Management* 8, no. 2 (1989).

109. An occurrence counted each time it appeared in a speaker's statement. Each speaker could make more than one problem statement, but each problem

statement was counted once per block of speech. Sometimes speakers had several opportunities to make a statement in the course of a transcript, and I counted each statement per block of speech regardless of whether the person had spoken before. Because debates are essentially arenas in which storylines compete, repetition serves to promote particular understandings of a problem, solution, and defense of policy. Thus, I have focused on what is being said, and how many times it is being said regardless of who speaks.

110. See also Deborah Stone, *Policy Paradox: The Art of Political Decision Making,* revised ed. (New York: Norton, 2002), 204–9.

111. Roe, *Narrative Policy Analysis.*

112. Teun A. van Dijk, "Text, Talk, Elites and Racism," *Discours Social/Social Discourse* 1, no. 2 (1992); Teun A. van Dijk, *Elite Discourse and Racism* (Newbury Park, CA: Sage, 1993); van Dijk, "Principles of Critical Discourse Analysis"; Teun A. van Dijk, "Political Discourse and Racism: Describing Others in Western Parliaments," in *The Language and Politics of Exclusion: Others in Discourse,* ed. S. H. Riggins (Thousand Oaks, CA: Sage, 1997); van Dijk, "On the Analysis of Parliamentary Debates on Immigration."

113. Schneider and Ingram, "Social Construction of Target Populations."

114. Maarten A. Hajer, *The Politics of Environmental Discourse: Ecological Modernization and the Policy Process* (New York: Oxford University Press, 1995); van Dijk, "Principles of Critical Discourse Analysis"; van Dijk, "On the Analysis of Parliamentary Debates on Immigration."

NOTES TO CHAPTER 2

1. John Kingdon, *Agendas, Alternatives, and Public Policies* (Boston: Little, Brown, 1995).

2. Deborah Stone, "Causal Stories and the Formation of Policy Agendas," *Political Science Quarterly* 104 (1989); David A. Rochefort and Roger W. Cobb, *The Politics of Problem Definition* (Lawrence: University Press of Kansas, 1994); Edelman, *Constructing the Political Spectacle.*

3. Select Commission on Immigration and Refugee Policy, "U.S. Immigration Policy and the National Interest" (Joint Committees on the Judiciary, 97th Cong., 1st sess., 1981).

4. Ibid., 10.

5. John M. Crewdson, "New Administration and Congress Face Major Immigration Decisions," *New York Times,* December 28, 1980.

6. "Jobs for Illegal Aliens Stirs Same Opposition as in '77 Gallup Poll," *New York Times,* November 11, 1980.

7. Calavita, "California's 'Employer Sanctions'"; Select Commission on Immigration and Refugee Policy, "U.S. Immigration Policy and the National Interest."

8. U.S. Congress, Senate Subcommittee on Immigration and Refugee Policy, *The Knowing Employment of Illegal Immigrants* (97th Cong., 1st sess., #82-s521-32, September 30, 1981), 39–42.

9. Rep. Romano L. Mazzoli (D-KY), *Immigration Control and Legalization Amendments of 1985*, H9708, 99th Cong., 2nd sess., *Congressional Record* (October 9, 1986): H9708.

10. Rep. Romano L. Mazzoli (D-KY), ibid.

11. Elizabeth Rolph and Abby Robyn, *A Window on Immigration Reform: Implementing the Immigration Reform and Control Act in Los Angeles* (Santa Monica, CA, Washington, DC: RAND and Urban Institute, 1990).

12. Calavita, "Employer Sanctions Violations."

13. B. Lindsay Lowell and Zhongren Jing, "Unauthorized Workers and Immigration Reform: What Can We Ascertain from Employers?" *International Migration Review* 28 (Fall 1994).

14. Martin and Taylor, "The Paper Curtain"; Martin, "Good Intentions Gone Awry: IRCA and U.S. Agriculture"; David S. North, "Enforcing the Minimum Wage and Employer Sanctions," *Annals of the American Academy of Social and Political Science* (July 1994).

15. Hagan, *Deciding to Be Legal.*

16. Michael Fix, ed., *The Paper Curtain: Employer Sanctions' Implementation, Impact, and Reform* (Santa Monica, CA, Washington, DC: RAND and Urban Institute, 1991); Jorge Durand, Douglas S. Massey, and Emilio Parrado, "The New Era of Mexican Migration to the United States," *Journal of American History* 86, no. 2 (1999).

17. Durand, Massey, and Parrado, "The New Era of Mexican Migration to the United States"; Douglas S. Massey and Kristin E. Espinosa, "What's Driving Mexico-U.S. Migration? A Theoretical, Empirical and Policy Analysis," *American Journal of Sociology* 102 (January 1997); Katharine M. Donato, "Current Trends and Patterns of Female Migration: Evidence from Mexico," *International Migration Review* 27, no. 4 (1993).

18. Susan Gonzalez Baker, *The Cautious Welcome: The Legalization Programs of the Immigration Reform and Control Act* (Santa Monica, CA, Washington, DC: RAND and Urban Institute, 1990).

19. General Accounting Office, "Illegal Aliens: National Net Cost Estimates Vary Widely" (U.S. General Accounting Office, Health Education and Human Services Division, 1995).

20. For example, in the two premier studies of net costs offered by Donald Huddle, an economist at Rice University, and Jeffrey Passel at the Urban Institute, Huddle estimates that Social Security costs for illegal immigrants is $3.3 billion, whereas Passel estimates the same cost to be zero. The difference in the two estimates arises because Passel argues that a) Social Security does not pay for itself, and therefore all legal participants in the program participate at a net cost to the

federal government, and that b) commercial interests are subsidizing "both natives and immigrants." For more on the Passel and Huddle studies, as well as correspondence between both researchers and the GAO, refer to Appendices III–V of General Accounting Office, "Illegal Aliens."

21. The 1882 law stated that customs officials had the duty to deny entry to anyone who might become a public charge, such as convicts, prostitutes, "lunatics," and "idiots."

22. Timothy J. Dunn, *The Militarization of the U.S.-Mexico Border, 1978–1992* (Austin: CMAS Books, University of Texas, 1996).

23. Patrick McDonnell, "1,000 Flip Switches to 'Light Border,'" *Los Angeles Times*, March 17, 1990.

24. Patrick McDonnell, "Protesters Light Up the Border Again," *Los Angeles Times*, August 24, 1990. Participants in "Light Up the Border" regularly carried American flags and signs reading, "Wake Up America!"

25. California Field Institute, "*The California Field Polls*" (San Francisco, CA, 1994).

26. Lowell Sachs, "Treacherous Waters in Turbulent Times: Navigating the Recent Sea Change in U.S. Immigration Policy Attitudes," *Social Justice* 23, no. 3 (1996).

27. Lawrence C. Dodd and Bruce I. Oppenheimer, "Revolution in the House: Testing the Limits of Party Government," in *Congress Reconsidered*, ed. Lawrence C. Dodd and Bruce I. Oppenheimer (Washington, DC: CQ Press, 1997), 38–40.

28. James Bornemeier, "Congressman to Seek Cuts in Immigration," *Los Angeles Times*, February 17, 1995.

29. "CBPP: Immigrants' Use of Public Benefits Has Declined Since 1996; CIS Report Exploits Loose Definitions to Paint Misleading Picture," *US Newswire*, March 26, 2003.

30. This interpretation follows Kitty Calavita's 1996 assertion that Proposition 187 provided a symbolic referent for what she terms "balanced budget conservatism," pitting voters or "taxpayers" against the poor, and the most undeserving of the poor, illegal immigrants, who lack any standing in the public's mind.

31. Gimpel and Edwards, *The Congressional Politics of Immigration Reform*.

32. Paul Sabatier and Hank C. Jenkins-Smith, *Policy Change and Learning: An Advocacy Coalition Approach* (Boulder, CO: Westview, 1993).

NOTES TO CHAPTER 3

1. Tom Morganthau, Gloria Berger, Nikki Finke Greenberg, Elaine Shannon, Renee Michael, and Daniel Pederson, "Closing the Door?" *Newsweek*, June 25, 1984.

2. Ibid. The poll corroborated earlier findings (discussed in Chapter 2) showing a majority of the American public supportive of "penalizing companies that

knowingly hire" illegal immigrants (61 percent), and few supporting amnesty (34 percent). Many more supported arrest and deportation (55 percent). Most Americans did not think that border enforcement would solve illegal immigration problems (60 percent), while only 32 percent thought it would.

3. Schneider and Ingram, "Social Construction of Target Populations," 338–39.

4. Sen. Steve Symms (R-ID), *Immigration Reform and Control Act of 1985*, S11414, 99th Cong., 1st sess., *Congressional Record* (September 13, 1985): S11414.

5. Sen. Pete Domenici (R-NM), *Congressional Record* (September 16, 1985): S11502.

6. Sen. Lawton Chiles (D-FL), *Congressional Record* (September 13, 1985): S11414.

7. In the final law, employer violations are subject to civil penalties with criminal penalties reserved for repeat offenders.

8. Sen. Daniel J. Evans (R-WA), *Congressional Record* (September 17, 1985): s11590.

9. Sen. Pete Wilson (R-CA), *Congressional Record* (September 12, 1985): s11309.

10. Sen. Orrin Hatch (R-UT), ibid.

11. Sen. Slade Gorton (R-WA), *Congressional Record* (September 17, 1985): S11590.

12. Richard Hofstadter, *The Age of Reform* (New York: Vintage Books, 1955), 24.

13. Sen. Pete Wilson (R-CA), *Congressional Record* (September 12, 1985): S11309.

14. Sen. Slade Gorton (R-WA), *Congressional Record* (September 17, 1985): S11590.

15. Sen. Slade Gorton (R-WA), ibid.

16. Sen. Daniel J. Evans (R-WA), ibid.

17. Sen. Orrin Hatch (R-UT), *Congressional Record* (September 12, 1985): s11309.

18. Calavita, *Inside the State*; Martin, "Good Intentions Gone Awry: IRCA and U.S. Agriculture." Some historical examples demonstrate how growers have successfully manipulated regulation to suit their continued demand for foreign labor. Kitty Calavita, for example has documented how the INS became a captive of its grower clientele during the Bracero program; the agency ultimately *facilitated* illicit use of guest labor instead of managing temporary labor contracts. Another famous example would be the "Texas proviso" installed into the 1954 McCarran-Walter Act. The bill made it illegal to harbor or transport illegal immigrants, but southwest growers were able to secure the exclusion of "hiring" from the definition of "harboring and transporting."

19. Martin, "Good Intentions Gone Awry: IRCA and U.S. Agriculture."

20. Sen. Alan Simpson (R-WY), *Congressional Record* (September 17, 1985): S11590.

21. Rep. John Bryant (D-TX), *Congressional Record* (October 15, 1986): H10583. Statement from speech in support of S. 1200 conference report.

22. Rep. Matthew Martinez (D-CA), ibid., H10583. Martinez cast a vote against the S. 1200 conference report.

23. Sen. Howard Metzenbaum (D-OH), *Congressional Record* (September 17, 1985): S11590.

24. Sen. Edward Kennedy (D-MA), ibid. Statement made in opposition to the Wilson amendment to allow for 350,000 temporary agricultural workers annually.

25. Sen. Howard Metzenbaum (D-OH), ibid. Metzenbaum is speaking against the Wilson amendment.

26. Rep. James Sensenbrenner (R-WI), *Congressional Record* (October 9, 1986): H9708. Statement made in opposition to Eligio "Kika" de la Garza's (D-TX) amendment which extended Fourth Amendment protections to open fields.

27. Rep. John Bryant (D-TX), ibid.

28. Rep. Barney Frank (D-MA), ibid. Further on in the Fourth Amendment debate in the House, Frank entered into an exchange with Rep. Ron Packard (R-CA) who wanted the Fourth Amendment protection to apply to the glasshouse flower industry in San Diego County. Packard said to Frank, "That would be considered an open field . . . and what would you do?" Frank replied, "I would say to the gentleman that people who live in glass houses should not break laws."

29. The RAW program was eventually ended because it was rife with applicant abuse. For a full account, see Fix, ed., *The Paper Curtain*.

30. Rep. Norman Mineta (D-CA), *Congressional Record* (October 15, 1986): H10583.

31. Rep. Robert Garcia (D-NY), ibid. Garcia, while voicing concerns, was still supporting the bill.

32. Sen. Jeff Bingaman (D-NM), *Congressional Record* (September 13, 1985): S11414. Statement made in favor the Hart-Levin amendment.

33. Rep. Steve Bartlett (R-TX), *Congressional Record* (October 9, 1986): H9708.

34. Rep. Esteban Torres (D-CA), ibid. Torres spoke in favor of the Bartlett amendment.

35. Sen. Pete Domenici (R-NM), *Congressional Record* (September 13, 1985): S11414.

36. Sen. Dennis DeConcini (D-AZ), ibid.

37. Sen. James McClure (R-ID), ibid. McClure introduced the amendment to extend Fourth Amendment rights to fields and agricultural processing areas. The amendment passed the Senate 51 to 39.

38. Rep. Leon Panetta (D-CA), *Congressional Record* (October 9, 1986): H9708.

39. Sen. Pete Wilson (R-CA), *Congressional Record* (September 13, 1985): S11414.

40. Sen. James McClure (R-ID), *Immigration Reform and Control Act—Conference Report,* S16879, 99th Cong., 2nd sess., *Congressional Record* (October 17, 1986): S16879.

41. Sen. William Armstrong (R-CO), ibid.

42. Rep. Carlos Moorhead, (R-CA), *Congressional Record* (October 15, 1986): H10583. Note that this is excerpted from statements made generally in support of the S. 1200 conference report. Moorhead says that "while there are features of the bill, including those I just mentioned, which trouble me and I am sure trouble other members in this House, I believe we should vote to approve this conference report. . . ."

43. Rep. Hal Daub (R-NE), ibid.

44. Sen. James McClure (R-ID), *Congressional Record* (October 17, 1986): S16879.

45. Chavez, *Covering Immigration,* 73–74, 218–36.

46. Sen. James McClure (R-ID), *Congressional Record* (October 17, 1986): S16879.

47. Rep. Carlos Moorhead (R-CA), *Congressional Record* (October 15, 1986): H10583.

48. Sen. Dennis DeConcini (D-AZ), *Congressional Record* (September 17, 1985): S11590. This statement was a preamble to a bill he co-sponsored with Sen. Levin to allow immigrants eligible for amnesty to continue working in the United States without penalty of deportation.

49. Sen. William Armstrong (R-CO), *Congressional Record* (October 17, 1986): S16879. A legal immigrant who resides in the United States for a period of five years (three if married to a U.S. citizen) can initiate the naturalization process.

50. Rep. Hal Daub (R-NE), *Congressional Record* (October 15, 1986): H10583.

51. Dorothee Schneider, "'I Know All about Emma Lazarus': Nationalism and Its Contradictions in Congressional Rhetoric of Immigration Restriction," *Cultural Anthropology* 13, no. 1 (1998).

52. Rep. Romano Mazzoli (D-KY), *Congressional Record* (October 15, 1986): H10583.

53. Rep. Peter Rodino (D-NJ), ibid.

54. Rep. Peter Rodino (D-NJ), *Congressional Record* (October 9, 1986): H9708.

55. Rep. Dan Lungren (R-CA), ibid.

56. Rep. Howard Berman (D-CA), ibid.

57. Rep. Lawrence Smith (D-FL), ibid.

58. Rep. Leon Panetta (D-CA), ibid.

59. Rep. Leon Panetta (D-CA), *Congressional Record* (October 15, 1986): H10583.

60. Sen. Pete Wilson (R-CA), *Congressional Record* (September 12, 1985): S11309. Wilson's entire statement introduced a guest-worker amendment that would increase temporary agricultural labor from the proposed caps and shorten the application period for farmers requesting worker approval from the DOL than provided in the H-2 program of S. 1200. This bill, to ensure the return of workers to their country of origin, would require 20 percent wage withholding. While the statement may represent posturing to garner support for this amendment and the benefits for growers in his state, it does so by addressing the fears among legalization supporters that undocumented workers have faced the worst abuses in the agricultural sector.

61. Rep. John Bryant (D-TX), *Congressional Record* (October 15, 1986): H10583.

62. Rep. Peter Rodino (D-NJ), *Congressional Record* (October 9, 1986): H9708.

63. Ibid.

64. Rep. Romano Mazzoli (D-KY), ibid.

65. In another debate on October 15, 1986, Clay Shaw (R-FL) reminded the House that Congress would expect the INS to enforce employer sanctions, which would make a huge deportation policy an unreasonable mandate for the INS.

66. Gutiérrez, *Walls and Mirrors*.

67. Calavita, *Inside the State*; Gutiérrez, *Walls and Mirrors*. Both Calavita and Gutiérrez contend that the deportation program was also a way for growers to reinstate the contract labor (Bracero) program, a system preferable to growers because of the control it gave them over their laborers.

68. Gutiérrez, *Walls and Mirrors*. Gutiérrez points out that Operation Wetback was elemental in galvanizing Mexican-American protests against this and later repatriation campaigns, as even those Mexican-American organizations typically taking a hard-line stance against immigrants (e.g., the League of United Latin American Citizens and the American GI Forum) were distressed at the widespread disruption of families with mixed U.S. and Mexican nationalities.

69. Schneider and Ingram, "Social Construction of Target Populations," 339.

NOTES TO CHAPTER 4

1. In March of 1998 the law was declared unconstitutional in federal court. Upon taking office, Governor Gray Davis, a Democrat, dropped further appeals.

2. Seth Mydans, "Poll Finds Tide of Immigration Brings Hostility," *New York Times*, June 26, 1993.

3. Ibid.

4. Citrin et al., "Public Opinion toward Immigration Reform: The Role of

Economic Motivations"; Espenshade and Hempstead, "Contemporary American Attitudes toward U.S. Immigration."

5. John Dillin, "Republicans Sniff an Election Issue in Immigration," *Christian Science Monitor*, June 15, 1994.

6. Gimpel and Edwards, *The Congressional Politics of Immigration Reform*, 260–62.

7. Sachs, "Treacherous Waters in Turbulent Times."

8. William Branigin, "House Votes Curbs on Federal Benefits, Public Education of Illegal Immigrants," *Washington Post*, September 26, 1996.

9. Edsall and Edsall, *Chain Reaction*, 214.

10. Calavita, "The New Politics of Immigration."

11. HR 2202 Title IV, "Disqualification of Aliens Not Lawfully Present in the United States from Certain Programs," Sec. 602, "Authority of States." To clarify, the provision would not deny *citizen* children of illegal immigrants the right to an education.

12. Rep. Elton Gallegly (R-CA), *Congressional Record* (March 20, 1996): H2488.

13. Rep. Marge Roukema (R-NJ), ibid., H2489. The Supreme Court decision to which she refers is the 1982 5-to-4 ruling in *Plyler v. Doe*, which instituted the right of children illegally in the United Staes to be educated in public schools.

14. Rep. Newt Gingrich (R-GA), ibid., H2495.

15. Rep. Nathan Deal (R-GA), *Congressional Record* (September 25, 1996): 11098.

16. Rep. Lamar Smith (R-TX), *Congressional Record* (March 19, 1996): H2380. The analysis by George Borjas to which he refers was one of those surveyed by the 1995 GAO reports which led to the Office's general cautioning about utilizing existing studies in determining legislation, given the discrepancies in measurement and analysis in researchers' methodologies.

17. Rep. Gerald Solomon (R-NY), *Congressional Record* (March 19, 1996): H2364.

18. Rep. Tillie K. Fowler (R-FL), ibid.

19. Rep. Duncan Hunter (R-CA), ibid., 2367.

20. Rep. Cliff Stearns (R-FL), *Congressional Record* (September 25, 1996): H11089.

21. Rep. David Obey (R-WI), *Congressional Record* (March 19, 1996): H2366.

22. Tom Latham (R-IA), *Congressional Record* (March 20, 1996): H2476.

23. Rep. Greg Ganske (R-IA), ibid., H2479.

24. Rep. Brian Bilbray (R-CA), ibid.

25. Rep. Xavier Becerra (D-CA), ibid., H2477.

26. This is visible in the survey of causal statements documented in Table 3.3.

27. Rep. Randy "Duke" Cunningham (R-CA), *Congressional Record* (March 20, 1996): H2480.

28. Rep. Gerald Solomon (R-NY), *Congressional Record* (March 19, 1996): H2364.

29. Rep. Duke Cunningham (R-CA), *Congressional Record* (March 20, 1996): 2478.

30. Rep. Ed Bryant (R-TN), ibid., H2482.

31. Rep. Duke Cunningham (R-CA), ibid., H2486.

32. Rep. David Dreier (R-CA), *Congressional Record* (March 19, 1996): H2362.

33. Rep. Brian Bilbray (R-CA), *Congressional Record* (March 20, 1996): H2486.

34. Rep. Nathan Deal (R-GA), ibid., H2487.

35. Gus de la Vina, Western Regional Director, INS. U.S. Congress, "U.S. Border Patrol's Implementation of 'Operation Gatekeeper,'" ed. House Committee on Government Reform (Washington, DC: Government Printing Office, 1996), 62.

36. Ibid., 23.

37. Rep. Duncan Hunter (R-CA), ibid.

38. Ibid., 80.

39. Rep. Lamar Smith (R-TX), *Congressional Record* (March 20, 1996): H2497.

40. Rep. Ed Bryant (R-TN), ibid., H2499.

41. Rep. Steve Chabot (R-OH), ibid., H2497. Chabot and his co-sponsor, John Conyers, Jr. (D-MI), introduced an amendment to strike the extension of the 1-800 hotline for employer verification.

42. Rep. F. James Sensenbrenner, Jr. (R-WI), ibid., H2498.

43. The Pombo-Chambliss amendment (rejected) would have created a three-year pilot program for agricultural workers. Twenty-five percent of a worker's salary would be withheld in an account in the worker's country of origin to be claimed upon his or her return to that country. The Goodlatte amendment (passed) increased the cap on agricultural guest workers to 100,000 and streamlined the H2-A application process for growers. Goodlatte's H-2A did not stipulate any withholdings of a guest worker's paycheck.

44. Rep. Walter B. Jones, Jr. (R-NC), *Congressional Record* (March 21, 1996): H2612.

45. Rep. Bob Goodlatte, (R-VA), ibid., H2623.

46. Some members did not agree with the portion of Pombo-Chambliss requiring that a quarter of a worker's earnings be withheld. This provision was compared to the Bracero program and considered too vulnerable to grower abuses. The Goodlatte amendment made the streamlining changes as well as raising the numeric cap without the wage withholdings.

47. Rep. Anthony Beilenson (D-CA), *Congressional Record* (March 20, 1996): H2489.

48. Rep. Tom Campbell (R-CA), ibid., H2490.

49. Rep. Bill Clay (D-MO), ibid., H2490.

50. Rep. Bill Richardson (D-NM), ibid., H2493.

51. Rep. Pat Williams (D-MT), ibid., H2494.

52. Rep. Ros-Lehitinen (R-FL), ibid., H2491.

53. Rep. Nydia Velazquez (D-NY), ibid., H2485. Representatives Velazquez and Roybal-Allard (D-CA) co-sponsored an amendment to strike Section 607. The House ultimately rejected the amendment 267 to 151 (D 58–129; R 211–21).

54. Rep. Tom Campbell (R-CA), ibid., H2486. The amendment to the bill to which Campbell refers is the Velazquez/Roybal-Allard amendment to strike Section 607.

55. Rep. Howard Berman (D-CA), ibid.

56. Rep. Sheila Jackson-Lee (D-TX), ibid., H2478.

57. Rep. Xavier Becerra (D-CA), ibid.

58. Rep. John Conyers, Jr. (D-MI), ibid., H2497.

59. Rep. Michael P. Flanagan (R-IL), ibid., H2500.

60. Rep. Esteban Edward Torres (D-CA), ibid., H2501.

61. The verification program survived these and similar critiques. Initially, the vote on Chabot-Conyers was delayed and the amendment was modified to strike H.R.2202's provisions for increasing INS and Department of Labor inspectors to specialize in employer violations. The House defeated the modified Chabot-Conyers amendment 159 yeas to 260 nays (R 79–152; D 79–108). *H.R.2202 Bill Tracking Report. Immigration and the National Interest Act of 1995*, 104th Cong., 1st sess., *Congressional Record* (1996): Roll Call No. 76.

62. Schneider and Ingram, eds., *Deserving and Entitled*, 8.

63. "USDA Announces Restoration of Food Stamp Eligibility for Qualified Legal Immigrant Children," *States News Service*, October 1, 2003; Anderson, "Senate OKs Reinstating Food Stamps; Bill Restores '96 Cutbacks"; Mike Allen, "Bush Signs Bill Providing Big Farm Subsidy Increases," *Washington Post*, May 14, 2002.

64. Allen, "Bush Signs Bill Providing Big Farm Subsidy Increases." Since Food Stamps are administered by the Department of Agriculture, a farm bill is a logical home for such a provision. The primary reason the bill was signed without much fanfare was that it supplied substantial farm subsidies, and therefore threatened President George W. Bush's credibility as fiscally responsible. The President, however, referred to it as "not perfect" but "compassionate."

65. Bachrach and Baratz, "Two Faces of Power."

66. Edelman, *The Symbolic Uses of Politics*; Edelman, *Constructing the Political Spectacle*.

67. Schneider and Ingram, *Policy Design for Democracy*, 145.

NOTES TO CHAPTER 5

1. Schneider and Ingram, *Policy Design for Democracy*, 145.

2. Gimpel and Edwards, *The Congressional Politics of Immigration Reform*, 44.

3. Gilens, *Why Americans Hate Welfare*; Edsall and Edsall, *Chain Reaction*.

4. Gilens, *Why Americans Hate Welfare*; 3–4; Hancock, *The Politics of Disgust*, 1–18.

5. For a discussion of the emergence of this language in response to redistributive Great Society policies see Omi and Winant, *Racial Formation*, 113–18.

6. Van Dijk, "On the Analysis of Parliamentary Debates on Immigration," 110.

7. Van Dijk, "Political Discourse and Racism," 36–39.

8. Van Dijk, "Principles of Critical Discourse Analysis"; van Dijk, "Political Discourse and Racism"; van Dijk, "On the Analysis of Parliamentary Debates on Immigration."

9. Rep. Peter Torkildsen (R-MA), *Congressional Record* (March 21, 1996): H2597.

10. Rep. Philip Crane (R-IL), ibid., H2593.

11. Freeman, "Modes of Immigration Politics."

12. Rep. Barbara Vucanovich (R-NV), *Congressional Record* (March 21, 1996): H2594.

13. Rep. Jane Harman (D-CA), ibid.

14. Rep. Greg Ganske, (R-IA), *Congressional Record* (March 19, 1996): 2369.

15. Van Dijk, "Political Discourse and Racism."

16. Rep. Bob Dornan (R-CA), *Congressional Record* (October 9, 1986): H9708.

17. Sen. Jesse Helms (R-NC), *Congressional Record* (October 17, 1986): S16879.

18. Rep. Gene Taylor (D-MS), *Congressional Record* (March 21, 1996): H2619. Again, the Pombo amendment provided for an expanded agricultural guest-worker program.

19. James P. Smith and Barry Edmonston, eds., *The New Americans: Economic, Demographic, and Fiscal Effects of Immigration* (Washington, DC: National Academies Press, 1997).

20. Ibid.

21. Sen. Lloyd Bentsen (D-TX), *Congressional Record* (October 17, 1986): S16879.

22. Rep. Brian Bilbray (R-CA), *Congressional Record* (March 20, 1996): H2492.

23. Rep. Ron Packard (R-CA), *Congressional Record* (September 25, 1996): H11103.

24. Prior to Section 110's enactment as part of the IIRAIRA, Canadians were exempt from visa requirements for visits to the United States. While Section 110 did not establish a visa requirement for Canadian entrants to the United States, it did require that border guards verify the address and citizenship of all "aliens" entering the country. The Canadian government, with the assistance of U.S. representatives from states along the northern border, lobbied for the repeal of 110 because it harmed trade between the two nations. H.R.2920, which would have repealed Section 110, passed in the Senate on July 30, 1998. However, by the time

it was added to the appropriations bill, it had changed. Instead of the repeal, it directed that Section 110 be enforced at land borders and that it not disrupt trade, tourism, and other "legitimate traffic."

25. James Scheuer (D-NY), *Congressional Record* (October 9, 1986): H9708.

26. Earl Pomeroy (D-ND), *Congressional Record* (September 25, 1996): 11094.

27. Sen. Jesse Helms (R-NC), *Congressional Record* (October 17, 1986): S16879.

28. Martinez, *Border People*, 22.

29. Mike Davis, *Magical Urbanism: Latinos Reinvent the U.S. City* (London: Verso, 2001), 70–71.

30. For rankings, see Jack Jedwab, "Canadian Aliens: The Numbers and Status of Our 'Illegals' South of the Border" (paper presented at the Canadian-American Research Symposium [CARS] on Immigration, Niagara Falls, Ontario, April 26, 2003).

31. Sen. Phil Gramm (R-TX), *Congressional Record* (October 17, 1986): S16879.

32. Sen. Don Edwards (D-CA), ibid.

33. Brown, "The Fourth Member of NAFTA: The U.S.-Mexico Border," 114–15.

34. Sen. Dennis DeConcini (D-AZ), *Congressional Record* (October 17, 1986): S16879.

35. Douglas S. Massey, "March of Folly: U.S. Immigration Policy after NAFTA," *American Prospect* 37, no. 22 (1998).

36. Dianne Schmidley, "Profile of the Foreign Born in the United States: 2000" (U.S. Census Bureau Special Studies/Current Population Reports, 2001).

37. Sen. Paul Simon (D-IL), *Congressional Record* (October 17, 1986): S16879.

38. Sen. Lloyd Bentsen (D-TX), ibid.

39. Rep. James Scheuer (D NY), *Congressional Record* (October 9, 1986): S9708.

40. Roberts, "Who May Give Birth to Citizens?" 208–15.

41. Sen. Lloyd Bentsen (D-TX), *Congressional Record* (October 17, 1986): S16879.

42. Rep. Nathan Deal (R-GA), *Congressional Record* (March 20, 1996): 2487. This appeared as statement 23 in Chapter 4.

43. Phyllis Pease Chock, "Ambiguity in Policy Discourse: Congressional Talk," *Policy Sciences* 28, no. 2 (1995): 4–5.

44. Ibid., 6.

45. Rep. Sheila Jackson-Lee (D-TX), *Congressional Record* (March 21, 1996): H2597.

46. Durand, Massey, and Parrado, "The New Era of Mexican Migration to the United States."

47. Donato, "Current Trends and Patterns of Female Migration: Evidence from Mexico"; J. Reichert and D. S. Massey, "Patterns of U.S. Migration from a

Mexican Sending Community: A Comparison of Legal and Illegal Migrants," *International Migration Review* 13, no. 4 (1979). Of course, actual rates of labor force participation for women vary by national origin, language, skills, and employment opportunities, though Nancy Foner notes that in New York, the 1990 census revealed 60 percent of immigrant women participated in the labor force, with the highest participation rates being those of Filipino and West Indian women Nancy Foner, *In a New Land: A Comparative View of Immigration* (New York: New York University Press, 2005), 95–103. Additional research demonstrates that Hispanic immigrant women who are married with children have higher labor force participation rates than their native born white counterparts. Haya Stier and Marta Tienda, "Family, Work and Women: The Labor Supply of Hispanic Immigrant Wives," *International Migration Review* 26, no. 4 (1992).

48. Pierrette Hondagneu-Sotelo, *Domestica: Immigrant Workers Cleaning and Caring in the Shadows of Affluence* (Berkeley: University of California Press, 2001).

49. Edsall and Edsall, *Chain Reaction*; Omi and Winant, *Racial Formation*.

50. Rep. Dana Rohrabacher (R-CA), *Congressional Record* (March 20, 1996): H2489.

51. Eduardo Porter, "Illegal Immigrants Are Bolstering Social Security with Billions," *New York Times*, April 5, 2005.

52. Kris Axtman, "IRS Seminars, IDs Help Illegal Immigrants Pay U.S. Taxes," *Christian Science Monitor*, March 21, 2002.

NOTES TO THE CONCLUSION

1. Charles K. Lindblom, *Politics and Markets: The World's Political Economic Systems* (New York: Basic Books, 1977); see Chapter 13.

2. Calavita, "Employer Sanctions Violations"; Calavita, "California's 'Employer Sanctions'"; Gimpel and Edwards, *The Congressional Politics of Immigration Reform*; Martin and Taylor, "The Paper Curtain."

3. Tichenor, *Dividing Lines*.

4. Arnold, *Logic of Congressional Action*.

5. Alejandro Portes and Ruben G. Rumbaut, *Immigrant America, a Portrait*, second ed. (Berkeley: University of California Press, 1996).

6. Matthijs Kalmijn, "The Socioeconomic Assimilation of Caribbean American Blacks," *Social Forces* 74, no. 3 (1996); Model, "Caribbean Immigrants"; Portes and Rumbaut, *Immigrant America*; Alejandro Portes and Min Zhou, "The New Second Generation: Segmented Assimilation and Its Variants among Post-1965 Immigrant Youth," *Annals of the American Academy of Political and Social Science* 530 (1993); Mary C. Waters, *Black Identities: West Indian Immigrant Dreams and American Realities* (New York: Russell Sage Foundation, 1999; reprint, Cambridge, MA: Harvard University Press, 2001); Min Zhou, "Segmented Assimila-

tion: Issues, Controversies, and Recent Research on the New Second Generation," *International Migration Review* 31, no. 4 (1997).

7. Migration Policy Institute, "DataHub: Country and Comparative Data," http://www.migrationinformation.org/datahub/countrydata/data.cfm (accessed July 22, 2007).

NOTES TO THE EPILOGUE

1. Bob Deans, "Bush Open to 'Regularization'; Immigration Is Mexican's Top Priority," *Atlanta Journal-Constitution*, September 7, 2001.

2. Sharon McNary and Chris Richard, "The Minuteman Project: Citizens Patrolling the Border; Private Protection; Protest," *Riverside Press-Enterprise*, April 2, 2005.

3. Michael Coronado, "Minutemen Monitor, Get Monitored at Arizona-Mexico Border," *Orange County Register*, April 14, 2005.

4. "Mexican Government Threatens Legal Action against Anti-Immigration Project on U.S. Border," *Associated Press Worldstream*, March 29, 2005.

5. Ibid.

6. Lou Dobbs, *Lou Dobbs Tonight*, CNN, April 18, 2005, broadcast transcript, LexisNexis.com, electronic resource #041801cn.v19 (accessed November 1, 2006).

7. Beth Barrett, "Fewer Slip Past Border; U.S. Officials Credit Mexican Troops, Not American Minuteman Volunteers," *Daily News of Los Angeles*, April 7, 2005.

8. "Across the Nation," *Seattle Times*, May 1, 2005.

9. James Gilchrist ran for Congress in Orange County, CA, in 2005, but lost.

10. Initiative and Referendum Institute, "Election Results 2006" (University of Southern California School of Law, 2006).

11. "Immigrant Laws Dubious," *Pittsburgh Post-Gazette*, August 20, 2006.

12. Michael Rubinkam, "Hispanics Flee Pa. Town in Advance of Nearing Crackdown," *Associated Press State & Local Wire*, October 30, 2006.

13. American Civil Liberties Union, "Coalition Gains Immediate Halt to Unconstitutional Ordinance in Hazleton, PA," http://www.aclu.org/immigrants/discrim/26644prs20060901.html. The law was overturned by a federal court on July 26, 2007. Judge James Munley, who heard the case, *Lozano v. Hazelton* (2007), found the city's ordinance to be unconstitutional in that it violated the supremacy clause and the equal protection and due process clauses. American Civil Liberties Union, "Federal Court Strikes Down Discriminatory Anti-Immigrant Law in Hazleton, Pennsylvania," http://www.aclu.org/immigrants/discrim/31057prs20070726.html.

14. *Border Protection, Antiterrorism, and Illegal Immigration Control Act of 2005*, H11800, 109th Cong., 1st sess., *Congressional Record* (December 15, 2005).

15. Statement of Senator Richard Durbin (D-IL), during a *Face the Nation* interview. Bob Schieffer, "Congressman James Sensenbrenner and Senator Dick

Durbin Discuss Controversies over Illegal Immigration," *Face the Nation*, April 2, 2006.

16. Dan Balz, "Incumbent Reaches beyond His Base," *Washington Post*, January 8, 2004. Scott Shepard, "Democrats Unveil Election-Year Immigration Bill," *Cox News Service*, May 4, 2004. Despite disagreements that it spawned within the Republican Party, the President's plan would be included in the party platform. The Democrats, for their part, offered their own plan that coupled a guest-worker program with a broader legalization program. The immigration, amnesty, and guest-worker issues, however, would barely surface during the final months of the 2004 presidential race.

17. Bill Sammon, "Backers Say Bush Plan Goes beyond Immigration; Polls Reveal 'Amnesty' Plan Has Few Friends," *Washington Times*, January 12, 2004.

18. President George W. Bush, National televised address, CNN transcript, May 15, 2006, "Bush: 'U.S. a Lawful Society and a Welcoming Society,'" http://www.cnn.com/2006/POLITICS/05/15/bushimmigration.text/ (accessed May 16, 2006).

19. Statement of Rep. James Sensenbrenner, Jr. (R-WI) on *Face the Nation*. Schieffer, "Congressman James Sensenbrenner and Senator Dick Durbin Discuss Controversies over Illegal Immigration."

20. Niclole Gaouette and Noam N. Levey, "Immigration Bill Careens toward Vote," *Los Angeles Times*, June 28, 2007.

21. Michael Karnish, "Bush Removes Provision Requiring Back Taxes from Illegal Immigrants," *Boston Globe*, May 19, 2007.

22. Robert Pear and Laurie Flynn, "High-Tech Titans Strike Out on Immigration Bill," *New York Times*, June 25, 2007.

23. Molly Hennessy-Fiske, "Unions Square Off over Immigration; Some Welcome New Workers, and Others See Only Unwelcome Competition. The Split Could Doom the Bill," *Los Angeles Times*, June 1, 2007; Robert Pear, "Failure of Senate Immigration Bill Can Be Lesson for Congress, Experts Say," *New York Times* June 30, 2007. For example, South Asian immigration advocates felt that the status quo better meets their needs than a bill that both de-prioritized family reunification and slashed H 1B visas. Ketaki Gokhale, "Immigration Debate Ends, Reaction Mixed," *India West*, July 6, 2007.

24. Robert Pear, "Senate Takes Up a Revised Immigration Bill, but Obstacles Remain," *New York Times*, June 27, 2007; Niclole Gaouette, "Immigration Bill Ignites a Grass-Roots Fire on the Right," *Los Angeles Times*, June 24, 2007.

25. Andrew Kohut and Roberto Suro, "No Consensus on Immigration Problem or Proposed Fixes: America's Immigration Quandary," ed. Pew Research Center for the People and the Press and The Pew Hispanic Center (Washington, DC, 2006).

26. Richard Simon, "Immigration Bill Faces a Wall of Opposition," *Los Angeles Times*, May 18, 2007. The "return" to which the congressman refers is a provision

that an illegal immigrant who wishes to sponsor other illegal family members "touchback" to their country of origin to make applications on behalf of the other family members.

27. The Legal Immigration Family Equity Act was largely a corrective policy response to a series of suits filed against the INS on behalf of unauthorized immigrants who qualified and filed for legalization under the IRCA, but whose applications had been wrongly denied by the INS. Participation in the LIFE Act's legalization allowance required that petitioners file for membership in one of three class-action lawsuits (*CSS v. Meese, LULAC v. Reno,* or *INS v. Zambrano*) prior to 2000, prove they had a working knowledge of English and civics, and show continuous though unlawful residence in the United States between January 1982 and May 1988. The number of eligible petitioners, their spouses, and minor children reached 300,000 at the 2002 deadline.

28. Both an October 2006 and a post-election exit polling conducted by CBS News showed that Latinos like other Americans ranked the Iraq War and national security far higher than immigration among their "most important issues."

29. Images of signs appearing in rallies in Los Angeles, Atlanta and New Orleans available on: http://la.indymedia.org/news/2006/05/155803.php. Signs held by protesters in Boston were covered as well in Ralph Ranalli, "On Common, 2,500 Rally for Immigrants," *Boston Globe*, March 28, 2006.

References

"Across the Nation," *Seattle Times*, May 1, 2005.

Alba, Richard. "Immigration and the American Realities of Assimilation and Multiculturalism." *Sociological Forum* 14, no. 1 (1999): 3–25.

———. "Mexican Americans and the American Dream." *PS: Political Science and Politics* 4, no. 2 (2006): 289–96.

Allen, Mike. "Bush Signs Bill Providing Big Farm Subsidy Increases." *Washington Post*, May 14, 2002.

Almaguer, Tomas. *Racial Fault Lines: The Historical Origins of White Supremacy in California.* Berkeley: University of California Press, 1994.

American Civil Liberties Union. "Coalition Gains Immediate Halt to Unconstitutional Ordinance in Hazleton, PA," 2006, http://www.aclu.org/immigrants/discrim/26644prs20060901.html.

———. "Federal Court Strikes Down Discriminatory Anti-Immigrant Law in Hazleton, Pennsylvania," 2007, http://www.aclu.org/immigrants/discrim/31057prs20070726.html.

Ancheta, Angelo. *Race, Rights and the Asian American Experience.* New Brunswick, NJ: Rutgers University Press, 1995.

Anderson, Curt. "Senate OKs Reinstating Food Stamps; Bill Restores '96 Cutbacks." *Chicago Sun-Times*, May 13, 1998.

Andreas, Peter. *Border Games: Policing the U.S.-Mexico Border Divide.* Ithaca, NY: Cornell University Press, 2000.

Arnold, Douglas. *The Logic of Congressional Action.* New Haven, CT: Yale University Press, 1990.

Associated Press Worldstream. "Mexican Government Threatens Legal Action against Anti-immigration Project on U.S. Border." March 29, 2005.

Axtman, Kris. "IRS Seminars, IDs Help Illegal Immigrants Pay U.S. Taxes." *Christian Science Monitor*, March 21, 2002.

Bach, Robert. "Mexican Immigration and the American State." *International Migration Review* 12, no. 4 (1978): 536–57.

Bachrach, Peter, and Morton S. Baratz. "Two Faces of Power." *American Political Science Review* 56, no. 4 (1962): 947–52.

Balz, Dan. "Incumbent Reaches beyond His Base." *Washington Post*, January 8, 2004.

Barrett, Beth. "Fewer Slip Past Border; U.S. Officials Credit Mexican Troops, Not American Minuteman Volunteers." *Daily News of Los Angeles*, April 7, 2005.

Baumgartner, Frank R., and Bryan D. Jones. *Agendas and Instability in American Politics*. Chicago: University of Chicago Press, 1993.

Bean, Frank, Susan K. Brown, and Ruben G. Rumbaut. "Mexican Immigrant Political and Economic Incorporation." *PS: Political Science and Politics* 4, no. 2 (2006): 309–13.

Bornemeier, James. "Congressman to Seek Cuts in Immigration." *Los Angeles Times*, February 17, 1995.

Branigin, William. "House Votes Curbs on Federal Benefits, Public Education of Illegal Immigrants." *Washington Post*, September 26, 1996.

———. "Immigration Employment Provisions Dropped; Sen. Simpson Blasts Business Community in Attempt to Keep Overhaul Bill Intact." *Washington Post*, March 8, 1996.

Briggs, Vernon. *Mass Immigration and the National Interest*. Armonk, NY: M.E. Sharpe, 1984.

Brimelow, Peter. *Alien Nation: Common Sense about America's Immigration Disaster*. New York: Random House, 1995.

Brown, Timothy C. "The Fourth Member of NAFTA: The U.S.-Mexico Border." *Annals of the American Academy of Political and Social Science* 550 (1997): 105–21.

Brubaker, William Rogers, ed. *Immigration and the Politics of Citizenship in Europe and North America*. Washington, DC: University Press of America, 1989.

Bustamante, Jorge. "The 'Wetback' as Deviant." *American Journal of Sociology* 77, no. 4 (1971): 706–18.

Cain, Bruce M., and Karin McDonald. "Nativism, Partisanship and Immigration: An Analysis of Prop 187." Paper presented at the annual meeting of the American Political Science Association, San Francisco, CA, 1996.

Calavita, Kitty. "California's 'Employer Sanctions': The Case of the Disappearing Law." Center for U.S.-Mexican Studies, University of California, San Diego, 1982.

———. "Employer Sanctions Violations: Toward a Dialectical Model of White-Collar Crime." *Law and Society Review* 24, no. 4 (1990): 1041–69.

———. "Immigration, Law, and Marginalization in a Global Economy: Notes from Spain." *Law and Society Review* 32, no. 3 (1998): 529–66.

———. *Inside the State: The Bracero Program, Immigration and the I.N.S.* New York: Routledge, 1992.

———. "The New Politics of Immigration: 'Balanced-Budget Conservatism' and the Symbolism of Proposition 187." *Social Problems* 43, no. 3 (1996): 284–305.

California Field Institute. "*The California Field Polls*." San Francisco: Machine-readable data file, 1994.

California Secretary of State. *Statement of Vote, November 8, 1994 General Elections.* Secretary of State, Elections Division, Sacramento, CA, 1994.

Campbell, Andrea L. *How Policies Make Citizens: Senior Political Activism and the American Welfare State.* Princeton, NJ: Princeton University Press, 2003.

"CBPP: Immigrants' Use of Public Benefits Has Declined Since 1996; CIS Report Exploits Loose Definitions to Paint Misleading Picture," *U.S. Newswire,* March 26, 2003.

Chavez, Leo R. *Covering Immigration: Popular Images and the Politics of the Nation.* Berkeley: University of California Press, 2002.

Chavez, Leo R. "The Power of the Imagined Community: The Settlement of Undocumented Mexicans and Central Americans in the United States." *American Anthropologist,* no. 96 (1994): 52–73.

Chock, Phyllis Pease. "Ambiguity in Policy Discourse: Congressional Talk." *Policy Sciences* 28, no. 2 (1995): 165–84.

Citrin, Jack, Donald P. Green, Christopher Muste, and Cara Wong. "Public Opinion toward Immigration Reform: The Role of Economic Motivations." *Journal of Politics* 59, no. 3 (1997): 858–81.

CNN. "Bush: U.S. 'A Lawful Society and a Welcoming Society.'" *CNN.com,* May 15, 2006. http://www.cnn.com/2006/POLITICS/05/15/bush.immigration.text/ (accessed May 16, 2006).

Cobb, Kim. "Oklahoma Bill Casts One of the Widest Nets." *Houston Chronicle,* April 23, 2007.

Coronado, Michael. "Minutemen Monitor, Get Monitored at Arizona-Mexico Border." *Orange County Register,* April 14, 2005.

Coutin, Susan Bibler, and Phyllis Pease Chock. "'Your Friend the Illegal': Definition and Paradox in Newspaper Accounts of U.S. Immigration Reform." *Identities: Global Studies in Culture and Power* 2, nos. 1–2 (1995): 123–48.

Crewdson, John M. "New Administration and Congress Face Major Immigration Decisions." *New York Times,* December 28, 1980.

Dahl, Robert A. *On Democracy.* New Haven, CT: Yale University Press, 1998.

———. *Who Governs? Democracy and Power in an American City.* New Haven, CT: Yale University Press, 1961.

Davis, Mike. *Magical Urbanism: Latinos Reinvent the U.S. City.* London: Verso, 2001.

Deans, Bob. "Bush Open to 'Regularization'; Immigration Is Mexican's Top Priority." *Atlanta Journal-Constitution,* September 7, 2001.

DeLeon, Peter. "Social Construction for Public Policy." *Public Administration Review* 65, no. 5 (2005): 635–37.

Dillin, John. "Republicans Sniff an Election Issue in Immigration." *Christian Science Monitor,* June 15, 1994.

Dobbs, Lou. *Lou Dobbs Tonight.* CNN, April 18, 2005. www.lexis-nexis.com (accessed November 1, 2006).

Dodd, Lawrence C., and Bruce I. Oppenheimer. "Revolution in the House: Testing the Limits of Party Government." In *Congress Reconsidered*, edited by Lawrence C. Dodd and Bruce I. Oppenheimer. Washington, DC: CQ Press, 1997.

Donato, Katharine M. "Current Trends and Patterns of Female Migration: Evidence from Mexico." *International Migration Review* 27, no. 4 (1993): 748–71.

Dunn, Timothy J. *The Militarization of the U.S.-Mexico Border, 1978–1992*. Austin: CMAS Books, University of Texas, 1996.

Durand, Jorge, Douglas S. Massey, and Emilio Parrado. "The New Era of Mexican Migration to the United States." *Journal of American History* 86, no. 2 (1999): 518–36.

Edelman, Murray. *Constructing the Political Spectacle*. Chicago: University of Chicago Press, 1988.

———. *The Symbolic Uses of Politics*. Urbana: University of Illinois Press, 1974.

Edsall, Thomas Byrne, and Mary D. Edsall. *Chain Reaction: The Impact of Race, Rights and Taxes on American Politics*. New York: Norton, 1991.

Espenshade, Thomas J., and Katherine Hempstead. "Contemporary American Attitudes toward U.S. Immigration." *International Migration Review* 30, no. 2 (1996): 535–71.

Feagin, Joe R. "Old Poison in New Bottles: The Deep Roots of Modern Nativism." In *Immigrants Out! The New Nativism and the Anti-Immigrant Impulse in the United States*, edited by Juan Perea. New York: New York University Press, 1997.

Feldman, Paul. "62% Would Bar Services to Illegal Immigrants." *Los Angeles Times*, September 14, 1994.

Fix, Michael, ed. *The Paper Curtain: Employer Sanctions' Implementation, Impact, and Reform*. Santa Monica, CA, Washington, DC: RAND and Urban Institute, 1991.

Foner, Nancy. *In a New Land: A Comparative View of Immigration*. New York: New York University Press, 2005.

Fraga, Luis R., and Gary M. Segura. "Culture Clash? Contesting Notions of American Identity and the Effects of Latin American Immigration." *PS: Political Science and Politics* 4, no. 2 (2006): 279–87.

Freeman, Gary P. "Modes of Immigration Politics in Liberal Democratic States." *International Migration Review* 29, no. 4 (1995): 881–902.

Gaouette, Niclole. "Immigration Bill Ignites a Grass-Roots Fire on the Right." *Los Angeles Times*, June 24, 2007.

Gaouette, Niclole, and Noam N. Levey. "Immigration Bill Careens toward Vote." *Los Angeles Times*, June 28, 2007.

Garcia Bedolla, Lisa. *Fluid Borders: Latino Power, Identity and Politics in Los Angeles*. Berkeley: University of California Press, 2003.

Gilens, Martin. *Why Americans Hate Welfare: Race, Media, and the Politics of Antipoverty Policy*. Chicago: University of Chicago Press, 1999.

Gimpel, James, and James Edwards. *The Congressional Politics of Immigration Reform*. New York: Longman, 1998.

Gokhale, Ketaki "Immigration Debate Ends, Reaction Mixed." *India West*, July 6, 2007.

Gonzalez Baker, Susan. *The Cautious Welcome: The Legalization Programs of the Immigration Reform and Control Act*. Santa Monica, CA, Washington, DC: RAND and Urban Institute, 1990.

Gutiérrez, David. *Walls and Mirrors: Mexican Americans and Mexican Immigration*. Berkeley: University of California Press, 1995.

Hagan, Jacqueline Maria. *Deciding to Be Legal: A Maya Community in Houston*. Philadelphia: Temple University Press, 1995.

Hajer, Maarten A. *The Politics of Environmental Discourse: Ecological Modernization and the Policy Process*. New York: Oxford University Press, 1995.

Hancock, Ange-Marie. *The Politics of Disgust: The Public Identity of the Welfare Queen*. New York: New York University Press, 2004.

Hartmann, Edward George. *The Movement to Americanize the Immigrant*. New York: Columbia University Press, 1948.

Harwood, Edwin. "American Public Opinion and U.S. Immigration Policy." *Annals of the American Academy of Political and Social Science* 487 (1986): 201–12.

Hendricks, Tyche. "Bush Guest Worker Plan Recalls Bracero Program." *San Francisco Chronicle*, January 16, 2004.

Hennessy-Fiske, Molly "Unions Square Off over Immigration; Some Welcome New Workers, and Others See Only Unwelcome Competition. The Split Could Doom the Bill." *Los Angeles Times*, June 1, 2007.

Higham, John. *Strangers in the Land: Patterns of American Nativism 1860–1925*. New York: Atheneum, 1969.

Hofstadter, Richard. *The Age of Reform*. New York: Vintage Books, 1955.

Hollifield, James. *Immigrants, Markets, and States: The Political Economy of Postwar Europe*. Cambridge, MA: Harvard University Press, 1992.

Hondagneu-Sotelo, Pierrette. *Domestica: Immigrant Workers Cleaning and Caring in the Shadows of Affluence*. Berkeley: University of California Press, 2001.

Honig, Bonnie. *Democracy and the Foreigner*. Princeton, NJ: Princeton University Press, 2001.

Huber, Gregory A., and Thomas J. Espenshade. "Neo-Isolationism, Balanced-Budget Conservatism, and the Fiscal Impacts of Immigrants." *International Migration Review* 31, no. 4 (1997): 1031–54.

Huntington, Samuel P. "The Hispanic Challenge." *Foreign Policy* (March/April 2004): 30–45.

———. *Who Are We? The Challenges to America's National Identity*. New York: Simon & Schuster, 2005.

"Immigrant Laws Dubious," *Pittsburgh Post-Gazette*, August 20, 2006.

Ingram, Helen, and Anne Schneider. "The Choice of Target Populations." *Administration and Society* 23, no. 3 (1991): 333–56.

Initiative and Referendum Institute. "Election Results 2006." University of Southern California School of Law, November 2006. www.ballotwatch.org.

Jedwab, Jack. "Canadian Aliens: The Numbers and Status of Our 'Illegals' South of the Border." Paper presented at the Canadian-American Research Symposium (CARS) on Immigration, Niagara Falls, Ontario, April 26, 2003.

"Jobs for Illegal Aliens Stirs Same Opposition as in '77 Gallup Poll." *New York Times*, November 11, 1980.

Johnson, Kevin R. *The "Huddled Masses" Myth: Immigration and Civil Rights.* Philadelphia: Temple University Press, 2004.

Jonsson, Patrik. "Federal Court Eyes Local Crackdown of Illegal Migrants." *Christian Science Monitor*, March 15, 2007.

Kalmijn, Matthijs. "The Socioeconomic Assimilation of Caribbean American Blacks." *Social Forces* 74, no. 3 (1996): 911–30.

Karnish, Michael. "Bush Removes Provision Requiring Back Taxes from Illegal Immigrants." *Boston Globe*, May 19, 2007.

Kim, Claire Jean. "The Racial Triangulation of Asian Americans." *Politics and Society* 27, no. 1 (1999): 105–38.

King, Desmond. *Making Americans: Immigration, Race, and the Origins of the Diverse Democracy.* Cambridge, MA: Harvard University Press, 2000.

Kingdon, John. *Agendas, Alternatives, and Public Policies.* Boston: Little, Brown, 1995.

Kohut, Andrew, and Roberto Suro. *No Consensus on Immigration Problem or Proposed Fixes: America's Immigration Quandary.* Washington, DC: Pew Research Center for the People and the Press and The Pew Hispanic Center, 2006.

Lee, Erika. *At America's Gate: Chinese Immigration during the Exclusion Era, 1882–1943.* Chapel Hill: University of North Carolina Press, 2003.

Lieberman, Robert C. "Social Construction (Continued)." *American Political Science Review* 89, no. 2 (1995): 437–46.

Lindblom, Charles K. *Politics and Markets: The World's Political Economic Systems.* New York: Basic Books, 1977.

Lorey, David E. *The U.S.-Mexico Border in the 20th Century.* Wilmington, DE: Scholarly Resource, Inc., Imprints, 1999.

Lowell, B. Lindsay, and Zhongren Jing. "Unauthorized Workers and Immigration Reform: What Can We Ascertain from Employers?" *International Migration Review* 28 (Fall 1994): 427–48.

Martin, Philip L. "Good Intentions Gone Awry: IRCA and U.S. Agriculture." *Annals of the American Academy of Social and Political Science* 98, no. 1 (1994): 44–57.

Martin, Philip L., and J. Edward Taylor. "Immigration Reform and Farm Labor Contracting in California." In *The Paper Curtain: Employer Sanctions Imple-*

mentation, Impact and Reform, edited by Michael Fix. Santa Monica, CA, Washington, DC: RAND and Urban Institute, 1991.

Martinez, Oscar J. *Border People: Life and Society in the U.S.-Mexico Borderlands.* Tucson: University of Arizona Press, 1994.

Massey, Douglas S. "March of Folly: U.S. Immigration Policy after NAFTA." *American Prospect* 37, no. 12 (1998): 22–33.

Massey, Douglas S., and Kristin E. Espinosa. "What's Driving Mexico-U.S. Migration? A Theoretical, Empirical and Policy Analysis." *American Journal of Sociology* 102 (January 1997): 939–99.

McDonnell, Patrick. "1,000 Flip Switches to 'Light Border.'" *Los Angeles Times,* March 17, 1990.

———. "Protesters Light Up the Border Again." *Los Angeles Times,* August 24, 1990.

McNary, Sharon, and Chris Richard. "The Minuteman Project: Citizens Patrolling the Border; Private Protection; Protest." *Riverside Press-Enterprise,* April 2, 2005.

Meier, Matt S., and Feliciano Ribera. *Mexican Americans/American Mexicans: From Conquistadors to Chicanos,* rev. ed. New York: Hill and Wang, 1993.

Mettler, Suzanne. *Dividing Citizens: Gender and Federalism in New Deal Policymaking.* Ithaca, NY: Cornell University Press, 1998.

Migration Policy Institute. DataHub: Country and Comparative Data. http://www.migrationinformation.org/datahub/countrydata/data.cfm (accessed July 22, 2007).

Model, Suzanne. "Caribbean Immigrants: A Black Success Story?" *International Migration Review* 25, no. 2 (1991): 248–76.

Montejano, David. "Who Is Samuel P. Huntington? Patriotic Reading for Anglo Protestants Who Live in Fear of the Reconquista." August 13, 2004. http://www.texasobserver.org.

Morganthau, Tom, Gloria Borger, Nikki Finke Greenberg, Elaine Shannon, Renee Michael, and Daniel Pederson. "Closing the Door?" *Newsweek,* June 25, 1984.

Mydans, Seth. "Poll Finds Tide of Immigration Brings Hostility." *New York Times,* June 26, 1993.

Nevins, Joseph. *Operation Gatekeeper: The Rise of the "Illegal Alien" and the Making of the U.S.-Mexico Boundary.* New York: Routledge, 2002.

Newton, Lina. "'It's Not a Question of Being Anti-Immigration': Categories of Deservedness in Immigration Policymaking." In *Deserving and Entitled: Social Constructions and Public Policy,* edited by Anne Schneider and Helen Ingram. Albany: State University of New York Press, 2005.

Ngai, Mae. "The Architecture of Race in American Immigration Law: A Reexamination of the Immigration Act of 1924." *Journal of American History* 86, no. 1 (1999): 67–92.

Ngai, Mae. *Impossible Subjects: Illegal Immigrants and the Making of Modern America*. Princeton, NJ: Princeton University Press, 2004.

――――. "The Strange Career of the Illegal Alien: Immigration Restriction and Deportation Policy in the United States, 1921–1965." *Law and History Review* 21, no. 1 (2003): 69–107.

North, David S. "Enforcing the Minimum Wage and Employer Sanctions." *Annals of the American Academy of Social and Political Science* 534 (July 1994): 59–68.

Omi, Michael, and Howard Winant. *Racial Formation in the United States from the 1960s to the 1990s*. New York: Routledge, 1994.

Passel, Jeffrey S., and Roberto Suro. *Rise, Peak, and Decline: Trends in U.S. Immigration 1992–2004*. Washington, DC: Pew Research Center for the People and the Press and The Pew Hispanic Center, 2005.

Pear, Robert. "Failure of Senate Immigration Bill Can Be Lesson for Congress, Experts Say." *New York Times*, June 30, 2007.

――――. "Senate Takes Up a Revised Immigration Bill, but Obstacles Remain." *New York Times*, June 27, 2007.

Pear, Robert, and Laurie Flynn. "High-Tech Titans Strike Out on Immigration Bill." *New York Times*, June 25, 2007.

Perea, Juan, ed. *Immigrants Out! The New Nativism and the Anti-Immigrant Impulse in the United States*. New York: New York University Press, 1997.

Porter, Eduardo. "Illegal Immigrants Are Bolstering Social Security with Billions." *New York Times*, April 5, 2005.

Portes, Alejandro, and Ruben G. Rumbaut. *Immigrant America, a Portrait*, second ed. Berkeley: University of California Press, 1996.

Portes, Alejandro, and Min Zhou. "The New Second Generation: Segmented Assimilation and Its Variants among Post-1965 Immigrant Youth." *Annals of the American Academy of Political and Social Science* 530 (1993): 74–98.

Ranalli, Ralph. "On Common, 2,500 Rally for Immigrants." *Boston Globe*, March 28, 2006.

Reichert, J., and D. S. Massey. "Patterns of U.S. Migration from a Mexican Sending Community: A Comparison of Legal and Illegal Migrants." *International Migration Review* 13, no. 4 (1979): 475–91.

Roberts, Dorothy E. "Who May Give Birth to Citizens? Reproduction, Eugenics, and Immigration." In *Immigrants Out! The New Nativism and the Anti-Immigrant Impulse in the United States*, edited by Juan Perea. New York: New York University Press, 1997.

Rochefort, David A., and Roger W. Cobb. *The Politics of Problem Definition*. Lawrence: University Press of Kansas, 1994.

Rodriguez, Nestor P. "The Social Construction of the U.S.-Mexico Border." In *Immigrants Out! The New Nativism and the Anti-Immigrant Impulse in the United States*, edited by Juan Perea. New York: New York University Press, 1997.

Roe, Emery. "Narrative Analysis for the Policy Analyst: A Case Study of the

1980–1982 Medfly Controversy in California." *Journal of Policy Analysis and Management* 8, no. 2 (1989): 251–73.

———. *Narrative Policy Analysis: Theory and Practice*. Durham, NC: Duke University Press, 1994.

Rolph, Elizabeth, and Abby Robyn. *A Window on Immigration Reform: Implementing the Immigration Reform and Control Act in Los Angeles*. Santa Monica, CA, Washington, DC: RAND and Urban Institute, 1990.

Rubinkam, Michael. "Hispanics Flee Pa. Town in Advance of Nearing Crackdown." *Associated Press State & Local Wire*, October 30, 2006.

Rudolph, Christopher. "Security and the Political Economy of International Migration." *American Political Science Review* 97, no. 4 (2003): 603–20.

Rytina, Nancy F. "U.S. Legal Permanent Residents: 2004." U.S. Department of Homeland Security, Office of Immigration Statistics, June 2005. http://www.dhs.gov/xlibrary/assets/statistics/publications/FlowReportLegalPermResidents2004.pdf (accessed July 20, 2007).

Sabatier, Paul, and Hank C. Jenkins-Smith. *Policy Change and Learning: An Advocacy Coalition Approach*. Boulder, CO: Westview, 1993.

Sachs, Lowell. "Treacherous Waters in Turbulent Times: Navigating the Recent Sea Change in U.S. Immigration Policy Attitudes." *Social Justice* 23, no. 3 (1996): 125–37.

Sammon, Bill. "Backers Say Bush Plan Goes beyond Immigration; Polls Reveal 'Amnesty' Plan Has Few Friends." *Washington Times*, January 12, 2004.

Sassen, Saskia. "America's Immigration 'Problem.'" *World Policy Journal* 6, no. 4 (1989): 811–32.

Schieffer, Bob. "Congressman James Sensenbrenner and Senator Dick Durbin Discuss Controversies over Illegal Immigration." *Face the Nation*, April 2, 2006.

Schmidley, Dianne. "Profile of the Foreign Born in the United States: 2000." U.S. Census Bureau Special Studies/Current Population Reports, 2001. http://www.census.gov/prod/2002pubs/p23-206.pdf (accessed July 2, 2007).

Schneider, Anne, and Helen Ingram, eds. *Deserving and Entitled: Social Constructions and Public Policy*. Albany: State University of New York Press, 2005.

———. *Policy Design for Democracy*. Lawrence: University Press of Kansas, 1997.

———. "Social Construction of Target Populations: Implications for Politics and Policy." *American Political Science Review* 87, no. 2 (1993): 334–47.

Schneider, Dorothee. "'I Know All about Emma Lazarus': Nationalism and Its Contradictions in Congressional Rhetoric of Immigration Restriction." *Cultural Anthropology* 13, no. 1 (1998): 82–99.

Schram, Sanford. "Putting a Black Face on Welfare: The Good and the Bad." In *Deserving and Entitled: Social Constructions and Public Policy*, edited by A. Schneider and H. Ingram. Albany: State University of New York Press, 2005.

Schuck, Peter, and Rogers Smith. *Citizenship without Consent*. New Haven, CT: Yale University Press, 1985.

Sears, David O., and Jack Citrin. *Tax Revolt: Something for Nothing in California.* Cambridge, MA: Harvard University Press, 1982.

Sears, David O., Carl P. Hensler, and Leslie K. Speer. "Whites' Opposition to 'Busing': Self-Interest or Symbolic Politics?" *American Political Science Review* 73, no. 2 (1979): 369–84.

Select Commission on Immigration and Refugee Policy. *U.S. Immigration Policy and the National Interest.* Washington, DC: Government Printing Office, 1981.

Shapiro, Michael J. "Winning the West, Unwelcoming the Immigrant: Alternative Stories of 'America.'" In *Tales of the State: Narrative in Contemporary U.S. Politics and Public Policy,* edited by S. Schram and A. Neisser. New York: Rowman and Littlefield, 1997.

Shepard, Scott. "Democrats Unveil Election-Year Immigration Bill." *Cox News Service,* May 4, 2004.

Sidney, Mara S. "Contested Images of Race and Place: The Politics of Housing Discrimination." In *Deserving and Entitled: Social Constructions and Public Policy,* edited by A. Schneider and H. Ingram. Albany: State University of New York Press, 2005.

———. *Unfair Housing: How National Policy Shapes Community Action.* Lawrence: University Press of Kansas, 2003.

Simon, Richard. "Immigration Bill Faces a Wall of Opposition." *Los Angeles Times,* May 18, 2007.

Smith, James P., and Barry Edmonston, eds. *The New Americans: Economic, Demographic, and Fiscal Effects of Immigration,* edited by the National Research Council. Washington, DC: National Academies Press, 1997.

Smith, Rogers. "Beyond Tocqueville, Myrdal and Hartz: The Multiple Traditions in America." *American Political Science Review* 87 (1993): 549–66.

———. *Civic Ideals.* New Haven, CT: Yale University Press, 1998.

Stepick, Alex. *Pride against Prejudice: Haitians in the United States,* edited by N. Foner. New Immigrants Series. Needham Heights, MA: Allyn and Bacon, 1998.

Stern, Seth. "An Uneasy Deal with an Illegal Workforce." *CQ Weekly,* March 14 2005.

Stier, Haya, and Marta Tienda. "Family, Work and Women: The Labor Supply of Hispanic Immigrant Wives." *International Migration Review* 26, no. 4 (1992): 1291–1313.

Stoddard, Ellwyn R. "A Conceptual Analysis of the 'Alien Invasion': Institutionalized Support of Illegal Mexican Aliens in the U.S." *International Migration Review* 10, no. 2 (1976): 157–89.

Stone, Deborah. "Causal Stories and the Formation of Policy Agendas." *Political Science Quarterly* 104 (1989): 281–300.

———. *Policy Paradox: The Art of Political Decision Making,* rev. ed. New York: Norton, 2002.

Suro, Roberto. "States Take Immigration Woes to Capitol with Pleas for Relief; Lawmakers Offer Governors Everything but Money." *Washington Post*, June 25, 1994.

Tatalovich, Raymond. *Nativism Reborn? The Official English Language Movement and the American States*. Lexington: University Press of Kentucky, 1995.

Tichenor, Daniel. *Dividing Lines: The Politics of Immigration Control in America*. Princeton, NJ: Princeton University Press, 2002.

Tyner, James A. "The Geopolitics of Eugenics and the Exclusion of Philippine Immigrants from the United States." *Geographical Review* 89, no. 1 (1999): 54–73.

"USDA Announces Restoration of Food Stamp Eligibility for Qualified Legal Immigrant Children." *States News Service*, October 1, 2003.

U.S. Congress. *Congressional Record*. "Senate Consideration of S. 1200." 99th Cong., 1st sess. (September 12, 1985). Vol. 131.

———. *Congressional Record*. "Immigration Reform and Control Act of 1985." 99th Cong., 1st sess. (September 13, 1985). Vol. 131.

———. *Congressional Record*. "Immigration Reform and Control Act of 1985." 99th Cong., 1st sess. (September 16, 1985). Vol. 131.

———. *Congressional Record*. "Immigration Reform and Control Act of 1985." 99th Cong., 1st sess. (September 17, 1985). Vol. 131.

———. *Congressional Record*. "House Consideration of H.R. 3810, Consideration and Passage of S. 1200." 99th Cong., 2nd sess. (October 9, 1986). Vol. 132.

———. *Congressional Record*. "Immigration Control and Legalization Amendments of 1985." 99th Cong., 2nd sess. (October 9, 1986). Vol. 132.

———. *Congressional Record*. "Conference Report on S. 1200: Immigration Reform and Control Act of 1985." 99th Cong., 2nd sess. (October 15, 1986). Vol. 132, pt. 2.

———. *Congressional Record*. "House Consideration of the Conference Report on S. 1200." 99th Cong., 2nd sess. (October 15, 1986). Vol. 132, pt. 2.

———. "Immigration Reform and Control Act—Conference Report." 99th Cong., 2nd sess. (October 17, 1986). Vol. 132.

———. *Congressional Record*. "H.R. 2202 Bill Tracking Report. Immigration and the National Interest Act of 1995." 104th Cong., 1st sess. 1996.

———. *Congressional Record*. "Immigration in the National Interest Act of 1995." 104th Cong., 2nd sess. (March 19, 1996). Vol. 142.

———. *Congressional Record*. "Providing for Consideration of H.R. 2202, Immigration and the National Interest Act of 1995." 104th Cong., 2nd sess. (March 19, 1996). Vol. 142.

———. *Congressional Record*. "Immigration in the National Interest Act of 1995." 104th Cong., 2nd sess. (March 20, 1996). Vol.142.

———. *Congressional Record*. "Immigration in the National Interest Act of 1995." 104th Cong., 2nd sess. (March 21, 1996). Vol. 142.

———. *Congressional Record*. "Authorizing States to Deny Public Education

Benefits to Certain Aliens Not Lawfully Present in the United States." 104th Cong., 2nd sess. (September 25, 1996). Vol. 142.

U.S. Congress. *Congressional Record.* "Conference Report on H.R. 2202, Illegal Immigration Reform and Immigrant Responsibility Act of 1996." 104th Cong., 2nd sess. (September 25, 1996). Vol. 142.

——. *Congressional Record.* "Border Protection, Antiterrorism, and Illegal Immigration Control Act of 2005." 109th Cong., 1st sess. (December 15, 2005). Vol. 151.

——. House Committee on Government Reform. *U.S. Border Patrol's Implementation of "Operation Gatekeeper."* Washington, DC: Government Printing Office, 1996.

——. Senate Subcommittee on Immigration and Refugee Policy. *The Knowing Employment of Illegal Immigrants.* 97th Cong., 1st sess. (September 30, 1981).

U.S. General Accounting Office, Health, Education, and Human Services Division. *Illegal Aliens: National Net Cost Estimates Vary Widely.* Washington, DC: GAO, 1995.

van Dijk, Teun A. *Elite Discourse and Racism.* Newbury Park, CA: Sage, 1993.

——. "On the Analysis of Parliamentary Debates on Immigration." In *The Semiotics of Racism: Approaches to Critical Discourse Analysis*, edited by M. Reisigl and R. Wodak. Vienna: Passagen Verlag, 2000.

——. "Political Discourse and Racism: Describing Others in Western Parliaments." In *The Language and Politics of Exclusion: Others in Discourse*, edited by S. H. Riggins. Thousand Oaks, CA: Sage, 1997.

——. "Principles of Critical Discourse Analysis." *Discourse and Society* 4, no. 2 (1993): 249–83.

——. "Text, Talk, Elites and Racism." *Discours Social/Social Discourse* 1, no. 2 (1992): 37–62.

Wacquant, Loic. "The Penalization of Poverty and the Rise of Neo-Liberalism." *European Journal on Criminal Policy and Research* 9 (2001): 401–12.

Walzer, Michael. *Spheres of Justice: A Defense of Pluralism and Equality.* New York: Basic Books, 1983.

——. *What It Means to Be an American.* New York: Marsilio, 1992.

Waters, Mary C. *Black Identities: West Indian Immigrant Dreams and American Realities.* New York: Russell Sage Foundation, 1999. Reprint, Cambridge, MA: Harvard University Press, 2001.

Wong, Carolyn. *Lobbying for Inclusion: Rights Politics and the Making of Immigration Policy.* Stanford, CA: Stanford University Press, 2006.

Zhou, Min. "Segmented Assimilation: Issues, Controversies, and Recent Research on the New Second Generation." *International Migration Review* 31, no. 4 (1997): 975–1008.

Index

About the Author

Lina Newton is Assistant Professor of Political Science at Hunter College, City University of New York.